Curriculum and the Holocaust

Competing Sites of Memory and Representation

Studies in Curriculum Theory

William F. Pinar, Series Editor

jagodzinski • Postmodern Dilemmas: Outrageous Essays in Art&Art Education

jagodzinski • Pun(k) Deconstruction: Experifigural Writings in Art&Art Education

Huebner • The Lure of the Transcendent: Collected Essays by Dwayne E. Huebner. Edited by Vikki Hillis. Collected and Introduced by William F. Pinar

Pinar (Ed.) • Queer Theory in Education

Reid • Curriculum as Institution and Practice: Essays in the Deliberative Tradition

Westbury/Hopmann/Riquarts (Eds.) • Teaching as a Reflective Practice: The German Didaktic Tradition

Joseph/Bravman/Windschitl/Mikel/Green • Cultures of Curriculum

Doll • Like Letters In Running Water: A Mythopoetics of Curriculum

Morris • Curriculum and the Holocaust: Competing Sites of Memory and Representation

Curriculum and the Holocaust

Competing Sites of Memory and Representation

Marla Morris
Georgia Southern University

LEA
2001

LAWRENCE ERLBAUM ASSOCIATES, PUBLISHERS
Mahwah, New Jersey London

Lawrence Erlbaum Associates, Inc., Publishers
10 Industrial Avenue
Mahwah, NJ 07430

Cover design by Kathryn Houghtaling Lacey

Cover art by Rose Imhoff

Library of Congress Cataloging-in-Publication Data

Morris, Marla, 1962-
Curriculum and the Holocaust : competing sites of memory and representation / by Marla Morris
p. cm.—(Studies in curriculum theory)
Includes bibliographical references and index.
ISBN 0-8058-3812-0 (cloth : alk. paper)
1. Holocaust, Jewish (1939-1945)–Study and teaching.
2. Holocaust, Jewish (1939-1945), in literature. 3. Memory.
4. Holocaust, Jewish (1939-1945)–Historiography. I. Title.
II. Series.
D804.33 .M67 2001
940.53'18'071—dc21 00-062261
CIP

Books published by Lawrence Erlbaum Associates are printed on acid-free paper, and their bindings are chosen for strength and durability.

Printed in the United States of America
10 9 8 7 6 5 4 3 2 1

Contents

Preface

I never thought that I would write a book about the Holocaust. Not consciously anyway. This book came about after many years of not wanting to think about the Holocaust. When I would daydream about the possibility of writing a book, I often wished to grapple with the most abstract topics I could think of. At one point I thought I would write a book on Hegel. Hegel would have been a great place for me to hide. At another point, I thought I would write a book on A. N. Whitehead. Whitehead would have been yet another great place for me to hide. Then I thought I would write a book on the history of beauty and aesthetics. Another great place for me to hide. For me, interpretations around Hegel, Whitehead, and the philosophical treatment of beauty would not require emotional engagement. Maybe for some scholars, these kinds of texts evoke emotion and feeling. But for me, they seemed to provide a safe haven of no feeling, nothing. I did not want to be engaged emotionally. Before encountering curriculum theory and psychoanalytic literature, before taking the plunge out of the site of numbness, I did not really think about repression; I really had no idea what it was or why I was so invested in repressing my feelings. Intellectualization has always been one of my hiding places. Anna Freud (1966/1993) teaches that intellectualization is dangerous because it splits feeling and emotion off from thought.

I really cannot say how I came to write this book. I believe that it wrote me. I am convinced that it came out of a place in my unconscious, a place of deeply repressed memory: some place haunting and troubling, forgetting that my shelves are lined with Holocaust novels, not Hegel; forgetting that my shelves are lined with historiographies of the Holocaust, not Whitehead. The Holocaust is not about abstractions and beauty but ugliness and real life brutality. Repression. Forgetting and remembering.

My encounter will Bill Pinar changed my life, both intellectually and emotionally. My scholarship finally came home. Curriculum theory is the place/site that allows me to come home to myself, both emotionally and intellectually. Bill has taught me that scholarship should have something to do with one's life. Aha! What a breakthrough for me. For some reason I never made that connection. It seems obvious. But for me it was not.

My coming home to myself through curriculum theory means that I have to come home to my Jewish identity, to my repression, and to all that I have refused to deal with as a scholar and as a third generation American Jew after Auschwitz. I have come home late, perhaps belatedly, perhaps too late. I have a lot of catching up to do and much work ahead of me. This book I have written is only the beginning of a long journey. I have only just begun.

This book is not easy to read. It is not a straightforward accounting of the Holocaust because there is nothing straightforward about that horror. Each chapter plunges the reader a little further into the heart of darkness. Scattered throughout the text are the voices of the victims. What readers will hear might give pause. My first reader, my partner, mentor, lover, and best friend, Mary, told me that when she read my chapter on Holocaust historiography she began to have nightmares. This book might trigger these kinds of unconscious reactions. This is not a happy book and certainly I do not offer a happy ending. The book was not liberating to write, nor is it liberating to re-read. While writing the book, I too had my share of nightmares. The Holocaust is horrible. This memory is still with us and will remain. It is not something far off in the distant past; it will be with us in memory for generations to come. This book is my testament to keeping its memory alive.

My treatment of the Holocaust is multilayered, drawing on curriculum theory, psychoanalytic literature, philosophy, fiction, and historiography. The overall structure was inspired by listening to a Mahler symphony. Mahler often gives clues, fore-shadows, bits and pieces of what is to come later. This gives his symphonic movements a sense of recursivity. I wanted this text to have a sense of recursivity, not linearity. One of the misleading things about Holocaust representation is that texts often give readers the impression that there was a clear beginning, middle, and ending to the events that transpired between 1933 and 1945. But witnesses to this event suggest that they experienced murkiness, ambiguity, ambivalence, and confusion. The vortex of time and the vortex of lived experience are never clear. Not that my text is unclear because, of course, there is a logical structure to the text overlaid with some fore-shadowing. These fore-shadows perhaps give the reader time to gather up psychological readiness. A readiness is needed because Holocaust narratives are horrific. The plunge into the Holocaust gives a sense of a vortex. This vortex is termed, by many who write about the Holocaust, *the black sun of Auschwitz*, a term that may not be familiar to curriculum scholars. But Holocaust narratives are replete with this reference. The black sun is literally a reference to the thickness of black smoke rising up from the crematoriums. The smoke was so thick that it turned the sun black. The smoke was so thick that it covered the walls of the train station at Auschwitz.

Within the chapters, I take time to unpack and think through curricular, psychoanalytic, historical, and fictive writing on the Holocaust, because I feel that without carefully thinking through, little understanding is gained. However, the difficulty with grappling with Holocaust representation is that, at the end of the day, we have to understand that we cannot understand after all. The aporias of understanding, thinking through, and thinking about the Holocaust remain. These texts are Other; I suggest we keep them that way. And so this book is about what I call a *dystopic curriculum*. Dystopia is critical of the concept of hope. If readers want to find something hopeful here they will be disappointed. However, readers, I must stress that I am not a nihilist. This book is driven by an ethical responsibility to respond to the dead and to the victims of this Jewish tragedy called the Holocaust. This book is, ultimately, an ethical project.

IN MEMORY

This book is in memory of my father, Meyer Morris, who died August 22, 1999. In your absence you are present. And yet you are gone. You lived just the way you wanted to. You died the way you wanted to. And I thank God you died peacefully in your sleep. I respond to the call to remember you.

Along with my father, I have written this book in memory of the following people: George Gabris, Ida Gabris, Irwin Glick, Richard Kendrick, Milton Morris, Sally Morris, Bea Schwartz, Hershey Schwartz, Hyme Schwartz, Mary Schwartz, Rebekah Sneidermen, Harry Stiller. And the 6 million others.

ACKNOWLEDGMENTS

I acknowledge the many people who have helped me move my thinking along over the years. The conversations I have had with all of these wonderful souls have helped me grow intellectually, emotionally, and spiritually.

Ronna Burger. Ronna taught me about Aristotle and the importance of thinking ethically. Dr. Burger introduced me to the amazing work of Edith Wyschogrod. Alan Block. Alan has taught me much about what it means to be a Jewish intellectual. Alan has taught me about lost objects. Deborah P. Britzman. Deborah has taught me much about psychoanalysis and led me to the writings of Anna Freud. Toby Daspit. Toby and I struggled through graduate school together. Toby has taught me much about popular culture. Brent Davis. Brent has taught me much about issues of culture and curriculum. Brent has taught me to think culturally. Mary Aswell Doll. Mary has taught me to think through language, to think around and into language. Mary has taught me much about literature and the importance of reading fiction. Mary has been my constant companion, my teacher, my mentor, my best friend, my lover. Mary has also taught me what it is like to live the scholarly life and to live the teacherly life. Mary Doll is an amazing person. Mary is a much better writer than I will ever be. William Doll Jr. William has taught me the importance of thinking through postmodernism. Vivus Dorwin Jr. Vivus has taught me about the importance of music and friendship. Tibby Dubois. Tibby has taught me much about Holocaust narratives. Father Steven Duffy. Steve influenced my thinking theologically. He always inspired in me a sense of rigor. Elizabeth Ellsworth. Liz taught me about the notion of discontinuity and modes of address. James Gaffney. Jim influenced my thinking on ethics and Dante. Denis Janz. Denis was there the day I said I wanted to write a book on Hegel. We were sitting in the faculty lounge at Loyola University. Denis said, but who would you study with, who does Hegel anymore? Denis influenced my thinking on Martin Luther. Rosan Jordan. Dr. Jordan was the best outside examiner the graduate school could have assigned to me when defending my dissertation. Harisimran Khalsa, my long-time friend. We have had 20 years of conversations on music and friendship. One day I will write a book on friendship. Joe Kincheloe. Joe has taught me about the notion of thinking contextually. I couldn't have written in a contextual way without reading Joe's work. Wendy Kohli. Wendy has taught me about the Frankfurt School. Wendy led me to critical theory. Wendy has taught me how to integrate philosophy into curriculum studies. Janet Miller. Janet has taught me the value of autobiography and writing well. Petra Munro. Petra influenced my historiographical turn. Petra has a way of pushing my thinking in new directions. Petra always asks questions that I can't answer. Marshall Parks. Marshall and I have had many conversations about Richard Rorty and John Dewey. Marshall is my co-conference paper reader and dear friend. Marshall certainly understands philosophy in a way that far surpasses me. William F. Pinar. Bill has helped me grow as a scholar. Bill has given me the freedom to think the way I want to. Bill has led me back to myself. Bill led me to curriculum theory and psychoanalytic literature. Bill taught me the value of thinking autobiographically. Bill made it possible for me to get a Ph.D. Bill is an amazing mentor. Andrew Reck. Professor Reck gave me the opportunity to learn about the history of philosophy. It was in his class on American philosophy that I discovered A. N. Whitehead. Dr. Reck also introduced me to Hegel and the Western philosophical tradition. Maybe I will write those books on Whitehead and Hegel one day. Paula Salvio. Paula has led me to the works around post-Freudian analysis. Paula influenced my thinking on repression and led me to the writings of Maria Torok and Nicolas Abraham. Shirley Steinberg. Shirley has always supported my work and my struggles with Jewish identity. Shirley has also taught me the value of popular culture. Mike Siddoway. Mike and I spent many hours together in the hot summer without air conditioning in New Orleans. Mike inspired me to become a scholar. Mike was the first person I had ever met who had a Ph.D. I watched him struggle through his dissertation on mathematics. He taught me that it is more than just stick-to-itness that makes a mathematician. Naomi Silverman. Naomi is one of the few people I have met who doesn't like the idea behind the film *Life is Beautiful*. A kindred spirit. Naomi believed enough in my work to make this book become a reality. Roger Simon. Dr. Simon's work on the Holocaust influenced my thinking on the concept of hope. Joshua Steinert. Josh is the computer genius. Thanks for making my technological struggles easier. Dennis Sumara. Dennis has taught me much about hermeneutics, language, literature, and whippets. Peter Taubman. Peter is one of the few people who has written against hope in the field of curriculum. Finally, a kindred spirit. Peter is one of the few people who has actually asked me how I am doing since the death of my father. Mary B. Virre. Mary taught me more about the concepts of psychoanalysis than any book on the subject. Mary taught me about notions of repression and helped me to re-structure my ego so that I could feel again. This book could not have been written without her influence. The many years of working together with Mary helped me to get it together psychologically. I would not have been able to treat the Holocaust psychoanalytically without working with Mary. Delese Wear. Delese has taught me much about writing and fiction. Delese led me to the work of Cynthia Ozick. John Weaver. John knows more about the vicissitudes of German historiography than most in the field of curriculum. John led me early on to issues of the *Historikerstreit* in Germany and to the writings of Jeffrey Herf. John has been particularly helpful on East German politics. Philip Wexler. Dr. Wexler's encouragement has meant much to me. Professor

Wexler has helped me to think socially. Dr. Wexler's work on Jewish mysticism has meant much to me. Michael Zimmerman. Professor Zimmerman has helped me to understand the importance of grappling with Heidegger's Nazism. Dr. Zimmerman's words of encouragement have helped me think through some tough issues on subjects that I would rather avoid. Finally, thanks to my mother, Rhoda Gilpin, my grandmother, Sally Stiller, and my sisters Cathy Binstock and Lisa Snider, who all shaped me as a person.

—*Marla Morris*

ONE

Curriculum Theory and the Holocaust

> So the curriculum that we study is the presence of an absence. Present is the curriculum, the course of study, the current compliance, general education .... Present is the window. Absent is the ground from which these figures are drawn, negation, and aspiration. Absent is the laugh that rises from the belly, the whimper, the song. Suppressed is the body count, Auschwitz.
>
> —*(Grumet, 1988, p. xiii)*

Madeleine Grumet tells us that curriculum is the presence of an absence. The absence of Auschwitz, the silence around this dreadful memory in my own educative experience, is like a gaping hole in the heart of memory. Silence around the Holocaust in my own education has not, however, silenced memory. In fact, silence has allowed this memory to speak to me in haunting ways. It has called me out of the site of my unconscious. The repressed has returned. As Emmanuel Levinas (1996) might say, the other, or the memory of my ancestors, has "summoned" (p. 6) me.

Grumet (1988) remarks that "Absent is the ground from which these figures are drawn" (p. xiii). The ground she refers to is that of lived experience, and it is lived experience that is absented from school life. Erasing lived experience, erasing human subjectivities in school life, endangers students and teachers alike because we have no sense of who we are. This absenting erases our histories, memories, and our situatedness. Repressed human subjectivities and continual erasures deaden. William Pinar (1991) warns that "Repression of memory and history is accompanied by distortions of various kinds, including political, social, racial, and psychological distortions" (p. 177). The Holocaust is a memory that has been repressed for me. School was not a place in which I encountered this memory. Home was not a place that I encountered this memory, either. Hauntings of this memory have emerged because of this silence. The date was November 1937. This date marks my mother's birth. Exactly 1 year later, November 1938, marks the date of *Kristallnacht*. Efraim Sicher (1998) comments that,

> The breaking of crystal obscures any clear understanding of the meaning of what has happened, so that meaning itself is not easily recoverable. The breaking of crystal might therefore be a fit metaphor for a continuous crisis in the post-Holocaust generation. (p. 3)

Kristallnacht signifies a turning point in Jewish and German history. Isaiah Trunk (1979) reminds us that it was immediately after this event that Jews began to realize that their lives were in danger. *Kristallnacht* marks the event after which many Jews committed suicide.

The date of my mother's birth, November 1937, is significant for me. It situates my family historically at the heart of this crisis. But because my parents and grandparents are American, they were saved from this nightmare. My maternal great-grandparents had the foresight to leave Austria at the turn of the century. My paternal great-grandparents had the wisdom to leave Russia. But distant relatives stayed in Europe. However, tracing these distant relatives is impossible. With the exception of my maternal grandmother, all of my grandparents are dead.

I ask my grandmother to tell me what she remembers about my family. I ask her to tell me about my great-grandparents. Why did they leave Europe, I ask. What about the others who stayed behind? She says she does not know. Tell me about my great-grandparents, I say to her. She says my great-grandmother spoke in broken English, she spoke mostly Yiddish. My great-grandfather was president of a synagogue in Pittsburgh. Both of my grandfathers were religious men. For women, religious ritual, except in the home, was not thought to be important. This is the extent of the oral history my grandmother passes down to me. This is all I know about my people.

My mother is a secular Jew. My father, who recently passed away, was a secular Jew as well. I grew up knowing little of my own religious tradition. Talking about the Holocaust is taboo in my family. No one breathes a word about it. My older sister tells me that she cannot bear it, she cannot read anything about the Holocaust, it is just too depressing and too awful. And so the silence continues into the third generation after Auschwitz. Esther Rashkin (1992), drawing on the work of Nicolas Abraham and Maria Torok, who are Holocaust survivors and psychoanalysts, comments that family silences and family secrets become "suspended within the adult [and are] … transmitted silently to the child in 'undigested' form and lodge within his or her mental topography as an unmarked tomb" (p. 28). "What returns to haunt is the 'unsaid' and 'unsayable' of an other" (p. 28). The memory of Auschwitz, that silent, absent presence about which Madeleine Grumet speaks, has become lodged in my psyche. It is the profound silence, both educative and familial, that has marked me. The silence has called me toward the other, toward the memory of the other, and toward the other of memory. Emmanuel Levinas (1996) says,

> This tie to the Other (*autrui*) which does not reduce itself to the representation of the Other (*autrui*) but rather to his invocation, where invocation is not preceded by comprehension, we call religion. The essence of discourse is prayer. (p. 7)

The invocation I hear, the call of the other of memory, the call of my ancestors, demands a response. And this response will be a prayerful one. Like Levinas, James Macdonald (1995) suggests that "theory is a prayerful act." Thus, I offer up this study as a prayerful act, as a response to the call of my ancestors, as a responsibility to my own conscience. I am driven by an ethical imperative to remember. And this ethical imperative is not marked off from my life in the academy. As John Dewey (1909/1975) says, "There cannot be two sets of ethical principles, one for life in the school [or the university], and the other for life outside of the school" (p. 7). The call to remember is an ethical commitment, a public testimony of an academic struggling to grapple with the Holocaust. This commitment is also a private testimony of a third generation Jew after Auschwitz, as a private testimony to my ancestors.

I have, however, suffered much resistance to thinking about my own Jewishness and what this Jewishness means against the backdrop of the Holocaust. I wrote my master's thesis on Christology, the study of who and what Jesus was. I did not understand fully why I chose this as a master's thesis topic. At bottom, I felt deeply troubled by the anti-Semitism Christology perpetuated, but still I was not psychologically ready to embrace my own Jewishness.

Doing curriculum theory, William Pinar (1994) stresses, is most fundamentally an autobiographical act. Academic work, if it is to progress, must have something to do with one's own lifework. Thus, it is through curriculum theory that I have been able to return to myself, I have returned to my Jewishness. My intellectual and spiritual return to Judaism, to the synagogue, to *shul*, has not been without difficulty, however. The return and the work on the Holocaust have sent me back and down into the terrifying depths of the unconscious. Ten years ago, previous to this return, I plunged into psychoanalytic-oriented therapy primarily because I suffered from a sense of numbness. I experienced an uncanny speechlessness. I felt haunted by phantoms. Some analysts might call speechlessness resistance. And I certainly resisted these phantoms. Ten years later, during my work on the Holocaust, these phantoms returned and so too did I to psychoanalytically oriented therapy.

At the start of my research on the Holocaust I fiercely resisted utilizing psychoanalytic theory. I did not know why I felt this way. But I suppose I intuited, at some dimly conscious level, that engagement with psychoanalytic theory opens one to vulnerability because it unleashes the unconscious. Finally, after overcoming this initial resistance, I decided that it was psychoanalytic theory as it intersects with curriculum theory that would help me to untangle issues around the Holocaust. Many argue that curriculum theory and psychoanalytic theory are not incompatible (Appelbaum & Kaplan, 1998; Atwell-Vasey, 1998; Benzaquen, 1998; Britzman, 1998; Gilbert, 1998; Grumet, 1988; Kaplan, 1998; Pinar, 1991; Pitt, 1998; Robertson & Todd, 1998; Salvio, 1998.) William Pinar (1991) suggests that "curriculum as a form of social psychoanalysis permits the student to emerge as a figure, capable of critical participation in a historical present hitherto denied" (p. 165). Drawing on Pinar's notion of social psychoanalysis, I offer up what I term a *social psychoanalytic hermeneutic* to recover Holocaust memory. I offer up a Holocaust curriculum, a memory text that lets me speak from my own situatedness.

It is curriculum theory which allows me to recover Holocaust memory across many registers. William Pinar says, "Curriculum becomes intensely historical, political, racial, gendered, phenomenological, postmodern, autobiographical, aesthetic, theological, and international" (1999, p. xvii). A psychoanalytic hermeneutic allows me to move across these curricular registers, to weave through the warp and woof of the educative landscape. A psychoanalytic hermeneutic is a form of interpretation that allows me to cut across and between these multitudinous sites. Madeleine Grumet (1999) says that curriculum is "hermeneutic activity [it is an] act of interpretation" (p. 233). Grumet tells us that the "prefix [of the word interpretation] "inter" means between, and the root is traced to its Sanskrit antecedent, prath—to spread abroad. Interpretation occurs at the junction of opposites" (p. 233). To move in between curricular sites in broad ways is my task. My task as a curriculum scholar is not unlike Michel Serres' image of the weaver. Serres (1982) says, "one must find the weaver, the proto-maker of space, the prosopopeia of topology and nodes, the weaver who works locally to join two worlds that are separated" (p. 52).

Holocaust scholarship tends to be divided into two worlds: the world of historical representations and the world of literary representations. William Paulson (1988) reminds us that C. P. Snow warned against what he called "the two cultures" (p. 4). "Snow denounced the consequences for intellectual ignorance of those who live by literature and those who live by science" (p. 4). I believe, like Snow, that curricularists must find a way to bridge the two cultures of social science and the humanities, especially when attempting to interpret the complexities around the Holocaust. However, merely adding one culture (history) to another (literature) is not my aim, either. My task is to synthesize these two cultures in ways unique to the discipline of curriculum theory. A psychoanalytic hermeneutic around different and competing representations of the Holocaust allows me to cut across curricular registers that are "intensely historical, political, racial, gendered, phenomenological postmodern, autobiographical, aesthetic, theological and international" (Pinar, 1999, p. xviii). The ways in which the Holocaust gets represented tells much about the ways in which this event will be remembered in generations to come.

Many different kinds of representations around Holocaust memory abound. Audio-visual testimony, diaries, memoirs, dance, poetry, music, art and film all represent the Holocaust in important ways. However, I choose to focus on two kinds of representations, the historical and the literary. History was always a subject I detested in high school; it seemed interminably boring. It seemed to be little more than memorizing dates. But in college, history began to fascinate me. Most of my scholarly papers that have been published since my entrance into graduate school have been historical treatments. Whatever curricular issue I have grappled with has been treated historically. I feel that historical representations of the Holocaust are indispensable guides toward understanding complexities around this event. Of course, historical accounts are not the most authoritative representations; historians are not the only keepers of memory. But I suggest that if we are to call ourselves educated people we have to know something about the history of this event.

Like history, English was a subject I also detested in high school. It seemed little more than memorizing plots. But literature, outside of school, has always been my great love. Without realizing it, I had been collecting Holocaust novels all during my high school years. In essence, I have been doing memory work around the Holocaust most of my life.

Doing interpretive work around historical and literary representations of the Holocaust does not mean that one can get a complete picture of this event. It does not grant a better understanding than, say, study of audio-visual testimony or poetry. Studying historical and literary accounts of the Holocaust offers a particular perspective that enables me to raise broad curricular questions across many kinds of registers of lived experience. Robin Barrow (1981) claims that "Education implies breadth of understanding rather than narrow specialism" (p. 39). And it is a broad picture of the Holocaust that I would like to paint. However, any understanding of this event is necessarily limited. It would be arrogant to suggest that an academic, who has never actually suffered Auschwitz, can really understand after all. In many ways, the Holocaust is beyond understanding and representation. And yet—cautiously and with humility—I proceed. Curricularists can approach the black sun of Auschwitz in spite of the limits of understanding. If we refuse the call of remembering this event altogether because of the ineffableness of Auschwitz, we lapse back into silence. Silence is not the place to which I wish to return. Silence kills. Evocation, speech, writing, dialogue and prayer beckon. I am driven by phantoms: the phantoms of the dead, the phantoms of my Jewish ancestors.

A Holocaust education pains. There is no doubt about that. There is no way to avoid the fear and trembling in the face of Auschwitz. Shoshana Felman and Dori Laub (1992) ask "whether there is a relation between crisis and the very enterprise of education" (p. 1). A Holocaust curriculum cannot avoid crisis because it evokes one. A Holocaust curriculum approaches what Deborah Britzman (1998) calls "difficult knowledges" (p. 6). But doing interpretive work around the Holocaust is not just about acquiring knowledge. Rather, it is about understanding the event while standing at the limits of understanding. It is an understanding that is necessarily aporetic; it is to understand that we cannot understand. It is impossible, especially for outsiders to the event, to understand in the same way as a Holocaust survivor. David Geoffrey Smith (1999) tells us that,

> While standing in the middle of things, interpretive pedagogy looks to the margins of collective life for the oracular word of signification ... it is exactly at the boundary of experience ... where we become available to that which addresses us. (p. 132)

We know that we cannot understand the event of the Holocaust no matter how much knowledge we may acquire. Studying historical and literary representations of Auschwitz does not mean we understand them. Reading history does not mean we understand it. Reading novels about the Holocaust does not mean that we understand it. Still, we understand at the limits of our own situatedness, at the limits of our own horizon.

It is on the psychological register, though, that understanding suffers most interference. The aporias of understanding are inextricably tied to the psychological. The psychological register is complexified by unconscious traces that emerge in the forms of resistances, repressions, projections, introjections, reversals, and denials. At the outset of my study, I believed that the task at hand was to get rid of these interferences, because I thought that they thwarted and distorted interpretations of the Holocaust. However, I came to realize that this position is not realistic. It presupposes that, at the end of the day, we could get a close reading of this event without too much psychological baggage. But, as I dwelled over my own intellectual resistances and emotional struggles with this material, I realized that this position was naive.

My encounter with the writings of Jean Laplanche (1973, 1985, 1999) altered my thinking. Laplanche (1999) suggests that psychological interferences always leave traces in the psyche, no matter how much one works through difficult emotional issues. Some amount of repression remains, no matter how aware or how conscious one becomes of one's inner psychic workings. "The message [of the other or of the text] is partly translated and partly repressed" (p. 94). The message of the text and its reception by the reader undergo repression and interference, no matter how much the reader thinks she understands the text. Some repression always remains. This complex interaction between reader and text is guided by an unconscious transferential relation. The reader transfers her own patterns of perception onto the text which are marked by a certain amount of resistance, repression, and anxiety. The reader dwells in the liminal space between her own unconscious transference and the unconscious inscriptions introjected into the text by the writer. Exactly what it is that transpires between reader and text, at the site of the unconscious, is not clear. Interpretations which are inadequate are symptomatic of too much repression. An adequate translation lifts repression as much as possible, but traces of repression remain.

Laplanche (1999) stresses that translations of an analysand by an analyst should leave intact the otherness of the analysand. I argue, drawing on Laplanche (1999), that translations of Holocaust texts should also leave intact the otherness, the alterity, of these texts. The complexity of doing interpretive work emerges as one's own otherness, which is marked by unconscious transference, co-mingles with the otherness of the text, which is marked by the unconscious inscription "implanted" (p. 258) in the text by the writer. Laplanche (1999) says that at the intersection between self and other (and I would add between reader and text) lies an "enigmatic message" (p. 258), or a "third reality" (p. 80) that is in some ways beyond translation. I argue that Laplanche's (1999) notion of an enigmatic message can be applied to studying Holocaust texts. The alterity of the text, the text as other, the text of the Holocaust, which is other to itself (as an inscription of the author's unconscious), and its "implantation" (p. 258) in the reader (the introjected message) must be maintained. Fletcher (1999) suggests a "failed translation" (p. 16) is marked by rigidity. Laplanche (1999) stresses that rigid interpretations are guided by the compulsion to repeat old patterns, old habits of perception. And it is this that analysts call transference. He argues that we cannot, however, get outside of transference; we cannot get outside of our old patterns of perception and interpretation. All we can do is work to "loosen" (p. 258) transference. Grumet (1988) suggests that we should avoid getting "trapped in transference" (p. 117). But perhaps this move is impossible. We are always already trapped. Thus, it is not a matter of getting rid of transference, rather, it is a matter of becoming aware of our own habits of interpretation and translation. We can work to lift repression and resistance somewhat and become more aware of our intellectual and emotional responses and trappings, and by doing so I think we can become more open to the alterity of Holocaust texts.

Historical and literary representations of the Holocaust are determined, in part, by the ways in which we approach epistemological and psychological interferences. Psychological resistances to the difficult memory of the Holocaust may determine what it is that gets represented in the first place. That which is not-said and not-represented may be absented because of the writers' resistances and repressions. What it is that historians and novelists choose to exclude becomes key to what it is they might be repressing.

GENERAL OVERVIEW OF STUDY

Generally speaking, this study examines what I call *curriculum as memory text*. I argue that memory is the larger category under which history is subsumed. History, then, is a systematization of memory. History, however, is not reducible to memory; for historians, although operating out of their own memories, draw on archives, documents, and testimonies and are constrained by the discipline of history. Personal memories, perhaps, effect historians' renderings, but personal memories are different from historical renderings because they are not constrained in the same ways. Psychological interferences such as repression, resistance, denial, projection, introjection, and transference shape memory and therefore may determine, to a certain extent, the ways in which historians select, imagine, deconstruct, and reconstruct documents.

Historical novels are also a form of memory; they are expressions of memory. Writers organize, select, and narrate. Novel writing, however, is not reducible to memory, because writers, even if drawing on their own memories, are constrained by the narrative form. Memory seems not to be constrained in the same way. Although memory is a stream, stream of consciousness novels seem more tightly woven and constructed than memory itself. Personal memories operate out of sites of repression, resistance, projection, introjection, denial, and transference and may determine, to a certain extent, the ways in which novelists select, imagine, construct, and reconstruct the past.

I argue that the writings of historians share certain features with the writings of novelists. But, at bottom, the writing of history is not the same as the writing of historical novels. History shares with literature its narrative and imaginative form. I maintain that historians construct the past by drawing on memory, perception, and imagination. Historians select and omit events and express their thoughts by narration. But historians are ultimately constrained by the methodology of the discipline of history. Novelists, however, do not have to draw on evidence and are not constrained by any methodology, so their task is different.

History writing and the writing of historical novels around the Holocaust, if they are to be considered adequate representations of this awful event, if they are to do justice to the memory of the Holocaust, might follow Edith Wyschogrod's (1998) lead, that the "promise of truthfulness" (p. 10) be maintained. Truthfulness, for me, is not the same as Truth with a capital T. Truth is nowhere absolute. But truthfulness does justice to the memory of the Holocaust because it approaches an approximation of this event through many different perspectives and keeps the alterity and otherness of the event intact. Whatever truths we may learn about the Holocaust are ultimately limited because of the enormity and horror of this event.

Pinar (1991) says that "The curricular task becomes to recover memory and history in ways that psychologically allow individuals to reenter politically the public sphere" (pp. 173–174). Recovering Holocaust memory means that the researcher might be able to become more reflexive and reflective, marking and re-marking her own responses, resistances, interferences, and repressions around doing this kind of work. Recovering Holocaust memory is guided by what I call a *dystopic curriculum*. A dystopic curriculum allows interferences, otherness, alterity, and strangeness to emerge out of the different sites of representations. Under the sign of a dystopic curriculum, memories emerge not as a promise of hope, but as a testament to despair and truthfulness. Following Lawrence Langer (1991), Geoffrey Hartman (1996), and Ofer and Weitzman (1998), I argue against hope. Langer (1991) says "Tainted memory seems inconsistent with the rhetoric of hope" (p. 128). I argue against discourse that "eliminates the noise of otherness" (Edgerton,

1996, p. 57). As Hartman (1996) says, "What we generally do is seek a redemptive perspective to save the good name of humanity.... Yet the Final Solution's man-made calamity is exceptionally resistant to such a perspective" (p. 39). Similarly, Ofer and Weitzman (1998) point out that there is danger when scholars attempt to shield readers from the horrors of the Holocaust. They suggest that,

> the need to find meaning in the events of the Holocaust, the need to shield the audience from the worst horror of the Holocaust, and the need to comfort ourselves with some "redeeming" message—lead to both popularization and banalization. (p. 15)

There is nothing meaningful about Auschwitz; there is nothing about Auschwitz which is redemptive, salvific, or hopeful. The title of the Holocaust film *Life is Beautiful* signals to me an offensive, trivializing banalization of Holocaust memory. There was nothing beautiful about Auschwitz. To say that there is turns suffering into pleasure. It was this that repulsed Adorno (1966/1995). Similarly, Langer (1998) criticizes Judy Chicago's artwork entitled *Holocaust Project* because her message seems to be that there is light at the end of darkness. Langer suggests that Chicago offers to us a redemptive memory. But Langer points out that redemptive strategies serve as psychological defense mechanisms against pain. The film *Tea with Mussolini*, a comedy about Italy's complicity with Germany during the Holocaust, is yet another offensive, redemptive representation which turns suffering into humor. This has to be the biggest insult of all. Langer (1995) comments that we have inherited "A tradition of avoidance ... how much of our language about the Holocaust is designed to console instead of confront" (p. 5). Avoidance is also marked, Deborah Britzman (1998) tells us, in readings of Anne Frank's diary which offer up messages of hope and courage. Britzman argues that these kinds of consoling interpretations reflect psychological resistances and defense mechanisms that serve to protect against pain. The fact is that Anne Frank died in Bergen-Belson and there is nothing hopeful or courageous about that. Britzman (1998) says that,

> If the pedagogy of the diary enacts the educator's desire for a rescue fantasy, stable truth, and the splitting of good and evil through the idealization of the good object, such strategies preclude the possibilities of the learner and teacher working through the ambivalences of their own conflict. (p. 134)

Representations of the Holocaust should not be made comfortable. And this comfort is what these redemptive strategies offer. But there is nothing comfortable about the Holocaust. The horrors of the Holocaust demand a certain psychological readiness on the part of the researcher. Psychological readiness means that Holocaust representations and responses should not be covered over with gloss, which serve only to make the strange familiar. There is nothing familiar about planet Auschwitz. Langer (1998) suggests,

> If Jewish experience in the Holocaust can be made to "stand for" something else, some "larger human experience" whether a testimony to the integrity of the moral self, as in Todorov, or, in the case of Judy Chicago, a positive statement about the human condition in general, then the intolerable might seem more tolerable.... Whatever the intention, the result is to dilute or diffuse the particularity of mass murder. (p. 15)

A dystopic curriculum allows the shadow of the object, the shadow of the Holocaust, to darken perspectives. But darkening perspectives does not mean sliding into nihilism. A dystopic curriculum is an ethical one, a response to the "invocation" (Levinas, 1996, p. 7) of the other. A dystopic curriculum is a promise of remembering that attempts to cut through lightness and inauthenticity toward the dark. A dystopic curriculum is not unlike what Ilan Gur-Ze'ev (1998) calls a "counter-education." Gur-Ze'ev comments that,

> Within counter-education no room exists for a positive utopia, and it does not promise collective emancipation.... Counter-education suggests possibilities for identifying, criticizing, and resisting violent practices of normalization, control. (p. 463)

There is nothing emancipating or liberating about doing memory work around the Holocaust. As Richard Rorty (1991) points out, it is coping with reality that matters, not solving or fixing it. Redemptive or emancipating strategies serve to fix this horrible reality by making it seem less horrible. But as Nel Noddings (1989) stresses, American education moves against the grain of anything that smacks of suffering or grief. Noddings says,

> Education has at least in modern times been guided by optimism and notions of progress (notions that are, I think, peculiarly masculine). Perhaps we should now consider an education guided by a tragic sense of life. (p. 244)

It is the Jewish tragedy, a particular tragedy to Jews, around which we need to attend.

In what way should we attend to this disaster? I suggest educators approach the Holocaust without repressing grief and suffering, although traces of repression will always already affect our work. Paula Salvio calls for an attending to the other through "empathetic identification." Salvio (1998) says that,

> empathetic identification, defined as the capacity for attending to how another person feels rather than merely imagining ourselves in his/her position, is a powerful index to the social attitudes of a given period. (p. 44)

But can we wholly empathize with Holocaust survivors? On one hand, I can say that I feel for the survivor; I feel for her suffering and am troubled by it. But on the other hand, I can never fully empathize because I really do not know how it feels to have suffered Auschwitz. Jonathan Boyarin (1992) cautions against what he terms the "hegemony of empathy" (p. 86). Empathy might have "repressive effects" (p. 87). Boyarin explains that we must become cautious of the way in which we use the notion of empathy. Boyarin argues that,

> The hegemony of empathy is an ethic of obliteration of Otherness. We might say that this occurs where humanism demands acknowledgment of the Other's suffering humanity, but where conditions do not allow the work involved in what Eric Cheyfitz calls "the difficult poetics of translation" ... that is, where the paradoxical linkage of shared humanity and cultural Otherness cannot be experienced. (p. 86)

Empathy can be a move toward making the strange familiar by saying, "I understand what it is you are suffering." But how can an outsider to the event of the Holocaust ever understand, in an emotional way, what this nightmare felt like? Outsiders to this horrific event will never understand what it was like, or what it felt like, to live and die under the black sun of Auschwitz. If empathy suggests that your suffering is the same as mine, that the Holocaust survivor's suffering is like my own, then empathy is false. Still, a cautious empathy, a limited empathy, must remain or else we cannot do work on this horrific memory. A limited sense of empathy must keep the alterity of Auschwitz intact. I can empathize with the other, but I cannot feel what she feels. I will never wholly be able to translate her suffering as if it were my own. Her suffering always remains a stranger suffering than mine. We must always remain strangers to one another in our grief. The memory of the Holocaust lies at the limits of understanding, representation, and empathy.

EDUCATION AND THE HOLOCAUST

In the field of education, there have been notable contributions to Holocaust scholarship that I would like to address. I hope to demonstrate the importance of some of the work that has already been done in the field. Although I draw on my predecessors, my work departs from that which has already been done. I offer a particular perspective of Holocaust education primarily because curriculum theory allows me to examine both historical and literary representations through a dystopic lens guided by what I term a *psychoanalytic hermeneutic.*

John Weaver's (in press) work, entitled *Rethinking Academic Politics in (Re)Unified Germany and the United States*, concerns the ways in which former East and West German historians shape memory. Weaver writes that historians, together with government officials in East Germany, shaped a particular memory of the Holocaust which suited their ideological and political agendas. Former East Germany has only recently (since reunification) begun to come to terms with their complicity during the Nazi era.

Former West German historians have been attempting to come to terms with their Nazi past since the end of World War II. Weaver (in press) explains that West German historians embraced what was termed *Vergangenheitsbewältigung*. This term means to grapple with loss or to grapple with that which passed. This term, then, signals that West German historians attempted to examine what had happened, to examine where Germany had gone wrong. West German historians, much earlier than East German historians, tried to look back with a critical edge. Whether or not they were successful is another issue. But at least there was a start to examine the past after the war had ended. Later, Weaver recounts, West German historiography shifted. *Doppelvergangenheitsbewältigung* signifies grappling with two pasts. Here, West German historians attempted to grapple with two dictatorial traditions. These two dictatorial traditions were labeled Fascism and Stalinism. Fascism in the West and Stalinism in the East needed to be unpacked. Weaver (in press) says that West German historians, unlike their counterparts in the East, claimed that the "former GDR was just as authoritative and destructive as the Nazi regime." West German historians always felt that their academic work was far superior to that of East Germans' work, for at least in the West historians got a head start in coming to terms with the past. West German historiography followed trends in the United States and Britain. Political and military histories were being written alongside cultural histories and the histories of everyday life, which is termed *Alltagsgeschichte*.

In contrast to West German historiography, East German historiography, Weaver (in press) explains, tended to become "rigid." Academics and state officials together decided what kind of history would be considered appropriate. As the keepers of official memory, historians wanted to be certain that East Germans would not be implicated in the rise of the Nazi regime. But since the opening of the Stasi archives, it is now well known that Communists in the East were complicit with the Holocaust, but they also perpetuated crimes against Jews even after the end of the war. The memory that these historians created was covered-over rhetoric that served to conceal the truth. Weaver (in press) says that historians conveniently "pass[ed] over working class collaboration with the Nazis." Calling this framing of collective memory an "issue of power" Weaver explains:

> East German historians would meet with SED [*Sozialistische Einheitspartei Deutschlands* or the United Socialist Party of Germany] officials at the party congresses to establish research agendas. At these congresses, historians would be given the task of creating history for the East German State with an emphasis on working class opposition during the Nazi regime, critiques of the West German historiographical tradition and the role of capitalism in the rise of fascism (in press).

The East German government has traditionally only honored Communist resisters of Fascism, while denying recognition that Jews were victims. The true victims of the East, according to this ideology, were anti-Fascist resisters, while Jews remained an afterthought. East Germany not only denied any responsibility for the Holocaust until 1991, it also denied paying restitution to Holocaust survivors. In a move of psychological reversal, Jews were seen, especially by the state, as enemies of Communism, typically associated with capitalism. East German historians and state officials have claimed, in one way or another, that the root cause of the Holocaust was capitalism. Capitalism led the way to Fascism. Although reunification has changed the East German party line, Jeffrey Peck (1996) is not confident that hard-liners have changed their views. Peck (1996) says, "The official disappearance of East Germany, however, does not make its response to the Holocaust a moot issue. The 40-year history of the German Democratic Republic (GDR) was not erased with the declaration of reunification" (p. 449). Weaver (in press) points out the ways in which collective memory is produced by politics and ideology. Academics shape collective memory and can become complicit in erasing unwanted memory. As seen later, fiction writers living in the former East Germany were not free to write anything. Like historians, they had to comply with the Socialistische Einheitspartei Deutschlands or the United Socialist Party of Germany (SED) mentality or fear accusations of espionage and arrest. Later, I discuss Christa Wolf's (1980) novel *Patterns of Childhood*, which evokes critics' suspicions that she was offering up a portrait of heroic East Germans. Wolf suggests that non-Jewish East Germans were victims of Nazism. But this portrayal omits the fact that the victims of history were Jews. This portrayal also omits the fact that East Germans were complicit in many ways with Nazism.

Weaver's (in press) work is important because we learn that collective memory is place-bound. Where we live has much to do with how we remember the Holocaust. Different places produce different kinds of Holocaust memory. Bystander countries like the United States and Britain frame Holocaust memory differently than collaborating countries like France and Italy. Bystanders and collaborators also produce different kinds of repressed memories to cover up or cover over their indifference, inaction, apathy, or outright complicity. Place is indeed an important factor in the work of memory.

In addition to Weaver's work, Gregory Wegner (1995) also emphasizes the importance of place around collective memory of the Holocaust. In the *Journal of Curriculum and Supervision*, in an article entitled "Buchenwald Concentration Camp and Holocaust Education for Youth in the New Germany," Wegner stresses the emotionally evocative power of doing historical work on site at the Buchenwald Memorial with high school students. Wegner (1995) tells us that, "Students arriving at Buchenwald from the *Weibelfeldschule* stepped into an environment heavily reinforced with the geographical significance of place. [The students studied] ... in a building once used as apartments for SS personnel" (p. 181). Wegner stresses that this high school history seminar was not just an intellectual exercise, but a real encounter, an emotional encounter with Germany's past. The intensity of actually being on the site at Buchenwald heightened students' sense of confrontation with the past. "One student could be heard to ask "why" over and over again as we proceeded to the upstairs rooms, where corpses were sorted ... gold teeth removed" (p. 183). Downstairs *meathooks* could be seen. Wegner explains that these were used to hang Jews. Buchenwald was "attached to a crematorium" (p. 183), which Wegner says was "one of the darkest and most haunting places" (p. 183).

Before reunification, Wegner (1995) writes that Buchenwald Memorial reflected the anti-Fascist rhetoric common among former East Germans. And so when the Memorial initially opened to the public, Buchenwald became a memorial to the heroes and resisters of Fascism. Carefully "omitted" from the "visitors guides" (p. 175) were stories about inmates who were not Communist. Also omitted was the story of Buchenwald after 1950. Under Stalinist control, approximately 10,000 prisoners died there. Wegner tells us that "mention of the Soviet Camp remained strictly forbidden in East German schools" (p. 175).

Like Weaver, Wegner (1995) points out how collective memories are inextricably tied to politics and ideology. The ways in which a memorial is remembered has much to do with power. The powerful shape memory for public consumption. After reunification, explanations of Buchenwald have since changed as the anti-Fascist rhetoric has changed. One of the important points Wegner raises is that collective memory is not static. Collective memory changes primarily because of politics.

Historians and novelists are not immune from the politics of memory. Academic politics influence whether one considers legitimate certain kinds of memory. Academic politics influences whether one considers legitimate literary and or historical representations of the Holocaust. Because some academics feel that historians are the keepers of memory and represent an authoritative voice of the past, historians' renderings of the Holocaust seem to be more legitimate than novelists' renderings. Historians are considered, by some, to be arbiters of truth and gatherers of hard facts, while novelists are considered mere dreamers. James Young (1988) writes that this attitude, which he claims is perpetuated by historians, deligitimates and denigrates literary representations of the Holocaust. Literary representations seem second rate, trivial, and unimportant. This unfortunate attitude on the part of some historians and others inside the academy who relegate the humanities to a second class status, has done much damage to the ways in which we create memory around the Holocaust. Literary representations are just as important to the memory of this event as historical accounts. It is not enough to read historical representations of the Holocaust. I argue that both historical and literary representations are crucial and should be read alongside each other. But the politics of the academy has much to do with what it is we remember and what becomes more valued as memory.

The politics of memory is what Elizabeth Ellsworth (1997) becomes concerned about in her book entitled *Teaching Positions: Difference, Pedagogy and the Power of Address.* Ellsworth (1997) draws on Shoshana Felman's interpretation of Claude Lanzmann's (1985) film *Shoah.* "The political labor of memory construction," (p. 178) writes Ellsworth, turns much on the ways in which we understand this event. Ellsworth argues that notions of communicative dialogue, representation, and understanding cannot help us fathom that which is discontinuous, that which moves beyond representation, and that which we really cannot understand after all. Concepts like communication, dialogue, and representation do not do justice to the memory of the Holocaust, Ellsworth suggests. These concepts attempt to know too much, attempt to promise too much. These concepts offer up closure where there is none, truth where there is none. Ellsworth (1997) declares that:

> This question [about the Holocaust] is not "about" truth or establishing warrants for action. The question is about the necessity, the right, the responsibility of participating in the ongoing, never completed historical, social, and political labor of memory construction. (pp. 177–178)

Lanzmann's film *Shoah* (1985) "teaches through analytic dialogue, through the discontinuity and the impossibility of full understanding" (Ellsworth, p. 115). Ellsworth stresses the discontinuity of this event.

The discontinuity of this event is not only due to differing perspectives of victims, bystanders, and perpetrators, but the discontinuity is also a psychological one. This discontinuity is because of "the splitness of my own psyche" (p. 124). Ellsworth argues that this splitness is "beyond any conscious control" (p. 124). Exactly what this split psyche is, Ellsworth does not elaborate. But I think she is suggesting that perhaps encounters with Holocaust texts create a split in the psyche because the event is so hideous. A split off part of the self is a repressed self. This repressed self attempts to protect the ego from being overwhelmed.

Ellsworth (1997) argues that what we should be concerned about are active engagements with Holocaust texts, with responses to these texts, and the aporetic nature of these responses. The consequences of responding to these texts in a certain way are not clear. We do not know what the implications of our response will be. Further, Ellsworth wants to "foreground the notion of performativity" (p. 136). "What has reading performed or let loose in the world?" (p. 128). What are the implications of our "mode[s] of address?" (p. 116). Ellsworth stresses again that these implications are not clear.

I believe that Ellsworth raises some important questions. She is right to point out the difficulties and uncertainties that abound when approaching Holocaust texts. Unsettling our notions of clarity or understanding, Ellsworth is on target. Representing the Holocaust is not an easy task and many questions remain about the effects of these representations on readers and researchers. I also agree with Ellsworth that the notion of response is important. Of course we must respond to these memories. My own work has emerged from an ethical sensibility around the notion of response.

Unlike Ellsworth, however, I claim that notions of representation and understanding, although problematic, do not always lead to closure or certainty. Unlike Ellsworth, I believe that notions of "truthfulness" (Wyschogrod, 1998, p. 10) are crucial in this discussion, especially in light of Holocaust deniers and so-called revisionists who operate to unwrite the Holocaust altogether. I contend that we work at the limits of understanding, empathy, and representation. Our perspectives are partial and situated. I suggest that understanding the Holocaust is always already an ambivalent undertaking. Representing this event in textual form does not necessarily imply mapping it onto a corresponding reality. But approximations of truthfulness are key if our representations are to be adequate to the memory of the victims and survivors. Further, I argue that understandings and representations are always already tenuous because of psychological interferences which guide interpretations. Ellsworth (1997) says that this event is haunted by discontinuities. I draw on the work of Jean Laplanche (1999) to try to untangle some of the psychological reasons why this event is discontinuous. Laplanche (1999) says that we have a "primordial split self" (p. 220). The self is split because of the otherness of the unconscious. The unconscious is not our center, rather it is perpetually and radically "decentered" (p. 52). Human subjectivity is marked by an "ex-centricity" because there is no center to the self (p. 52). The self is a stranger to itself. This stranger within, the stranger of the unconscious is what creates a split self. Extending Ellsworth's (1997) notion of the split psyche, I attempt to draw out in more detail what the implications of a split self might mean when interpreting Holocaust texts. Drawing on Freudian, Kleinian, Fairbairnian, and Laplanchian psychoanalytic theory, I hope to raise questions not only about the split self as it encounters Holocaust texts, I also hope to raise questions around symbiosis, internal objects, mental representations, alterity, and individuation. Thus, my study is more grounded in psychoanalytic theory than Ellsworth's and this theory helps me to understand why phantasy, good and bad objects, and projection and transference all play roles in the notion of split selves and why they are relevant to studying the Holocaust. A split-off self, a repressed self, a dissociated self, a detached self, could all have many implications when it is that self who is trying to untangle responses and "modes of address." The notion of the split self, though, is complex and demands interrogation.

Like Ellsworth, Deborah P. Britzman (1998), in her book *Lost Subjects, Contested Objects: Toward a psychoanalytic inquiry of learning* discusses how a "mode of address" (p. 119) is made complex by approaching what she terms *difficult knowledges* (p. 119). Like Ellsworth, Britzman (1998) suggests that the Holocaust demands,

> A patience with the incommensurability of understanding ... the ways meaning becomes ... fractured, broken and lost, exceeding the affirmation of rationality, consciousness and consolation. (p. 118)

Like Langer (1998), Hartman (1996), and Ofer and Weitzman (1998), Britzman worries that the very discourse we use to interpret Holocaust texts may become suspect. Britzman (1998) warns against consoling or comfortable language around "difficult knowledges" (p. 119). She suggests that words like courage and hope only reflect psychological defense mechanisms that serve to protect against pain. Britzman draws heavily on the problematics of the utilization of defense mechanisms and the ways in which these can protect readers from experiencing pain. "These mechanisms of defense ... are key ways the ego attempts to console itself" (p. 119). In my own work, I too draw on the problematics of defense mechanisms. However, I think my work differs from

Britzman's because I also worry about the complexities around the notion of transference and tease out different interpretations of this term.

Both Ellsworth and Britzman use Holocaust texts as examples of the ways in which educators might grapple with "difficult knowledges" (Britzman, 1998, p. 119). It seems to me that both writers suggest pedagogical strategies to cope with horrors beyond our imagination. Ellsworth (1997) suggests that the Shoah is "pertinent to all teaching situations" (p. 115). Against this position, I argue that learning about the Holocaust is not pertinent to all teaching situations; it is only pertinent to teaching and learning about the Holocaust. I do not think encounters of the Holocaust are generalizable, nor should they be. The Holocaust and our encounters with it should not be lumped together with Hiroshima or Stalinist crimes. There are no universal messages to be drawn. I argue for the radical alterity and uniqueness of the Holocaust. Any move toward comparability is a move which levels the horrors specific to the black sun of Auschwitz. Comparing Auschwitz to something else denigrates this Jewish tragedy. My approach also differs from Ellsworth and Britzman because I do not suggest pedagogical strategies. My work turns on the notion of understanding and what it means to be an educated person in a post-Holocaust era. The Holocaust is 'post' in a complex way. Although historically the Holocaust is an event that has ended, in many ways it is not located in the past, but rather, intersects with our current lived experience and will effect future generations. It effects us in ways that haunt; the ghost of the Holocaust is here to stay. There is an uncanny presence in its absence. Distance from the event seems to create an increasing weight, an increasing anxiety, in the hearts and souls of many as it lives on and seems to take on a life of its own. Thus, the teaching of the Holocaust will spring from our understanding of it. Curriculum theory is a call to understanding. In fact, "the field today is preoccupied with understanding" (Pinar, Reynolds, Slattery, & Taubman, 1995, p. 6). I am interested in examining what it is a curriculum theorist can understand about an event that is beyond understanding.

In *The International Journal on Audio-Visual Testimony*, in an article titled "The Contribution of Holocaust Audio-Visual Testimony to Remembrance, Learning and Hope," Roger Simon (1998) suggests that educators encounter audio-visual testimony alongside the reading of historical accounts. Simon (1998) argues that testimonies enable one to engage with Holocaust texts in a personal way "not limited to abstract and objectified forms of historical interpretation" (p. 148). Here, the viewer must "respond responsibly" (p. 147). Like Ellsworth, Simon is concerned about the importance of response. Recall that, for Ellsworth, responding is an ambiguous performative activity because one does not know beforehand the consequences of one's response. There are always discontinuities between one's response and the consequences of responding in a particular way. Like Ellsworth, Simon (1998) says that responding to testimony demands "an attending to alterity, to a difference not easily or ethically reduced to the terms of one's own self-understanding" (p. 147). I agree with Simon here. Like Simon, I argue that the alterity of the text, the otherness of the text of the Holocaust, must be kept intact. Unlike Simon, I suggest that this otherness is not only due to epistemological problems, but also to unconscious traces left or deposited in the text by the other and is co-complexified by my unconscious transferential relation to the text. Although Simon mentions that resistance to viewing testimony will prevail, he does not unfold the psychological reasons why this might occur.

Simon (1998) suggests that there are two kinds of responses to testimony: the "spectatorial" (p. 147) and the "summoned" (p. 148). Simon does not privilege one kind of response over against the other, but he maintains rather that these are different ways in which one may respond to Holocaust survivor testimony. The "spectatorial" (p. 147) reception of Holocaust testimony, is a "sensibility [that] embodies and enacts a capacity to group a given testimony within frames of understanding which render it intelligible and meaningful" (p. 148). It seems to me that the spectator's perception is marked by distance, by a detached and intellectualized engagement. At this level of reception, one could say that the viewer understands what the survivor says. However, at a deeper more psychological level, the observer who remains a stranger to this event cannot understand what the survivor says after all. Radical alterity mitigates against any clear understanding of what it is the survivor says. I think that Simon's spectator who can make sense of what she hears, and make intelligible what she sees, admits too much. The spectator's reception, to me, seems naive.

Drawing on the work of Levinas, Simon (1998) suggests that another kind of reception of Holocaust testimony is what he calls "the summoned" (p. 147). When one feels summoned to hear the call of the other, one engages in a response which opens toward the listener's "vulnerability" (p. 148) so as to be summoned, to open oneself to pain. Like Simon, I suggest that one needs to embrace a psychological readiness if one wishes to engage in this kind of work. I contend also that it is not just a question of the reader's or listener's vulnerability. What is at stake is even more than this. Researchers need to be prepared for the possibility of being traumatized. Of course, not everyone who does work on the Holocaust becomes traumatized. Certainly researchers will not experience trauma in the same ways as Holocaust survivors. But there are traces of trauma deposited in these texts, deposited deeply from the unconscious of the writer. The reader's own unconscious will interact with these complex psychodynamics and it is almost unavoidable that some sort of psychic upheaval will occur. The intensity of this psychic upheaval the researcher may experience has much to do with her own psychic makeup, family history, and her own personal memory in regard to the black sun of Auschwitz. What complexifies "intrapsychic trauma" according to Roth (1995b, p. 38) is that it might not happen at a conscious level. I will argue that Holocaust texts, because they are so hideous, cannot be assimilated consciously. As Freud (1915) pointed out, what transpires between one unconscious and another (the reader's unconscious and unconscious traces deposited in texts by the author) does not have to pass through consciousness at all. Thus the reading impacts the reader at the site of the unconscious in uncanny ways. Of course it is difficult to say when "intrapsychic" (Roth, 1995b, p. 38) trauma will emerge and in what form it might become manifest. Again, not every reader will experience this, but it is nearly unavoidable if one is truly emotionally and intellectually engaged with these difficult memories.

Simon (1998) calls the engagement with Holocaust testimony a "hopeful project" (p. 141). This is not a "utopian" (p. 141) hope, one that is pointed toward the future, but a "present" (p. 141) hope. This is a "proleptic" hope, as Slattery (1999, p. 30) might say, one that is intertwined in past, present, and future. Simon (1998) contends that our very "re-thinking" (pp. 146–147) of the Holocaust and its necessarily "unsettling" (pp. 146–147) nature, and our openness to "loss" (p. 149), gives us hope in the continued remembrance of the Holocaust. Opposing Simon, Britzman (1998), Langer (1998), Hartman (1996), and Ofer and Weitzman (1998) suggest that the notion of hope is incompatible with the memory of Auschwitz. I too argue against hope. I argue for a dystopic curriculum. A curriculum that is not nihilistic but guided by an ethical sensibility. There is nothing hopeful about the Holocaust. Langer (1998) says, "What [do] hope and grace have to do with a historical episode that ended in mass murder?" (p. xiv).

In summary, Weaver, Wegner, Ellsworth, Britzman, and Simon have all done noteworthy work on the Holocaust. Each of these scholars demonstrates an ethical sensibility. I have learned much from their work. However, my study departs from what these scholars have done in many ways. I offer to educators a Holocaust curriculum which is interpreted through dystopic lenses. Under the sign of a dystopic curriculum, competing memories (those memories inscribed in historical representations and those inscribed in literary representations) emerge not as a promise of hope, but as a testament to despair.

In chapter 2, I offer a psychoanalytic hermeneutic that might help us to understand the complexities involved when attempting to "recover memory" (Pinar, 1991, pp. 173–174). Generally speaking, I argue that unconscious processes may, in some way, determine what gets represented as Holocaust memory in the first place. I also suggest that unconscious psychological processes guide our responses to these difficult memories. More specifically, in chapter 2, I examine what I term the *vicissitudes* of classical psychoanalytic theory. I suggest that Freudian theory can be interpreted in a post-Freudian way. A post-Freudian reading of Freud avoids some of the pitfalls of pathologizing and reducing complex ideas to simple ones. Post-Freudian thinking helps to raise questions about the ways in which people respond to the Holocaust. I draw primarily on the writings of Jean Laplanche, who I consider to be one of the most important post-Freudian interpreters on the scene. Further, I draw on object-relations theorists, primarily Melanie Klein and Ronald Fairbairn, because these thinkers help raise questions that become pertinent to discussions on the Holocaust. Finally, I examine the disciplines of psychohistory and psychobiography in the context of the Holocaust and discuss potential promises and shortcomings of these discourses. I argue that psychohistory and psychobiography must not reduce people to categories, must not reduce suffering to labels, and must not pathologize. Psychohistories and psychobiographies are more useful when they work toward complexifying their subject matter. When psychoanalytic concepts are applied to historical events, overdetermination is key. A more adequate analysis of the Holocaust works to keep the otherness of suffering in place. I suggest that we are always strangers to the suffering of others.

In chapter 3, I examine what I term *classical* and *postmodern* notions of representation and discuss possible psychological effects for Jews, of anti-Semitic representations of Jewish subjects. I contend that although there were many reasons that the Holocaust occurred, one cannot reduce these causes to anti-Semitism. Still anti-Semitism played a large role in the rise of the Nazi era and the 'Final Solution.' Therefore, it becomes important for educators to grapple with anti-Semitic representations. Because the anti-Semite and the Jew have interconnected, and perhaps symbiotic, "representational trajectories" (Nochlin, 1995, p. 1), it is crucial to reflect on the relations of anti-Semitic projections and Jewish introjections of these representations.

In chapter 4, I unravel some complexities around the notions of memory and history. I suggest that memory is the larger category under which history may be subsumed, although history is not reducible to memory. I show how the discipline of history grew out of literature during the 17th century. It is important to understand the connections between history and literature. Although history shares certain features with literature, it is not reducible to it. Like history, I contend that literature is a form of memory, an expression of memory.

What I term the *memory text of Holocaust histories* will be fleshed out in chapter 5. Here I analyze perpetrator, victim, and bystander histories. The literature on perpetrators, in particular, is massive. Here, I highlight general trends in Holocaust historiography. My analysis is partial but I hope that it will untangle some of the key debates that have appeared in the literature since the 1960s.

The literature on Holocaust victims tends to be less systematized because it is scattered across many kinds of texts such as diaries, memoirs, biographies, and cultural histories. Moreover, victims have been, for the most part, erased from Holocaust historiography because it has traditionally been thought that victims' testimonies are unreliable. As Weaver (in press) points out, the very methodology of history has made Jewish victims invisible. I attempt to recover the most marginalized groups of victims of the Holocaust: women and gays and lesbians. I also turn to work that has been done by psychoanalysts with victims of the Holocaust.

In the third section of chapter 5, I examine bystander historiography. Here I am primarily interested in examining two collaborating countries, Italy and France, and two bystander countries, Britain and the United States. I stress that these countries responded (or did not respond) in complex and contradictory ways. Here I am interested in looking at the complexities of response and the ways in which repressed memory and psychological denial play a role in shaping the memories of the Holocaust.

Educators who are new to these conversations might object to the seemingly simplistic categories of victim, perpetrator, and bystander. However, I divide chapter 5 into these categories because these are the categories historians use to make sense of the event. It must always be kept in mind, though, that these categories can be reductionistic and might even obscure issues. However, I feel that these categories, for the most part, are helpful.

Chapter 6 deals with what I term the *memory text of Holocaust novels*. Here I examine current debates around the very act of writing these novels. I turn to literary critics. Then I turn to both Jewish and German non-Jewish Holocaust novels. I draw on psychoanalytic theory to interpret these works.

Chapter 7 is entitled "Under the Sign of a Dystopic Curriculum." The title is in memory of Bruno Schulz. Schulz's (1939/1979) novel, *Sanatorium Under the Sign of the Hourglass*, was written just a few years before he was killed by the Nazis. Schulz was a Jew, a teacher, a poet, and a novelist whom many consider to have been as great a writer as Kafka.

John Updike (1979) comments that Schulz's "panoramas disclose themselves ... through the lens of memory" (p. xiii). In this final chapter, I suggest that it becomes important to look at utopian discourse that historically has served to other. I contend that utopian thinking, generally speaking, is not able to manage difference. Two thousand years of utopian thinking created the conditions, in part, for the Holocaust to emerge. The Holocaust was Hitler's utopia. Of course, there are many complex reasons why the Holocaust happened. But utopian thinking was certainly part of the story. Hitler's (1923) *Mein Kampf* set the stage for a völkisch utopia which served to annihilate millions of Jews. Educators must become more critical of utopian thinking. In order to do this, one must first examine what it is that utopian thinking teaches. After examining some utopian models, I tease out the notion of dystopia. I argue that this might be a more adequate way to frame discussions around the Holocaust. Of course, frames limit; they can only offer up partial pictures. So the final chapter is not a conclusion in any formal sense. Perhaps the conversation has just begun. In the final chapter I tease out what I call a *dystopic curriculum*. Dystopic thinking is skeptical, critical. Dystopic thinking is a way of looking suspiciously at happy texts or utopias. Through a dystopic lens, I argue that the psychological process of transference is key to understanding why interpretations of this hideous event may turn it into yet another story with a happy ending. The Holocaust should never be the story of happy endings. Happy endings sound the cry of "hope."—I am suspicious of this word. Hope signifies something that makes little sense in a post-Holocaust era. We must keep the memory of Auschwitz difficult, hideous. There is nothing hopeful about the annihilation of 6 million Jews. A dystopic lens keeps the otherness of this memory intact. We must work to keep "planet Auschwitz" strange and never make it into something familiar or comfortable. Through the lens of a dystopic curriculum, educators might engage in memory work and this memory work is tough, not soft. This call to remembrance is a testament to suffering.

TWO

A Psychoanalytic Hermeneutic

To interpret competing memories of the Holocaust as they are represented in the writings of historians and novelists, I draw on psychoanalytic theory. It becomes important for educators to understand the complexities of psychoanalytic theory and some of the differences between classical Freudian theory, post-Freudian interpretations, and object relations theory and how these theories have been applied to Holocaust scholarship in what is termed *psychohistory*. In this chapter, my aim is to offer a brief historical overview of some general trends in psychoanalytic thinking so that we might be able to raise questions around the Holocaust in complex ways. Freudian, Laplanchian, Kleinian, and Fairbairnian psychoanalytic theory help raise questions around the ways in which we deal with the Holocaust. I want to point out that when we are talking about complex responses to difficult memories, complexifying the subject matter becomes key. I think reducing psychoanalytic terms to simple ones does not help to unpack Holocaust texts. Moreover, I think it is crucial to grasp a sense of the historical developments in psychoanalytic thinking in order to better contextualize and situate my own post-Freudian position. Psychoanalysis is a form of hermeneutics that offers insights helpful for understanding the ways in which we might psychologically frame memories, especially when these memories are repressed. The way in which we frame memories might be a clue to our own resistances and limitations when grappling with this horrific event called the Holocaust.

The task of recovering Holocaust memory, however, becomes difficult because researchers are subject to their own resistances, reversals, intellectualizations, projections, and denials. Many kinds of unconscious psychological mechanisms can alter the way we construct and reconstruct memory. A step toward recovering memory is to grapple with our own unconscious responses to difficult texts. Adequate interpretations of the Holocaust take account of the limits of interpretation due to psychological resistances. Adequate interpretations must do justice to victims and survivors. Yet attempts to tell and re-tell Holocaust memory must be made, keeping the limits of interpretation in mind. Justice is done if the re-telling approximates truthfulness and keeps intact the otherness of this memory. But interpreters cannot represent the Holocaust adequately if they are unaware of their own unconscious psychological resistances and repressions.

Transferential relations with texts complexify these responses. We transfer old patterns of perception onto new texts. These old patterns, perhaps established in early childhood, shape the ways in which we interpret and translate texts. Our awareness of these old habits helps to undo habitually complacent readings, readings that do not allow for the otherness of the text to emerge, readings that do not allow for interference, discontinuity, and difference to emerge. Reading Holocaust texts interferes with complacency because psychic upheavals do not allow for assimilation into consciousness. These psychic upheavals get introjected into the unconscious and take on a life of their own.

THE VICISSITUDES OF CLASSICAL PSYCHOANALYTIC THEORY

A psychoanalytic hermeneutic is necessarily incomplete and ambivalent. Addressing Holocaust texts always keeps us at the limits of interpretation. It would be arrogant to suggest that a psychoanalytic hermeneutic could get it right or tell the absolute truth about the Holocaust. I want to emphasize that the call that has addressed me to do work around the Holocaust continually announces itself in interferences and ruptures. I am continually unsettled. Doing interpretive work around these texts causes unsettling ruptures in understanding and ruptures in representation. In working toward understanding these difficult memories, I realize how little an outsider to this event can understand. I stand outside this event because I am not a Holocaust survivor and thus I am always looking at this event through the memory text of others. At the moment I think I grasp Holocaust memory, this grasp is ruptured. Psychoanalytic theory can do only so much to help us understand. Saul Friedländer (1978) remarks that "A successful application of Freud's notions to history [or anybody else's notions for that matter] would lead to a partial explanation of a partial series of events" (p. 5). A psychoanalytic hermeneutic is indeed a partial explanation. Still, I argue that psychoanalytic notions can serve as powerful tools of interpretation.

Psychoanalytic theory is not monolithic. Edith Kurzweil (1998), comments that "the fragmentation of psychoanalytic theory proves, among other things, that the Freudians primarily are united by their profession rather than by their ideas" (p. ix). Deter Wyss (1961/1973) categorizes splits in the field of psychoanalysis as follows: The Freudian school, he suggests, includes Abraham, Ferenczi, and Fenichel. The New York Group includes Hartmann, Kris, Loewenstein, Erikson, Greenacre, Reich, Reick, Federn, and Alexander. The neo-Freudians include Adler, Horney, Fromm, Rado, and Sulliven. The British Group includes Glover, Jones, Anna Freud, and Klein. The British Group split because of disagreements between Melanie Klein and Anna Freud. Greenberg and Mitchell (1983) tell us that the British Group split into the A Group (followers of Anna Freud), the B Group (followers of Melanie Klein) and the Middle Group (followers of Winnicott and Fairbairn). Sandler and Sandler (1998) however, suggest that the A Group includes Kleinians and the B Group "contemporary Freudians" (p. ix). Sandler and Sandler refer to the Middle Group as the "Group of Independent Analysts" (p. ix). The British Group is known for what is called object relations theory. Sandler and Sandler (1998) suggest that object relations theorists include "Margaret Mahler, Rene Spitz, Ronald Fairbairn, Erik Erikson, Michael Balint, Donald Winnicott, Heinz Hartman, Edith Jacobson, Heinz Kohut, John Bowlby, Harry Guntrip, Arnold Modell, Otto Kernberg, Wilfred Bion" (p. ix). I would add to these lists post-Freudians like Christopher Bollas, Adam Phillips, Andre Green, Jean Laplanche, Martin Stanton, and Julia Kristeva. Post-Lacanians might include Bice Benvenuto, Dary Nubs, Filip Geer-a-dyn, and Judith Guruvich (Burgoyne & Sullivan, 1997). Kleinians, Fairbairnians, post-Freudians, and post-Lacanians agree on little. And interestingly enough, many of these splits in the field have been caused over interpretations of Freud's texts. Otto Kernberg (1998) points out that

> The interpersonal, intersubjective, and self psychoanalytic theorists feel that Freud and object relations are incompatible because it is impossible to reconcile drive theory with object relations. Conversely, Kleinian Independent [British Independent Group] and ego-psychology theorists feel that those theories are compatible. (p. xvi)

The question around whether or not theories like object relations are continuous or discontinuous with Freud's initial project has caused rifts within the field of psychoanalysis. However, this debate seems misguided because every new interpretation of Freud's texts alters his initial intentions, no matter how continuous, orthodox, or close the reading. There is no authoritative or definitive reading of Freud.

In part, difficulties around Freud's texts are due to James Strachey's English translation of Freud, which is referred to as the Standard Edition of the Complete Psychological Works of Freud, or simply, SE. Many scholars feel that Strachey's translation is the most definitive and authoritative one. Thus, Strachey's translation has become the "standard" reading of Freud. Scholars' loyalty to Strachey's translation presupposes that again, Strachey has gotten Freud right, that his is the closest reading. But some point out that Strachey's translation is skewed and re-presents a Freud which is more scientific and medicalized than Freud. Ilse Grubrich-Simitis (1996) tells us that

> For the past dozen years or so, James Strachey's English translation, as presented in the Standard Edition of the Complete Psychological Works of Sigmund Freud, has been the butt of vehement criticism. The criticism was brought to the attention of a wider public in 1983 by Bruno Bettleheim's book essay Freud and Man's Soul ... its author accuses Freud's English translations, including of course James Strachey, of corrupting Freud's humanistic project, set down in the vernacular ... by their scientistic, medicalized rendering. (p. 11)

The scientistic, medicalized rendering does pose problems for the reader. Strachey's translation gives the impression that Freud was even more prone to pathologize and medicalize than he was. Medicalized and scientistic language also give the impression that Freud's notions function in a way that reify and reduce. Notions that medicalize function as a diagnosis for an illness. Illnesses need to be cured. Certainly this is one way to read Freud.

However, a post-Freudian interpretation of Freud might sound different. A post-Freudian reading of Freud does not reify notions of self but points to complexities and ambiguities of self. Christopher Bollas, Adam Phillips, Andre Green, Martin Stanton, Jean Laplanche, and Jacques Derrida read Freud in a post-Freudian way. These scholars point out the ambivalences of Freud's texts. These scholars suggest that the project of Freudian analysis is not to reduce and pathologize, but to show, in fact, how strange and other we are, even to ourselves. The point here is not to use Freud to normalize and diagnose, but to use Freud to complexify notions around self and other. Instead of interpreting Freud as fixing problems and curing illness, Freud can also be interpreted through the lenses of ambivalence and uncertainty around who we are as human beings. Ambivalences concerning Freudian notions are something around which Jacques Derrida has remarked. Derrida (1996) comments that,

> Freud never managed to form anything that deserves to be called a concept ... [he offers to us] only an impression, a series of impressions associated with a word. To the vigor of the concept, I am opposing here the vagueness or the open impression, the relative indeterminacy of such a notion ... the unstable feeling of a shifting figure. (p. 29)

The Freudian notion of *introjection*, for example, is a slippery one. It is not something that is easily definable by Freud, or by anyone else for that matter. *Introjection* is a vague and shifting impression, as Derrida might say, pointing toward the ways in which we might internalize significant others into our psyche. Exactly how or why introjection happens is not clear. Freud suggests that after the resolution of the Oedipus Complex we introject images of our parents. How these significant others get internalized remains a mystery. What it is we do with these internal images is not clear either. Freud does not tell us, in any precise way, what it is we do with these internal images. Thus, a post-Freudian reading of Freud leaves open these kinds of questions. I suggest that we should use Freud's notions in a way that avoids pathologizing, diagnosing, or fixing, which reduces and reifies notions around identity and self.

Freud continually revised his texts and changed positions around many different ideas throughout his life. To say the least, Freud's texts are bewildering because of the contradictions, repetitions, and reversals readers find throughout his 24-volume masterpiece. Laplanche (1985) comments that

> It is above all certain large contradictions, traversing Freud's work from one end to the other, which must be interpreted dialectically, either as contradictions of thought—consequently referable to a certain "unspoken" dimension—or as contradictions of the object itself: such for instance, is the case for the major contradictions inherent in the notion of the "ego," at once a totality and a specific agency, a cathected love object that nevertheless arrogates to itself the position of a subject. (p. 1)

Laplanche is right to point out Freud's "unspoken" dimension. This unspoken dimension highlights Freud's own ambivalences around his work. These ambivalences, which result in the many contradictory positions one finds reading the vast landscape of Freudian theory, can become frustrating for the reader who wants clarity and certainty, but that is not what Freud's project was about. Certainly, to dismiss Freud because he tended to be contradictory is naive.

Freud seemed ambivalent about the nature of the psyche. It seems to me that the large change in Freud's own thinking turns on the notion of the unconscious. Early Freud divides the psychic apparatus into three systems. The *first topography* (Freud, 1932–1936b, p. 71) includes systems *Ucs.*, *Pcs.*, and *Cs.*, which are designated as the *unconscious*, *preconscious*, and *conscious*, respectively. Early on, Freud seemed to suggest that the unconscious played less of a role in our lives than consciousness. Freud became convinced later in his life that most of our lives are acted out unconsciously. Freud revises this first topography because he realizes that,

> Portions of the ego and superego [are] well unconscious ... we perceive that we have no right to name the mental region that is foreign to the ego the system Ucs; since the characteristic of being unconscious is not restricted to it. (p. 72)

Later Freud, therefore, designated these three areas of the psyche, or what is called the *second topography*, as *id*, *ego*, and *superego*. The id, or the unconscious, plays a much greater role in conscious life than initially assumed by Freud. The id covers over larger portions of both ego and superego than was once presupposed. Along with revising his mental topography, Freud changed his position around many other notions too. For example, the notion of anxiety, before 1926, suggests an overloading of stimulus. After 1926, the term *signal anxiety* appears and anxiety is considered "a device activated by the ego" (Laplanche & Pontalis, 1973, p. 422). Anxiety serves to ward off danger. Here anxiety plays a defensive role to protect the ego. This function of defense is the crucial change Freud makes around the notion of anxiety.

Along with revisions around the notions of topography and anxiety, Freud dropped the hypnotic method, dropped the term *defense hysteria*, and dropped the notion of *seduction theory*. Most notably, though, Freud became more pessimistic about human nature. In 1930, he began to talk about aggression and the death instinct; some suggest he was influenced by Melanie Klein. But it is against the backdrop of the rise of the Nazi era that Freud changed his mind about what it is that motivates human action. Peter Gay (1989) says, "Having long delayed the recognition of aggression as a fundamental human endowment, Freud, in his later years, confessed that he could no longer conceive of the mind without it" (p. xxviii). It is important to understand that Freud's later work was written against the backdrop of Hitler's ascendency to power. Hitler was elected in 1933, and Freud, subject to his own denial and resistances, "refused" (Gay, 1989, p. xlvi) to believe that the Nazis would overshadow all of Europe. While many Jewish psychoanalysts had already fled Europe by 1933, Freud refused to leave until his daughter

Anna was "summoned to [the] Gestapo" (Gay, 1989, p. xlvii). Finally, Freud fled to London and died in 1939. He was, however, not totally oblivious to what was happening. We read in the final lines of Freud's *Civilization and Its Discontents* that

> Men have gained control over the forces of nature to such an extent that with their help they would have no difficulty in exterminating one another. And now it is to be expected that the other of the two 'Heavenly Powers' ... eternal Eros, will make an effort to assert himself.... But who can foresee with what success and with what result? (p. 104)

James Strachey (1961) notes that the last sentence of *Civilization and Its Discontents* was added in 1931 when "the menace of Hitler was already beginning to be apparent" (p. 104).

No matter what objections one might have to reading Freud and utilizing his psychoanalytic notions, it must be acknowledged that Freud is a major figure of our time and has changed our language and the landscape of Western culture. Jacques Derrida (1996) says that

> The nearly unforgettable and incontestible, and undeniable impression (even above all for those who deny it) that Sigmund Freud will have made on anyone, after him, who speak of him or speak to him, and who must, accepting it or not, knowing it or not, be thus marked.... If one is under the impression that it is possible not to take into account, forgetting it, effacing it, crossing it out, or objecting to it, one has already confirmed ... even countersigned (thus achieved) a "repression" (pp. 30–31).

Freud suggests in his second topography that there are three places of mind: the id, ego and superego. The ego and superego are born out of the id, and to a great extent the id covers over both ego and superego. The id seeks "satisfaction" (Freud, 1914-1916a, pp. 122–123) of libidinal "aims." "The object [objeht] of an instinct ... may be changed any number of times" (pp. 122–123). The object around which the instinct aims is secondary, while the satisfaction of the libido is primary. The id, Freud (1932-1936b) tells us, "has no organization ... contrary impulses exist side by side.... There is nothing in the id that could be called negation ... [nothing] compares to time ... no alteration in its mental processes is produced by the presence of time" (p. 74). What is unconscious is not remembered. For Freud, there is no such thing as a dim unconscious or shadowy unconscious. What is unconscious cannot be remembered.

Freud (1959) says that "the ego is identical with the id, and is merely a specially differentiated part of it.... The same is true of the relation between the ego and superego. In many situations they are merged" (p. 17). However, Freud also says that the ego is not identical with the id because unlike the id, the ego is "an organization" (p. 17), which has the "impulsion to bind together" (p. 19). Hence, it seems Freud is saying that the ego is both identical and not identical with the id. Thus, the aporia of the ego. Most of the content of consciousness, Freud suggests, is unconscious; therefore, much of our lives are acted out unconsciously.

The *superego* for Freud is a later development than either id or ego. The superego develops after the resolution of the Oedipus Complex. Laplanche and Pontalis (1973) explain that the Oedipus Complex is

> A desire for the death of the rival—the parent of the same sex—and sexual desire for the parent of the opposite sex ... [or] love for the parent of the same sex, and jealous hatred for the parent of the opposite sex. (p. 283)

If the child does not resolve the Oedipus Complex she will develop relationships in later life that unconsciously repeat these early struggles. Whether or not the Oedipus Complex is resolved, however, the child still introjects mental representations of her parents into her psyche. These introjections sound the voice of conscience. If a too-harsh superego emerges, then Freud might suggest that the Oedipus Complex has not been resolved. A too-harsh superego can cause psychic upheavals in later life and become unsettling. Many suggest that a too-harsh superego is the root of sadism.

If the Oedipus Complex is not resolved, repression of unbearable thoughts about parents occur. Freud (1937/1991) says that,

> All repressions take place in early childhood; they are primitive defense mechanisms taken by an immature, feeble ego. In later years no fresh repressions are carried out; but the older ones persist ... new conflicts are disposed of by ... after repression. (p. 14)

After repressions, then, are uncanny repetitions of old conflicts in new forms. Repressed material pushes upward and has "an impulsion to break through" to consciousness (Freud, 1932-1936, p. 68). But the ego, which manifests resistances, pushes against repressed material, preventing it from being made conscious. Juan-David Nasio (1998) explains that

> The more the ego attacks the representation [which is intolerable] the more it isolates it. This defensive spirt of effort on the part of the ego is precisely what Freud calls repression ... repression primarily means isolation. It is because this representation has become radically separated from the other organized representations of psychic life that it becomes fundamentally unbearable. (p. 17)

That which is repressed returns. But it returns in the form of disguises and displacements. Hysteric, phobic, schizophrenic, depressive, or obsessional acting-out are signals that something old is not being remembered or has not been worked through. These are symptoms that signal the failure of repression. Repression has failed to keep these interferences pushed down into the unconscious registers. What is old and not worked through arrives at the conscious level in bizarre forms which take on their own trajectories and unfold in their own time.

Repression is considered by Freud (1914-1916a), as one of the "vicissitudes of the instincts" (p. 126). Instincts "undergo the following vicissitudes—reversal into its opposite, turning around upon the subject or self, repression, sublimation" (p. 126). These vicissitudes serve to protect the ego from the flooding of negative or unpleasurable stimuli. In her book, *The Ego and The Mechanisms of Defense* Anna Freud (1966/1993) fleshes out these so-called vicissitudes under the name *defense mechanisms*. Anna Freud expands her father's list of vicissitudes, terming defense mechanisms "regression, repression, reaction formation, isolation, undoing, projection, introjection, turning against the self, reversal ... displacement" (p. 44). She also mentions other kinds of defense mechanisms such as intellectualization and identification with the aggressor. Understanding defense mechanisms becomes key, especially when one attempts to deconstruct responses researchers might have reading Holocaust texts.

Defense mechanisms are used by the psyche to protect the ego from pain. We utilize them throughout life. They can help or hurt, depending on what they are used for. When examining Holocaust texts we need to understand some of the ways defense mechanisms work to shut off intolerable thoughts from conscious awareness. Thus, it becomes crucial to flesh out some of the defense mechanisms that are relevant to Holocaust memory work.

Denial is the most obvious form of defense. There are all types of denials. To deny, for instance, that the Holocaust happened is a form of defense against pain. Holocaust deniers are easy to dismiss as kooks, but it is frightening to realize that their numbers continually grow. So-called revisionists practice another form of denial by re-writing the Holocaust in ways that falsify. Some revisionists say that fewer than 6 million Jews were murdered; some argue that gas chambers did not exist. Some argue that only Nazis were complicit and not ordinary Germans, the *Wehrmacht* (the German army) or police reserve units. Some argue that the real culprits were the Russians, not the Germans, who merely imitated the Gulag system in order to prevent Russians from putting Germans in Gulags. The Russians, in other words, should be blamed for starting up concentration camps, while Germans merely imitated the

Russians so not to be killed themselves. Some claim that the Holocaust was a Jewish plot to acquire Israel. These bizarre rationalizations, reversals, and outright lies are all forms of denial. Although these revisionist beliefs seem crazy to me and to others doing work around the Holocaust, they seem perfectly reasonable to the revisionists. This is what is unsettling.

Another form of denial is prevalent among East Germans. Recall that East Germans have traditionally considered themselves, not Jews, to be the victims of history. Anti-Fascist rhetoric serves as a defense mechanism against pain, against the idea that Germans, East and West, were complicit. East German Communists persecuted Jews and perpetuated anti-Semitic crimes against Jews even after the close of World War II. Margaret Mitscherlich-Nielson (1989) points to the way in which Germans have generally been in denial since the end of the war. She says that

> After the defeat [of Germany] there was first an abrupt derealization; the past simply faded away like a dream. The switch of identity through identification with the victims, accomplished as it was without particularly noticeable signs of injured pride, reinforced the defense against any feelings of being implicated. The manic effect to undo, the enormous effort to rebuild, a kind of nationally accepted therapy, made permanent denial and repression possible for the majority of Germans. (p. 406)

The idea that Germans were victims of history is a form of defense, a denial that serves to protect the ego from pain. In Germany, many levels of this denial are still intact today.

One of the bizarre manifestations of denial for Germans concerns the arrival of *philosemitism* during the 1970s and 1980s (Rapaport, 1997). Against the backdrop of the Holocaust and Germany's long history of anti-Semitism, it seems odd that all things Jewish had suddenly become fashionable. German Jews seem to be, for the most part, skeptical of this; many say that they live in Germany but 'sit on their suitcases.' I would suggest that philosemitism, at least for Germans, could function as a reaction formation. Laplanche and Pontalis (1973) note this is a

> Psychological attitude or habitus diametrically opposed to a repressed wish, and constituted as reaction against it ... reaction-formation is the counter-cathexis of a conscious element equal in strength to the unconscious cathexis, it works in the contrary direction. (p. 376)

Philosemitism masks an anti-Semitism, and I think that I would subsume reaction formations as forms of defense. Underneath the love for all things Jewish is a more insidious hatred.

Projection is another defense mechanism that becomes useful to look at when studying the perpetrators of the Holocaust. *Projection* is a defense mechanism that perpetrators utilized to justify scapegoating and ultimately murdering Jews. When the ego cannot tolerate its own heart of darkness, its own negativity, it projects negativity onto the other to rid itself of intolerable thoughts. Andre Green (1986) says that "Projection is linked to a primary defense mechanism fundamentally defined by the action of expelling; of casting out (to project—to spit, to vomit) something within which is unpleasant" (p. 85). Green says further that projection is "closely linked to paranoia" (p. 85). The anti-Semite is paranoid because he feels, in a move of reversal, that the Jew is the persecutor. Anti-Semites throughout history, and especially during the Middle Ages, had bizarre phantasies about Jews. Jews had been thought to be the devil, Christ killers, bloodsuckers, and cannibals. Of course, these phantasies have absolutely no basis in reality, they are projected onto the Jew because the anti-Semite cannot tolerate his own heart of darkness: He projects it onto the Jew so as to rid himself of badness.

Along with the mechanism of projection, the defense mechanism of *splitting* might have allowed perpetrators to carry out murder, while repressing the emotional effects of killing. Lifton (1986) and Kelman (1976) point out that Nazi doctors and camp guards might have experienced a process of derealization and numbing, becoming desensitized to what they were doing. Sometimes this desensitization led to splitting, or what Lifton (1986) calls *doubling* (p. 6). Green (1986) points out that splitting and repression for Freud are two different things, but both serve to protect the ego from flooding of negative feelings. "In splitting the relationship [between id and ego] is horizontal; the reason of the ego and the reason of the instinctual demands coexist.... It says 'yes' and 'no' at the same time" (pp. 25–26). Unlike splitting, repression, for Freud, is a "vertical move" (p. 25) which pushes against the ego's resistances. Lifton and Kelman, when they talk of splitting, suggest the simultaneity of experiencing two selves at once. The man who kills experiences himself in two places at once. He pulls the trigger, but while doing so is split off from the act psychologically. From the site of his observing ego he watches himself, distancing himself from the act of murder.

For victims and survivors of the Holocaust, the utilization of the mechanisms of defense were crucial for survival. But let me make it clear that the experiences of victims and victimizers were radically different and should never be leveled. I am not suggesting here that victims' experiences were the same as the victimizers, because both groups utilized defense mechanisms. People use defense mechanisms for radically different reasons in radically different circumstances. Without utilizing defense mechanisms, we would lapse into a state of psychosis. According to Freud, everyone needs defenses to be ego syntonic. Without defenses, our egos would simply deteriorate. For victims and survivors of the Holocaust defense mechanisms became crucial. Those who could not turn to stone emotionally endangered their existence. Splitting, which serves to cut off emotions and stop the flow of feeling, became prevalent among Jews. Bruno Bettlelheim (1971) remarked, while being deported to Dachau, "What happened to me—for instance, the split within me onto one who observed and one to whom things happened—was a typical schizoid phenomena" (p. 114). Splitting might have prevented the ego from deteriorating. But, at the end of the day, it is hard to say whether these defenses saved anybody. Bettleheim comments that all of the teachings of psychoanalysis that he took with him into the concentration camp became irrelevant. People who seemed to demonstrate a psychological togetherness, before the war, those who seemed to have intact egos before the advent of Auschwitz, responded in ways that completely stunned Bettelheim. He points out that psychoanalytic theory came up short against the horrors of the Holocaust and what these horrors did to the human psyche. Psychoanalytic theory did not help Bettelheim understand the complex responses of Jews. I think this is a very important point to keep in mind. Psychoanalytic theory can only explain so much.

Repressed memory around the Holocaust, for Jews, serves as yet another form of defense against pain. The not-telling, the pact of silence around this horrific event, is still very much a part of Jewish culture, although more people talk about the Holocaust today than they did 20 years ago. Even if Jewish survivors talk about this memory, the re-telling haunts. It becomes difficult to say whether talking about it or repressing it is more harmful. Many Jewish fiction writers, after having written about the Holocaust, committed suicide. But many analysts would suggest that repressing the memory has bad effects too. Many analysts suggest that lifting repressed memory might help undo depression and depersonalization. Dori Laub (1992) comments that repressing Holocaust memory eventually becomes harmful to the psyche, for the repressed returns. The repressed haunts in all sorts of bizarre ways.

> Survivors who do not tell their story become victims of a distorted memory, that is, of a forcibly imposed "external evil." ... The "not telling" of the story serves as a perpetuation of its tyranny. The events become more and more distorted in their silent retention and pervasively invade and contaminate the survivor's daily life. (p. 74)

Karl Abraham and Maria Torok have suggested that repression is not total. Unlike Freud, they suggest that memory becomes, rather, "encrypted" (in Bellamy, 1997, p. 21). An encrypted memory is one that is not wholly forgotten nor wholly remembered. It manifests itself, Bellamy tells us, "in the form of a "crypt"—a kind of melancholia that must inhabit an obscure threshold between memory and forgetting" (p. 21). Kestenberg (1989) points out that Shatan and Rosenfeld suggest that memory of Holocaust survivors is "encapsulated" or "jailed" (p. 386). Memory gets stuck; it becomes lodged in the heart of the psyche. Repressed memory is located somewhere between the remembered and the forgotten; it becomes haunting and torments survivors because it never goes away. Repressed memory somehow gets intrapsychically passed down to the next generation. Intergenerational trauma is a result of not working through encrypted and repressed memory. But it is difficult to say if these memories can ever really be worked through. Laplanche (1999) argues that when the repressed returns, it does not return as a copy of the originary trauma; rather, it becomes "dislocated" (p. 104) and forms what he calls a "double inscription" (p. 36). Second- and even third-generation Jews who are children or grandchildren of Holocaust survivors, suffer these dislocations and displacements. It is not uncommon for children of Holocaust survivors to suffer nightmares, even if their parents never talk about their experiences in the camps. A belated and unwelcome suffering haunts intergenerationally, but analysts really do not understand how repressed memory gets introjected into the next generation. The unconscious works in uncanny ways.

Researchers of the Holocaust are subject to their own psychological resistances, repressions, denials, and projections while working on this difficult memory. In general, curriculum theorists and educators who do work on the Holocaust might be on the lookout for their own intellectualizations of this difficult material. Anna Freud (1966/1993) suggests that intellectual activity, when it is divorced from emotional registers, serves as a defense against pain. Intellectualization is an "ascetic flight from instinct" (p. 162). It is not enough to engage in "abstract intellectual discussions and speculations" (p. 162), although these abstractions are important. Freud is not arguing here for anti-intellectualism, which is something altogether different from intellectualization. Rather, intellectualization is one way the ego compartmentalizes overwhelming emotional affects by detaching and separating them from emotional life. Laplanche and Pontalis (1973) comment that the trouble with intellectualization is that it cuts one off from emotional life:

> Intellectualization is comparable to other mechanisms described by psychoanalysis, and particularly to rationalization. One of the main aims of intellectualizations is to keep the affects at arms length, to neutralize them. (p. 225)

This process of neutralizing emotions in analysis becomes evident, for example, when the analysand draws on theoretical knowledge, of, say, psychoanalytic literature, while ignoring emotional conflicts at hand during the encounter of working with the analyst. Drawing on abstractions may work to avoid emotional reactions from being analyzed. To intellectualize is a way to explain away emotions. This is very dangerous when doing work around the Holocaust. If researchers do not feel anything while studying these horrific texts, something is wrong. More than likely, the researcher has shut down her emotional register. Distance and detachment from memory work damages both the researcher and her subjects of research. However, it is important to engage in intellectual activity but not at the expense of one's emotional life.

Researchers of the Holocaust are subject not only to their own resistances and repressions around difficult texts, but they are also subject to unconscious transferential relations with texts. One's awareness of transferential relations with texts may alter the ways in which interpretative work is done. At this juncture, I would like to flesh out the notion of transference and its relevance to self and other, and then draw out some implications of transference for interpreting texts.

Freud (1911-1913) tells us that the "compulsion to repeat" (p. 151) old patterns of relationships, formed with primary others or significant others, like our parents, shape the ways in which we handle relations with new people who come into our lives. "Repetition is a transference of the forgotten past" (Freud, p. 151). The forgotten past is most fundamentally an unconscious past. When a new person arrives on the scene, under the influence of transference, one tends to attribute qualities and feelings, thoughts, and phantasies that are, in essence, transferred from the past, from some other significant other who has become internalized in the psyche, onto the new person. The old and the new can get blurred. Sometimes one may even unconsciously seek out others who in some uncanny way, remind one of significant others from childhood, especially and ironically, if the relations one had with these significant others, were bad. Freud says that transference relations turn on "prototypes" (1966/1990, p. 29) from childhood which were primarily "unsatisfied," "libidinal cathexis" (p. 29). These prototypes "attach" themselves to "stereotype plates" (p. 29). Because the compulsion to repeat bad relations continues for some throughout life, and because it seems that the unconscious seeks its own destruction, Freud connects the compulsion to repeat with the death instinct.

The purpose of analysis, says Freud, is to help us undo transferences by becoming conscious of what is unconscious so that the cycle of abusive relations can stop. Arnold Cooper (1990) comments that Freud "believed that the transference represents a true reconstruction of the past, a vivid reliving of earlier desires and fears that distort the patient's capacity to perceive the "true nature" of the present reality" (p. 513). In analysis, the analysand misperceives the analyst who becomes blurred with the internalized phantasies of significant others. These *internal objects*, then, get transferred onto the analyst. Freud's project, and the project of classical psychoanalysis, is to untangle these distortions and resolve the transference so that the analyst can appear as she actually is to the analysand. The object of analysis is to send internal objects back to their original source, to send these phantoms back where they belong, back home. Internal objects, or what Freud calls *stereotype plates*, usually represent the image of the mother or father or any other significant other who shaped one's childhood. But when these images get projected onto other people, the identities of the new people become blurred with the identities of the parents. The internal other, who is a sort of double of the original other or, say, the mother, must go back home. The analyst is not the mother, although the analysand may see her that way. The analyst may be a second mother figure, but she is not the mother. Analysis is supposed to untangle these confusions. But whether it can do this is questionable.

Freud uses the word transference in several senses. Generalized transference, Freud suggests, happens all the time and is not particular to the analytic situation. Transference at this level is a psychical process that is not, strictly speaking, induced only in the analytic situation. But in the analytic situation, the nature of transference changes. As analysis progresses, as anxiety is created by the analytic situation itself, the transference heightens and it changes from a generalized transference to a more specific one. This specific transference, which gets deposited onto the analyst, Freud called *transference neurosis*. Analyst Brian Bird (1990) explains, "When I think of transference, I think of feelings, of reactions, and of a repetition of past events; but when I think of transference neurosis, I think literally of neurosis. A transference neurosis is merely a new edition of the patient's original neurosis, but with me in it" (p. 343). When the analyst becomes the center of the analysand's anxieties, this is a signal that transference neurosis has arrived. Transference neurosis, according to Freud, can be experienced both as sexual and hostile. Freud suggests that both of these responses to the analyst serve as resistances to getting underneath the repressed unconscious. To sort out the actual from the phantasized images that blur relations due to transference, the activity of transference neurosis must be enacted. Otherwise, analysis will fail.

But transference is not that simple. The analyst, too, undergoes changes in her unconscious as a result of the patient's transference relations with her. Freud mentions only briefly that the analyst's unconscious is subject to what he terms *countertransference*. Freud suggests that countertransference should be avoided. Countertransference is seen by Freud primarily as sexual in nature and as an impediment to the analysand's treatment and the analyst's work.

In current psychoanalytic literature around the notion of transference analysts point out its complexities. Arnold Cooper (1990) remarks that "Today, the idea of transference has become so complex that we are no longer sure what in the analysis is not transference, and if it is not, what it is" (p. 527). If transference clouds lived experience, can we ever be in relation with others in a way that does not blur who these others are in our perception of them? Or are others always already blurred with patterns of perception inherited from childhood? Is any sorting out of transference possible? Or are we "trapped in transference" (Grumet, 1988, p. 117)? This blurring between self and other is thought by many analysts to be "inappropriate" (Greenson, 1990, p. 151) to the situation at hand, it is viewed as an "illusion" (Mackenzie Rioch, 1988, pp. 37–38), or as an "abnormal phenomena" (Tower, 1988, p. 155), and it is most fundamentally considered to be irrational. The trouble with transference is that it is mostly unconscious. As Margaret Little (1981) comments, "What is unconscious one cannot easily be aware of (if at all), and to try to observe and interpret something unconscious in oneself is rather like trying to see the back of one's own head" (pp. 35–36).

The question becomes whether these unconscious "stereotype plates" (Freud,1966/1990, p. 29) are irrational and inappropriate after all. Merton Gill (1988) suggests that this kind of thinking "does violence to the actual nature of the relationship between patient and analyst" (p. 314). Further, he claims that transference is not so much about distorted perceptions of the other as it is a question of seeing the other in preconceived and "rigid" frameworks (p. 320). The more we become aware of transferences the more "flexibility" (p. 32) we will have in our relations with others. It is not that transference will ever fully be resolved but if we are aware of it, we can undo rigid relations with others. Gill comments that transference functions as a way in which we "organize the field [of perception] to single out, for example, the particular item that others ignored but to which [one] attributes as idiosyncratic significance" (p. 320). As against Freud, Martin Stanton (1997) suggests that what is made conscious during analysis does not clarify anything. Stanton argues, conversely, that "Transference resists interpretation" (p. 50).

Like transference, countertransference is thought by many analysts to be inappropriate and irrational. Following Freud, some analysts believe countertranference disrupts treatment. Countertransference is signaled by the analyst's "anxiety" (Blake Cohen, 1988, p. 69) that emerges while in relationship with the analysand. According to Edward Tauber (1988), countertransference "represent[s] unanalyzed portions of the therapist's personality that ... interfere with the treatment" (p. 111). The point, then, for analysts, is to be analyzed enough before analyzing patients, so that the analyst's own issues get worked through.

However, some argue that traces of countertransference remain no matter how much working through an analyst may accomplish. Margaret Little (1981) explains the difficulties of countertransference.

> The ever-quoted remedy for countertransference difficulties—deepen and move through analysis of the analyst—one can at best only be an incomplete one, for some tendency to develop unconscious infantile countertransference is bound to remain. (p. 45)

Some analysts argue, as against Freud, that countertransference may be viewed not as an impediment, but as a "tool" (Blake Cohen, 1988, p. 67) that may be used to understand the ways in which an analysand evokes feelings in others. Paula Heimann was one of the first analysts to understand countertransference in a positive way. Mabel Blake Cohen (1988) comments that Heimann

> States that the analyst's emotional responses to his patients within the analytic situation represent one of the most important tools for his work, and that the analyst's countertransference is an instrument of research into the patient's unconscious. (p. 67)

It becomes important to understand that the analyst should not act out her countertransference anxieties, but that she should become aware of her own feelings toward the analysand. The feelings evoked tell the analyst much about the ways in which the patient evokes these kinds of feelings in others.

Lucia Tower (1988) contends that the term *countertransference neurosis* has also emerged on the scene. This term is not unlike transference neurosis. Countertransference neurosis might emerge in late stages of the analysand's analysis. Here the analysand becomes the center of anxiety for the analyst. If the analysand reminds the analyst of someone else, and the analysand becomes blurred in the analyst's psyche with someone else from the analyst's past, something has not been worked through. Tower, however, is uncomfortable with the term countertransference neurosis, thinking it a "misnomer" (p. 140). Perhaps she is uncomfortable with the term because it suggests a weakness on the part of the analyst. For some, the very notion of countertransference seems taboo and has traditionally been thought to be destructive for both analysand and analyst. But analysts are not simply mirrors to the analysand's unconscious. Analysts are human beings who are subject to their own psychic interferences. Freud was well aware of this, but still he thought countertransference a negative response to the analysand.

Another point of contention among analysts around transference concerns the notion of *transference neurosis*. Some collapse transference neurosis onto generalized transference. *Generalized*, or *floating transference* (Greenson, 1990, p. 151), according to some analysts, is all that analysands experience during analysis. Brian Bird (1990) points out that

> Most analysts nowadays work only with transference feelings. They either ignore the transference neurosis or believe ... that there are no significant differences between transference neurosis and other transference reactions. For myself, I believe just the opposite: there are differences, and they are significant. (p. 342)

Analysts who refuse to believe that transference neurosis signals a significant shift during analysis may fear their own anxiety and countertranference responses. This fear may result in simply ignoring the patient's transference neurosis, as Bird points out, explaining it away. According to Freud, transference neurosis is different from generalized transference and should be paid attention to. In fact, Freud argues that analysis will end in failure if the analysand does not move through the stage of experiencing transference neurosis. If transference neurosis is not enacted in the analytic situation, the gritty stuff of the unconscious never comes up. But it is up to the analyst to allow these intense feelings to surface. Transferential relations with others, whether inside or outside the analytic situation, remain elusive, especially when transference reactions may provoke responses in the other and cause the other to experience countertransference. Identities are built in relation, and relations are complex. Thus, the translation of transference is anything but transparent. Whether in therapeutic or nontherapeutic relations, interpretation with others and of others signifies strangeness. Analysis, if anything, points to this strangeness of self and other. As Jean Laplanche (1999) stresses, analysis points to our "ex-centric" (p. 62) and idiosyncratic subjectivity.

I suggest that transferential relations continue to emerge not just with people but also with texts. The text of transference, then, is broader than a one-on-one relation with an analyst. Freud claimed that generalized transference happens all the time. Transferential relations with texts have to do with the ways in which old patterns of perception mark interpretive work. Gill (1988) contends that the problem with transference is primarily rigidity. Whenever preconceived frames of reference continually haunt interpretations, whenever the interpreter finds herself repeating over and over again the same kinds of thoughts that keep the interpreter from thinking through the text in broader ways, transference could be the culprit. When researchers read Holocaust texts and are not psychologically ready to deal with horrific violence, the tendency is to gloss over the text or pull from the text ideas that in some way match preconceived notions or prearranged feelings about violent encounters. Transferential relations with texts are not unlike those experienced with people. Researchers need to become aware of their emotional responses to difficult texts, they need to become aware of the ways in which old patterns of perception overlay new scholarly projects. It is not that researchers can clearly translate texts, or clearly interpret texts; but reorganization of perception, and the undoing of resistances of our own emotional responses, may alter what it is that we see in these texts. I am not arguing for clarity or getting a close reading. I am arguing for a closer examination of inner psychic upheavals, numbness, and rigidity when approaching texts. Interpreters should be aware that readings of texts do something to the psyche as interpreters do something to the translation. As Green (1986), suggests that "when all is said and done, it is the interpretation that he must give himself of the effect of the text in his own unconscious" (p. 338). As the reader translates the text, the text changes the reader. This is especially difficult when dealing with texts around the Holocaust. These texts change interpreters, and many of these changes are belated. How difficult memory texts change readers and researchers is elusive, but change is inevitable. It is important that curricularists mark these changes because these changes effect the present work at hand and the work that is to come in the future.

Although researchers may transfer a "stereotype plate" (Freud, 1966/1990, p. 29) onto new texts, and although there may be a certain amount of rigidity and resistance while doing work on the Holocaust, because traces of transference will always remain; still, work to construct, interpret and re-interpret Holocaust texts can do justice to the memories of victims and survivors. Transference is inevitable, but I think that it is possible to translate a text in a certain way that is less rigid, less bounded by one's previous experiences and handling of violence. But perhaps researchers are never fully ready to do this kind of work. No matter how much time is spent around the black sun of Auschwitz, constant ruptures in understanding occur, psychic upheavals continue. Transferential relations with texts may determine beforehand what a Holocaust historian or a Holocaust novelist will choose to write about. Transference, Freud (1920/1989) suggests, is brought on by a "compulsion to repeat" (p. 603) which "overrides the pleasure principle" (p. 605). In fact, Freud argues that the compulsion to repeat is a manifestation of the death instinct. An examination of Freud's notion of the death instinct and aggression raises many questions for the Holocaust researcher. Let us now turn, then, to Freud's (1930/1961) notion of the death instinct.

Aggression is "the main representative of the death instinct" (p. 71). Aggression can either be introjected and "sent back toward" the ego (pp. 78–79), or it can be projected out onto other people. It manifests itself as self hatred or hatred of the other. And Freud remarks that hatred is older than love. But the death instinct, Freud insists, is enmeshed with the life instinct or eros. Eros and thanatos are inextricably bound.

Individuals who are aggressive can become dangerous. Groups can become especially dangerous when thanatos and eros are unleashed. When a group is led by a "tyrannical leader," Freud (1920-1922) stresses that a "horde" mentality tends to overtake the group (p. 121). When thanatos and eros are unleashed, trouble is bound to occur. This trouble is caused primarily because of "contagion" and "imitation" (p. 89). Tyranny is unleashed because it undoes repressed impulses and allows "all that is evil" in humankind to emerge (p. 74). Rob Weatherill (1998), comments that for Freud,

> The catch-all term, the 'death instinct' tends to conflate sadism, aggressiveness, assertiveness, destructiveness, mastery and the will for power, which are qualitatively different phenomena. Freud did see the differences between these qualities ... but in his final duality [eros and thanatos] he was forced to lump them all together. (p. 23)

Although Freud's notion of the death instinct has not been wholeheartedly embraced by the psychoanalytic community (Laplanche & Pontalis, 1973), he is not alone in his conviction that the death instinct is real. Melanie Klein (1937/1975), Christopher Bollas (1996/1997), Paul Russell (1998) and Rob Weatherill (1998) consider Freud's notion of the death instinct important because it can explain humankind's potential for aggression. Paul Russell (1998) declares

> We take the notion of the death wish quite seriously. It is not obviously wrong. One usually hears that aggression is the basic instinct, but that the idea of a death wish is mystical, unprovable. But this won't do. Freud's conception is a deeper one.... Hate is the death wish, and love and hate lie at the very core of what trauma is about. (p. 42)

I struggle with the notion of the death instinct because it suggests an essentialized, universal, innate thing which is lodged in the heart of humanity. On the other hand, I wonder why it is people who are not provoked, do bad things? From whence does their aggression spring? If people have an innate disposition toward destruction, can they be held responsible for committing crimes? Ernst Rappaport (1975) points out that

> One might object to Freud's theory of the death instinct inasmuch as by laying the blame on an inborn destructive instinct—man is freed—from the responsibility for his behavior and permitted to escape the fear of consequences. (p. 295)

Opponents of the death drive (Kohut, 1996a/1996b; Fairbairn,1943/1954) believe that aggression is caused by bad relations with parents. Aggression is not natural, it is provoked by others. Heinz Kohut (1996a) comments that "no purely destructive urge arises so long as the environment is reasonably empathetic and responsive" (p. 207). But counter examples abound. Many scholars argue that Germans were not provoked and were not coerced to act aggressively. It does not seem to make sense that an entire country was the product of bad parenting. Most Germans were not innately sadistic or victims of child abuse (Lifton, 1986; Kelman, 1976; Langer, 1998; Goldhagen, 1997). Why, then, did Germans murder Jews? What was the source of their aggression? Daniel Goldhagen (1997) argues that Germans killed Jews because they wanted to, they chose to, nobody coerced them. But Goldhagen's argument seems so simplistic. To say that Germans killed because they wanted to, still does not explain much. Rob Weatherill (1998) suggests that acts of aggression are due to both external provocation and internal conflict. He takes a middle position between Freud (1920-1922) and Fairbairn (1943/1954). Freud, recall, argued that the death instinct causes violence. Fairbairn suggests that aggression is caused by provocation and bad parenting. Weatherill (1998) comments that aggression is a mixture of both internal and external circumstances. At the end of the day, questions around why it is people kill remain open. Perhaps researchers may never get behind the complex motives of mass murderers.

Freud has much to teach about aggression, the unconscious, defense mechanisms, transference relations, and civilization and its discontents. But one of his shortcomings turns on dealing with the ways in which others get introjected into our psyches and become lodged. Object relations theorists pick up where Freud left off and develop notions of what they term *internal objects*. Object relations theorists flesh out the ways in which others get introjected into the psyche. Object relations theorists ask questions around the unconscious underpinnings of our inter-relations. Internal objects influence social relations.

OBJECT RELATIONS THEORY

Generally speaking, object relations theorists draw on Freud, in one way or another, to expand the notion of the "object." Freud (1914-1916) claims that "the object [*objeht*] of an instinct is the thing in regard to which the instinct is able to achieve its aim" (p. xiv). An object can be a person or a thing. Object relations theorists flesh out how objects get internalized and what these internalizations do to the psyche. When we interact with others we not only have a sense of the other as "an actual other" (Greenberg & Mitchell, 1983, p. 10) but as an "internal other" (p. 10) as well. These internal objects or internal representations of others "go under various names ... 'illusory objects,' 'introjections,' 'personifications'" (p. 11). Thomas Ogden (1994) stresses that object relations is not just about inter-relations with others, but it is about most "fundamentally a theory of unconscious internal object relations in dynamic interplay with current interpersonal experience" (p. 88). Thus, object relations theorists are interested in understanding the way in which these introjects complexify our inter-relations at an unconscious level.

At the start of this chapter, I suggested that there are many theorists who engage in what is termed *object relations*. Donald Winnicott, Wilfred Bion, Rene Spitz, Heinz Kohut, Heinz Hartman, Harry Guntrip, Edith Jacobson, Erik Erikson, Melanie Klein, and Ronald Fairbairn, to name a few, are considered object relations theorists. I have chosen, however, to examine here the work of Melanie Klein and Ronald Fairbairn. Klein was the first to do object relations theory and I think she offers much depth and insight especially around the notions of phantasies, projections, and paranoia. These issues become crucial when examining Holocaust perpetrators. For Holocaust texts, Fairbairn's ideas around the notion of introjection and reactive aggression become key. When examining Holocaust perpetrators, Fairbairn's theories become relevant.

Let us first turn to Melanie Klein's work. For Klein (1940/1975) the infant introjects the image of the mother into her psyche. This internal object is "bound up with the external one, of whom she is a 'double'" (p. 346). This 'double' becomes distorted because the infant's phantasies of her mother do not match the actual mother. The actual mother and the double, or introjected representation of the mother, become blurred. Klein suggests that the more blurred the mother becomes with the internal representation of the mother, the more split the ego becomes. Klein (1946/1984) remarks that

> Phantasies and feelings about the state of the internal object virtually influence the structure of the ego. The more sadism prevails in the process of incorporating the object, the more the object is felt to be in pieces. (p. 6)

Klein goes on to say that the more in pieces is the object the more likely the ego becomes split. Phantasies, for Klein, are the most primordial psychic reality. Thus, perceptions of the mother are always already distorted by phantasies. If phantasies are not worked through, the child cannot see the mother as mother, rather she sees the mother as a product of phantasy.

Phantasies, for Klein (1946/1984) emanate primarily out of the site of anxiety. Anxiety is brought on by the death instinct and the ego's fear of being "annihilated" (p. 4). "Persecutory anxiety" (Klein, 1950/1975, p. 43) emerges as a response to the intrusion of the mother as internal object. The child's image of the mother is split into the good and bad breast. "From the beginning the destructive impulse is turned against the object and is first expressed in phantasized oral-sadistic attacks on the mother's breast" (Klein, 1946/1984, p. 2). A key term for Klein is *projection*, because the child projects onto the mother what she phantasizes about the bad breast. The mother is potentially dangerous and is a possible persecutor. Klein calls this period in the child's life, which occurs from the beginning of life until about 18 months, the *paranoid–schizoid position*. And it is this persecutory anxiety and fear of annihilation that characterizes the child's phantasies. Most fundamentally, then, for Klein, object relations, from the very beginning of life, are primarily aggressive.

When the child reaches about 18 months, if she is able to work through the paranoid–schizoid position, she arrives at what Klein (1950/1975) calls the *depressive position*. Here, anxieties and guilt consume the child. Guilt arises due to the child's feelings toward the mother. "[D]epressive anxiety relates to dangers felt to threaten the loved object" (p. 43). In other words, the child feels guilt over projecting such hateful feelings onto the mother. Klein (1940/1975) states that the child experiences "a melancholia in *statu nascendi*: The object that is being mourned is the mother's breast" (pp. 344–345). During the depressive position a "reparative" phase announces itself if the child has been able to work through the paranoid–schizoid position. Klein (1946/1975) claims that reparation is possible and is perhaps

> a more realistic response to the feeling of grief, guilt, fear of loss resulting from the aggression against the loved object. Since the drive to repair or protect the injured object paves the way for more satisfactory object-relations. (p. 14)

For Klein, then, a psychologically healthy individual works through both the paranoid–schizoid position and the depressive position. If one gets stuck in either position, neurosis, psychosis, or both are bound to appear later in life. Klein suggests that the psyche introjects and projects both good and bad objects all throughout life and so the psyche is dynamic and fluid. But these two positions, if not worked through, sound the cry of repetition compulsion later in life. If these two positions are worked through, the ego is less likely to become split.

Greenberg and Mitchell (1983) point out that Klein "has a tendency to see bad objects as internally derived ... and good objects as absorbed from the outside" (p. 135). If the mother is good, it is the child who turns her into a bad object through phantasies. What is important here concerns the origin of aggression. Like Freud, Klein suggests that aggression and the death instinct are innate. Therefore, a predisposition toward aggression is natural. Mitchell (1994) comments that "For Klein, the root of evil lies in the heart of man himself" (p. 84). In other words, Klein (1940/1975) argues that there is lodged internally an innate desire toward aggression. There is something in human nature that leads to phantasies about aggressive and "terrifying objects" (p. 348). And if we cannot work through these phantasies, the tendency to act out aggression and paranoia becomes a real and dangerous potential.

For Klein, phantasies about the other, especially paranoid phantasies, have no basis in reality. So when we study, for example, the anti-Semite, it becomes clear that his phantasies are born out of this sense of paranoia; most scholars would agree that these phantasies about the Jew have no basis in reality. Phantasies tell more about the anti-Semite than about the Jew. Klein helps us to understand that paranoid phantasies have little to do with the other but have everything to do with the paranoic's own persecutory anxiety. Representations of Jews as devils on horseback, cannibals, child murderers, menstruating men (which were all popular during the Middle Ages) arrive on the scene out of a bizarre panorama of phantasies springing from paranoia. Paranoia also played a role in German culture during the rise of the Third Reich. A paranoid country needs a scapegoat. A paranoid country needs to blame someone for its problems. So the Jew became a convenient scapegoat. However, Sheldon Roth (1995a) argues that Germans did not suffer from paranoid–schizoid illness. The Germans' egos, he claims, were quite intact. They knew what they were doing. Klein's paranoid–schizoid position may suggest that someone who suffers from this is psychotic. But the Germans were not psychotic. Thus, Roth suggests that when applying psychoanalytic notions to perpetrators, caution becomes necessary.

Some questions around Klein's work might be raised here. Whether we can divide the psyche into two positions is questionable and seems reductionistic. Whether children phantasize bad thoughts about their mothers universally is questionable. And whether children phantasize at the very beginning of life is impossible to determine. Mitchell (1994) claims that Klein's "critics (e.g. Guntrip [who was a Fairbairnian]) accuse Klein of depicting the objects of human passion as phantasmagoric, solipsistic creations, with no necessary connection to the outside world" (p. 69). However, I think phantasy life for both children and adults plays a much larger role in our lives than most would like to admit. So I think Klein is right to emphasize phantasy. Laplanche (1999) suggests that one of the problems with theories like Klein's is that it offers up a "subjectivist" position whereby the other is always reduced to a perception of the other (p.73). But how does one get outside one's perceptions? Can we ever really see the other as other? Does perception always blind?

W. R. D. Fairbairn is often overlooked. Many curriculum theorists and educators might not be familiar with Fairbairn's work simply because he only wrote one book and his work has been overshadowed by Heinz Kohut. Some claim that Kohut has taken many of his ideas directly from Fairbairn without crediting Fairbairn. James Grotstein and Donald Rinsley (1994) have accused Kohut of stealing Fairbairn's ideas. "It is ironic, therefore, that the recent contributions of Heinz Kohut, which bear a striking resemblance to those of Fairbairn, never refer to Fairbairn's work. The same irony unfortunately applies to Winnicott, who never acknowledged Fairbairn's anticipations of his work" (p. 6). And so Winnicott and Kohut have become perhaps the most well known object relations theorists, and Fairbairn remains somewhat obscure. I think Fairbairn is one of the most important psychoanalytic thinkers of our time and I would like to bring him out of obscurity.

Fairbairn (1941/1954; 1943/1954; 1944/1954; 1946/1954) tried to get beyond Klein's solipsistic position. Fairbairn suggested that the child can see the mother as other, therefore, the mother does not become reduced to the perception or representation of the mother. The mother is bad only if she neglects and/or abuses the child. She is not bad because of the child's perception, or projection, or phantasy about a bad breast; rather, she is bad because she may be so in actual reality. Fairbairn's fundamental message was that children are innocent; they become ill because of abusive parents. Grotstein and Rinsley (1994) tell us that, interestingly enough, Fairbairn's name is significant:

> Fairbairn's name, like Freud ("joy" in German), describes an important aspect of his contributions—that of acknowledging "fairness" to the child at a time when such a view could not be taken for granted. At the same time, his name represents the acknowledgment of the sense of a "blessing" offered to the "fair" child ("bairn"). (p. 3)

Unlike Freud, Fairbairn (1943/1954) suggests that it is not instinctual "impulses" (p. 62) which seek satisfaction. But rather that "libidinal "aims" are of secondary importance in comparison with object relationships … that a relationship with the object, and not gratification of the impulse, is the ultimate aim of libidinal striving" (p. 60). Here, Fairbairn turns Freud on his head. For Freud, the object of libidinal satisfaction serves as a means to an end; whereas for Fairbairn, the object is the end itself. What is primary for Fairbairn, then, are object relations, not instinctual satisfactions.

Unlike Freud and Klein, Fairbairn dismisses the notion of drives and the death instinct. To account for aggression, Fairbairn (1944/1954) turns to actual relationships between mother and child, not phantasized ones. Accordingly, if the child is in some way neglected and or abused by the mother, a "basic endopsychic structure" (p. 114) is set in place by forces of repression. Repression is put in motion by "a certain volume of aggression" (p. 114). Like Klein, Fairbairn claims that the mother's image is split into the good and bad mother. Recall, for Klein, both good and bad breast get introjected. But Fairbairn (1943/1954) stresses that there is no need to introject a good object. Only bad objects get introjected. Bad object gets introjected not because the child has phantasized that she has a bad mother, but rather the mother is bad in actuality and bad objects seep into the psyche. Initially, bad objects "are simply banished to the unconscious" (p. 65). Along with bad objects, "parts of the ego" (1944/1954, p. 89) get repressed as well. "What are primarily repressed are neither intolerably guilty impulses nor intolerably unpleasant memories, but intolerable bad internalized objects" (1943/1954, p. 62). Thus, bad memories are bad because they are attached to bad objects and it is because of the bad objects that memories get repressed. When "repression fails" (pp. 65–66) what comes up from the unconscious, where the bad object was initially "banished" (p. 65), are distorted and "psychopathological defenses" (pp. 65–66). The abused child, later on, expresses herself in "phobic," "obsessional," "hysterical," or "paranoid" ways (pp. 65–66). These defenses serve to protect the ego from pain. These modes of being serve to distance the self from itself. Obsessional thinking is a way to not think about things that are bothersome. Ruminating obsessively over the number 5 for instance, keeps the self from getting underneath this desire to repeat words over and over again. Underneath these ruminations lurks some repressed memory and some kind of bad object that has gotten internalized in the psyche.

For Fairbairn there are three egos. Fairbairn (1944/1954) suggests that there is the *central ego*, the *libidinal ego,* and the *superego*, plus what he termed an "internal saboteur" which "differs from the superego ... [because] it is in no sense conceived as an internal object. It is wholly an ego structure" (p. 106). Fairbairn explains that "The subsidiary egos are of course, ordinarily unconscious; and their unconscious status at once raises the suspicion that they are subject to repression" (p. 108). Unlike Freud's second topography (id, ego, superego), whereby the ego and superego are born out of the id, Fairbairn claims that the endopsychic structure of the mind develops because of the ways in which subsidiary egos split off from the central ego, especially if one has introjected bad objects. "The central ego is conceived as a primary and dynamic structure, from which ... other mental structures are ... derived" (p. 106). The libidinal ego, unlike Freud's id, is not "a mere reservoir of instinctual impulse, but as a dynamic structure ... [has] greater devotion to internalized objects" (p. 106). Hence, the central ego, libidinal ego and superego are all "dynamic ego structures" (p. 132). While the internalized objects are "objects of the dynamic ego structures ... [they are] endopsychic structures which are not themselves dynamic" (p. 132). Odgen (1994) explains that for Fairbairn, internal objects are not images, they are structures. Internal objects

> Are not simply mental representations of objects, but are active agencies whose activity is perceived by itself and by other dynamic structures [which become] organized and registered as stable mental representations. (p. 95)

Fairbairn's insistence that internal objects become endopsychic structures suggests that internal objects lodge themselves in the heart of the psyche and become very difficult, if not impossible, to remove primarily because these objects are structures, not images. Grotstein and Rinsely (1994) explain that

> By postulating the obverse of classical and Kleinian theory, he [Fairbairn] helped us to understand the well-known conundrum that the worse one's internal objects are experienced to be, the less one is able to leave them! (p. 7)

Bad objects which become internalized as endopsychic structures also are the root of self destruction and self hatred because the child believes that she must have somehow provoked her mother's wrath. Fairbairn (1941/1954) declares that "the reaction provoked in the child conforms to the idea that he is not loved because of the badness and destructiveness of his hate" (pp. 55–56).

Fairbairn argues, most fundamentally, for the goodness of the child. He believes that no one is a natural born killer. It is here that Fairbairn departs from both Klein and Freud. Aggression, for Fairbairn is born of provocation. Heinz Kohut (1996a), whose work is derivative of Fairbairn, suggests that "no purely destructive urge arises so long as the environment is reasonably empathetic and responsive" (p. 200). Kohut claims that "when the self is shattered ... you have the fragment of utter destructiveness" (p. 223).

When one examines early psychohistories and psychobiographies of the Nazi era, many early works suggest that Germans acted out because of bad parenting. But again, I stress that it cannot be the case that the whole of German society was a product of bad parenting. I find this claim counterintuitive. Children who are abused often continue the cycle of abuse. This is, for the most part, true. However, many children who are abused, do not act out this cycle. Universal claims about human behavior always come up short against the complex landscape of lived experience. Even if many German children were victims of child abuse, it still does not explain why they turned into killers. Most victims of child abuse never kill. Rob Weatherill (1998) critiques reactive explanations of aggression because "the claim that all aggression is environmental and reactive does not seem to answer the obvious: namely, the unbelievable cruelty and destructiveness that erupts in human behavior" (p. 25). Reactive positions around aggression, Weatherill suggests, overlook "internal psychic realities" (p. 26). Here, I think Weatherill is referring to the death instinct or a death wish. Something springs from within the psyche that has little to do with the external world and pulls the self toward destruction. Ultimately, I think none of these explanations complete. But they do offer up partial answers, or at least raise questions that perhaps have no resolution.

Fairbairn argues that only bad objects get introjected into the psyche. The question is what does the self do with these bad objects once they get installed? The psyche cannot seem to get rid of them. This introjective mechanism may explain why it is that bad relations later in life manifest if the compulsion to repeat gets acted out. That is, the compulsion to repeat the originary bad object's internalization may shape later relations and the psyche may continue throughout life to introject bad objects. Transferential relations with others may turn on this kind of introjective mechanism. One may unconsciously seek out others who are bad because they remind one of the initial bad object. The psyche tends to act in ways that are comfortable and familiar, even if these familiar ways are bad. Patterns of acting out become rigid especially when one seeks bad objects.

Introjecting others' badness can occur even when reading texts. The Jew who reads anti-Semitic texts, who introjects representations of Jews as monsters, devils, or evil people harms the psyche. It may become quite devastating to read texts which represent Jews as devils, as Christ-killers. A certain amount of distance becomes necessary for Jewish readers, if they encounter anti-Semitic literature or do research around it. The point here is that Jewish readers must work to not introject these bad representations; they must read in ways that puts psychological distance between themselves and the texts. But it becomes difficult to say just how this mechanism works. It becomes difficult to say what exactly the effects of introjection are on Jewish readers. Ultimately, it is not clear how these bad objects work on Jewish subjects.

From Freud, Klein, and Fairbairn we learn how primal our early relations are with significant others. We tend to repeat patterns of response and behavior that were evoked with these originary relations with others later in life. It is not just that early object relations shape our perceptions; rather, they become part of the very structure of our psyche. Phantasies, splitting of the ego, change the very structure of our psyche. So the ways in which we perceive others and texts written by others, to some extent, are products of early experiences in life. The more integrated the ego, Freud, Klein, and Fairbairn would agree, the better able we are to get an approximation of the person or text or event we are trying to understand and deconstruct. But for Jean Laplanche (1999), what is at stake is not getting an approximation of the other, but loosening up the transference so that we are able to see the other as other, as radically different from the self. The other is stranger. John Fletcher (1999) states that Laplanche's notion of otherness demands attention. He

> Writes 'otherness' as a neologism in French—not just *étrangeté*, strangeness, foreignness, alienness, but *étrangèreté*, strange-ness, foreigner-ness ... 'alien-ness' (p. 47).

Thus for Laplanche (1999) our perceptions of the other are not reduced to a mental representation of the other which might get housed in a solipsistic realm. The other becomes stranger through language, through "the enigmatic message," (p. 80), the "third reality" (p. 80) that ensures a distance between self and other. So for Laplanche, relations with others and with texts do not turn on getting a likeness, but on remembering to keep strangeness of the other and of the self intact.

THE LIMITS OF PSYCHOHISTORY

Applying psychoanalytic notions to history is not new. In fact, a field of study called *psychohistory* has been established since the 1930s. Next, I briefly introduce some of the debates that have emerged around doing psychohistory. A study of these debates teaches about the limits of doing psychohistory in the first place. It is to these limits that we should turn.

Frank Manuel (1979) suggests that one can trace the roots of psychohistory to Vico, Herder, Michelet, Dilthey, and Febre. Albin (1980) argues that "psychohistory's birth pains occurred in the wake of Hitler" (p. xi). Reich (1933/1945), Fromm (1941/1969), Adorno (1950), Horkheimer (1950), and Erikson (1976) all grapple with the horrors of the Holocaust utilizing psychoanalytic tools. Some of these writers' works will be fleshed out in subsequent chapters. Psychohistories can broadly be divided into two kinds: *psychobiographies* (Binion 1976; Rappoport, 1975; Waite, 1977; Erikson, 1976) and *social psychohistories* (Lifton, 1986; Reich, 1933/1945; Lowenberg, 1983; Adorno, 1950; Horkheimer, 1950; Fromm, 1941/1969; Friedländer, 1978). Within the field of psychohistory there are, broadly speaking, two rival groups. Lawton (1988) explains that

> the radicals (basically the de Mause Group) tend to view psychohistory as an independent field.... The conservatives (basically GUPH) are more cautious about viewing our field as being separate from history. (p. 10)

Many historians dismiss psychohistory altogether because they feel that psychoanalysis is not scientific (Stannard, 1980), and when it is applied to history much of it tends to be reductionistic and simplistic (Stannard, 1980; Albin, 1980) or "too speculative" (Kren & Rappoport, 1976). Kren and Rappoport (1976) suggest that "most efforts to apply psychology and particularly psychoanalysis to history have at best been interesting failures" (p. 66). These "failures," as traditional historians might call them, are due to "lack of rigor" (Friedländer, 1978, p. 7). Friedländer counters these claims and offers up some important insights on the ways in which Freud's notions can be useful for the historian. Peter Gay (1985) says that traditional historians complain that "researchers cannot psychoanalyze the dead" (p. 3). And the discourse of psychoanalysis, for the traditional historian might seem obfuscating or beside the point of historical research. Gay (1985) says that the traditional historian

> Is likely to find the techniques of psychoanalysis esoteric, its language deplorable, and its propositions, to put it generally, remote from his researches into the past. (pp. 43–44)

Although the discourse of psychoanalysis is, no doubt, difficult, I would argue, and I think Gay would support my claim, that psychoanalytic notions could certainly help historians articulate and explain, partially, why it is people do what they do. Common sense explanations around complex motivations of perpetrators just will not do. The discipline of psychoanalysis has much to teach about the inner workings of the psyche. Moreover, without a background in psychoanalytic literature, the historian has no way to articulate her own anxieties around disturbing material. Without at least the awareness of what defense mechanisms are and what they do, the historian is at the mercy of her own repressions. These repressions and resistances will determine, to a certain extent, what it is the historian chooses to write about or not write about. What gets excluded from history, then, has much to do with what it is historians can psychically handle. It would, therefore, behoove the historian to have some understanding of her own psyche before attempting to recover the past.

The question becomes what are we using psychoanalytic notions to do? Do we use these notions to think through complex historical issues, or do we use them to shut thinking off? If we use psychoanalytic notions in reductionistic ways, we are using them incorrectly; we are using them to shut down thinking and emotion. But psychoanalytic notions do not have to be used reductionistically. In fact, Gay (1985) points out that both historians and psychoanalysts work against reductionism "As discoverers and documenters of overdetermination, psychoanalysts and historians, each in their own manner, are allies in the struggle against reductionism, against naive and crude monocausal explanation" (pp. 74–75). Pathologizing labels such as survivor syndrome, post-traumatic stress syndrome, and obsessive–compulsive disorder tend toward reductionism. These labels squash out the depth of the complexities around the human psyche. These categories gloss over the radical difference of suffering. It becomes problematic to box people into categories and attempt to fix them with a label. I find these practices normalizing and oppressive. Diagnostic categories can also scar because they stigmatize, and stigmas do not easily go away. But, as I have pointed out throughout this chapter, there is much more to psychoanalytic theory than labeling. If anything, psychoanalytic theory should point out how strange we are; human beings cannot be labeled.

Early psychobiographies on Hitler tended to demonize him. Rappaport (1975) diagnoses Hitler as an "ambulatory schizophrenic" (p. 210); Binion (1976) declared that Hitler suffered from "oral sadism" (p. 170); Waite (1977) argued that Hitler suffered from "anality and sadism" (p. 149); Langer suggested that Hitler was "neurotic bordering on schizophrenia" (cited in Rappaport, 1975, p. 208); Waite (1977), Erikson (1976), and Bromberg (cited in Rappaport, 1975) suggested that Hitler suffered from borderline personality disorder. But Waite (1977) cautions that when we demonize Hitler we exonerate him. "To dismiss Hitler or Himmler as mad men or fiends, incomprehensible to "normal" people, is to say that critical judgment of them is not possible" (1977, p. xvii). In later chapters, I analyze some of these studies in more detail. Next, I introduce certain trends in psychohistory. These trends are interesting to follow because they demonstrate a real shift in the ways in which psychoanalytic notions have been used when applied to the Holocaust.

Like psychobiographies, social psychohistories tended to pathologize Germans. Adorno (1950) and Fromm (1941/1969) argued that Germans suffered from sadomasochistic upbringings and had a tendency to develop authoritarian personalities. Some argue that Germans suffered from "infantile helplessness" and "passivity" (Reich, 1933/1945, p. 26). But these kinds of explanations are reductionistic and simpleminded. Not all Germans are obedient, passive, sadistic, or sadomasochistic.

A turn in Holocaust scholarship in the 1980s signals a complete reversal of some of these early theories. Browning (1998), Goldhagen (1997), Lifton (1986), and Kelman (1976) argue that Germans were not "inherently evil" (Lifton, 1986, pp. 4–5) and most Germans did not demonstrate sadistic tendencies. As Lawrence Langer (1998) suggests, "sadism or psychotic rage" do not explain mass murder (p. xii). Browning, Goldhagen, and Lifton declare that those who were complicit in crimes during the Holocaust were quite ordinary. It was the "ordinariness of most Nazi doctors" that stunned Lifton (1986, p. 4). Even the category "ordinary Germans," which is used by Browning, Goldhagen, and others does not help us understand much. What is an ordinary German? Who is ordinary? But I think the point here is that Holocaust scholars emphasize that sometimes mass murderers are not psychotic maniacs, or sadistic lunatics; they are sane, everyday human beings. Christopher Browning (1998) argues in the beginning of his study around Police Battalion 101 that his aim is not to demonize the perpetrators. Browning believes that historians must reject demonization.

My analysis departs from what has been done in the field of psychohistory in many ways. As a curriculum theorist, I argue that a broad understanding of the Holocaust is key. Both the memory text of history and the memory text of novels need to be examined. Curriculum theory allows me to cross borders and cut across narrow fields of inquiry. Again, I argue that it is not enough to read history. Literary representations are just as important to examine as historical ones. So my task is broader than the task of a psychohistorian. I think I bring unique insights to Holocaust texts because I am not merely adding historical insights to literary ones. From the perspective of curriculum theory, I am able to analyze these texts from a particular point of view. A social psychoanalytic hermeneutic around Holocaust texts turns on the notions of unconscious traces, transferences and countertransferences, and defense mechanisms. A post-Freudian reading of Freud, an analysis of Klein and Fairbairn, and the insights of Laplanche broaden the scope of my investigation by allowing me to ask questions which most psychohistorians have not asked because, for the most part, they only draw on Freud.

THREE

Representation and Anti-Semitism

To grapple with the Holocaust, educators need to have some kind of understanding around the complexities of representation and anti-Semitism. In this chapter, my aim is to point out the difficulties of interpreting these notions. I suggest that anti-Semitism signifies many different things in different historical periods. I argue that anti-Semitism is not monolithic. It is important to contextualize this term historically so educators understand it is a changeable, shifting creature. It is important to understand also that there were many complex reasons that the Holocaust emerged and anti-Semitism is only one reason among many. I think it is naive to reduce the Holocaust to anti-Semitism. Yet, it is also naive not to acknowledge its role during the Holocaust. The literature on anti-Semitism is separated from Holocaust historiography. The texts on anti-Semitism, that is, seem to form a separate and distinct canon which stands apart from Holocaust scholarship. Further, Holocaust scholarship is so balkanized that some historians tend to have difficulty treating anti-Semitism as part of their work. If they do treat anti-Semitism, it is done, sometimes, in superficial ways. In the chapter dealing with Holocaust historiography (chap. 5) I discuss Daniel Goldhagen's (1997) text *Hitler's Willing Executioners: Ordinary Germans and the Holocaust*. Here, I examine why historians have roundly criticized his treatment of anti-Semitism. Goldhagen's work signals that the notion of anti-Semitism is not well understood, even among historians. One of the problems in historians' analyses of anti-Semitism is that it is treated, ironically, ahistorically, and acontextually. My approach to anti-Semitism in this chapter is an historical and theological one. I attempt to contextualize anti-Semitism against the backdrop of the Holocaust.

But before tackling this difficult and disturbing history of Jew hatred, a turn to the subject and the vicissitudes of representation become necessary. The ways in which scholars think about the notion of representation shape their views on the notion of anti-Semitism. This twist further complicates what it is when we talk of anti-Semitism.

A TURN TO THE SUBJECT AND THE VICISSITUDES OF REPRESENTATION

Maxine Greene (1995) suggests that "the educative task is to create situations in which the young are moved to begin to ask, in all the tones of voice, 'why'" (p. 6). The "why" Greene refers to could point to questions around existence, being: why am I here? The "why" might also point toward the horizon of the self, identity. Why am I this way and not that? Why am I who I am? Why do I think this way about myself? Why do I experience the world in this way? Suzanne de Castell (1996) suggests that "the formation of self [is an educator's] project" (p. 28). The why of self concerns not only a self who thinks but a self who feels. The self who feels may not feel very well. The self who does not feel well may feel exiled, alienated, and marginalized. So the educator's task is to ask why.

Curriculum theorists might recognize that feeling bad about oneself affects the ways in which one interacts with others. But engagement with our world cannot be healthy if the self feels bad. Negative feelings about oneself may be co-complicated with how others define who we are and how we then internalize those negativities. The "why" of education might become, then, a question about naming. Why do others name or define me the way they do? Why do I internalize these negative namings?

Identities are produced not in isolation, but in relation. As Madeleine Grumet (1995) points out "Relation is basic to education" (p. 16). Relations between us, as we walk through our lives in schools and universities, tend to be unhealthy because they are not thought through deeply enough. Understanding relations is fraught with difficulties, of course. Understanding what we know about ourselves and others, and how we define others and how others define us, is a highly complex, problematic enterprise. The unhealthy self cannot relate in a productive way to the other. William Pinar (1995) explains:

> We are what we know. We are, however, also what we do not know. If what we know about ourselves—history, our culture, our national identity—is deformed by absences, denials, and incompletenesses, then our identity—both as individuals and as Americans, is fractured. This fractured self is a repressed self. Such a self lacks access both to itself and to the world. (p. 23)

Identity formation has to do with our relations with memory, history, and culture. Memory may be handed down to us through texts. "Deformed" selves, as Pinar points out, do not understand how interconnected they are to memory, history, and culture. Formation of self, then, has much to do with how we are always already inscribed in the texts of our culture before we arrive on the scene, how we interact with these texts, and how we might struggle against these texts. Susan Griffin (1992) remarks that "perhaps we are like stones; our own history and the history of the world are embedded in us.... It is said that the close study of stones will reveal traces from fires suffered thousands of years ago" (pp. 88–89). Memory, history, and culture webs us to events; pasts are sedimented in our very being. Thinking through these sedimented pasts, these traces, becomes necessary for the process of self formation.

Memory, history, culture, and identities are also co-produced, in part, in relation to textual representations. But, as Jan Jagodzinski (1997) explains, "Society is, at once, both an open and closed system; we are caught by our representations of it, at the same time we struggle to change these representations" (p. 25). We may try to push the stone of self up the hill, like Sisyphus, but upon arrival at the top of the hill, the stone of self may fall down again into the sedimentation and inscription of culture and memory. It is the educator's task to interrogate the struggle of Sisyphus as we are caught between culture and the re-invention of ourselves. This re-invention is continual and it is complex.

My own struggle concerns Jewish self formation against a backdrop of centuries of what I term *Jew hatred*. Therefore, I am interested in examining relations between those representations of Jews in texts that have already been handed down to us by Jew haters, and the process of Jewish self representation and self formation. The hermeneutic circle between how Jews are defined by others and how Jews define themselves may be insidious and difficult to break. Jews may introject cultural inscriptions by others and graft these inscriptions onto themselves in the form of self hatred. Although these circles of hatred are hard to break, I argue that there are ways around these difficulties. Opening spaces and rupturing places between representations by others and self-representation become key.

In Western culture since about the third century, it has been Christians who have had the power to define, name, and represent Jews. Educators must remember that students and teachers may be Jews and

Christians, and may come to the place we call school with traces of these very complex, theological memories sedimented and grafted onto their skin. Curriculum theorists cannot underestimate the importance of understanding how these theological memories, traces, emotionally and intellectually affect our lives in schools. Although school is the place that is supposed to be neatly separated from religion, it is not. Students and teachers grow up in traditions and bring them into the classroom, if only in quiet ways, even if the question of religion is never raised. The traces of these traditions mark the text of school life. These markings, these stains, cannot be ignored—ignoring these stains is dangerous.

The historical memory of Jewish–Christian relations has been stained with violence. Christians, since the third century, have represented Jews in violent and pejorative ways. Old, stoney representations of Jews remain in the collective unconscious or consciousness of many Christians. Jews have been exiled and marginalized for centuries, and we remain, in many ways, exiled in the classroom and in the academy by Jew hatred. Although there is much debate over the current climate for Jews in America, the presence of Jew hatred can never be underestimated. Under many unturned stones lie the bedrock of hatred. Jew hatred is like an invisible poison that permeates all of our relationships and damages us all. Most often, though, the problematics of Jew hatred remain hidden. These are stoney "silences our pedagogies ought somehow to repair" (Greene, 1995, p. 47). But the repair can never be complete. The damage done to Jews is centuries old, and Jew hatred pervades our culture in all sorts of insidious ways. Thus, I do not offer up a healing pedagogy; I only suggest some ways to better understand how representations of Jews by Jew haters have been introjected into the self-representations of Jews, and how this injection or introjection has been a dangerous one for Jewish self formation. These things have everything to do with life in schools and scholarly life. Scholars, too, are Jews and Christians and other religious denominations, carrying the rocks and webs of culture up and down the Sisyphusean hills in and beyond the academy. Grumet (1995) tells us that curriculum "is the process of making sense with a group of people [about] the systems that shape and organize the world that we can think about together" (p. 19).

Judaism and Christianity are complex theological social systems that have shaped us and have organized the ways we think about life. However, Judaism and Christianity have been strange bedfellows for centuries. Christianity is a complex system which, by and large, has had the power to name, control, suppress, define, and represent Jews. Ours has been, historically, an unhealthy relationship. I am skeptical that many of us have engaged in healthy dialogues around these complexities. Certainly, Jewish and Christian fundamentalists cannot dialogue at all. Ultimately, as Myles Horton (1990) points out, dialogues "don't change men's hearts" (p. 103). Still, Paulo Freire (1990a) suggests we must attempt to understand "the spirit of the culture ... the soul of the culture" (p. 131).

How I respond to representations of Jews in texts may determine how I feel about myself as a Jew and in relation to others. The tricky thing about reading texts is that we tend to merge psychologically with what we are reading. Wolfgang Iser (1978) comments that in the process of reading "text and reader ... merge into a single situation, the division between subject and object no longer applies" (pp. 9–10). If I merge with texts in the process of reading, how do I then protect myself, psychologically, from the assault and violence of representations of Jews by Jew haters. Can I protect myself? Self-identification with representations that are Jew hating produce self-hating Jews. I am certainly not immune from this phenomenon. Reluctance to grapple with my Jewish identity comes out of, perhaps, an unconscious self-hatred.

I argue that self-identification with Jew hating representations, however, can be disrupted. One way to disrupt these negative identifications is by first becoming outraged. Jagodzinski (1997) says that "The sense of outrage belongs somewhere at the limit of the frame ... for it signifies an almost unbearable desire, an uncontrollable temper, a body which cannot be contained" (p. xi). So it is the feeling of outrage that moves me to interrupt these negative representations of Jews. But these interruptions do not go without difficulties. The outrage must not harden one's heart and result in Christian-bashing. Outrage must move one to expose, though, texts written by writers who have perpetuated hateful representations of Jews. The dangers of representation are, perhaps, obvious as we live in a post-Holocaust age. Although, certainly, textual representations in themselves cannot account for the why of the Holocaust.

It is when textual encounters move me emotionally that I begin to find productive ways in which to deal with these kinds of issues. Ironically, though, as David Jardine (1995) points out, the encounter "does not begin with me. It only begins when something happens to me in my reading of a text, when something strikes me, tears me open, 'wounds' me and leaves me vulnerable and open to the world" (p. 110). Something has happened to me studying these texts, these violent representations. I have grown outraged but I realize that my outrage must move toward a systematic analysis around issues of representation and self formation. By a systematic analysis of these texts, I hope to undo stoney, rigid, simplistic representations of Jews. Hopefully my analysis may point toward ways that might "intervene in the dominant modes of representation" (Jagodzinksi, 1997, p. 139). Intervention becomes possible partly through what I term *jagged imaginings,* which move us to undo rigidity.

Deborah Britzman (1995) teaches that:

> Imaginative thinking can move us beyond the constraints of nostalgia and the anxious impulse to arrange history without an awareness of what it is that structures our destinies or how the inherited contexts and practices constrain our possibilities. (p. 76)

Jagged imagining is a way that might allow us to question culturally inherited representations. But re-imaginings cannot completely overturn that which we imagine against, for imagining against something implies a certain friction with that something. That something of tradition always remains, even as a trace or stain. Further, we must not simply re-place one static image with another. Doing this only causes paralysis. As Robert Musil (1914/1990) writes, we must attempt to avoid "paralysis and rigidification" (p. 56) in our thinking. Jagged imagining, re-inventing how we might represent ourselves, also means embracing a willingness to walk on or near a precipice. Imagining against tradition is risky. Paula Salvio (1997) remarks that

> Resistance to regulatory control and culture's continual attempts to grip the body is, in reality (and particularly in schools), wrought with forms of resistance that are marked by painful struggle, misunderstandings, confusions, and feelings of betrayal. (p. 248)

But we will always, in some ways, be gripped by culture, no matter how much we struggle against it. The grip of a stoney body—a stoney body of representations, however, can be disrupted by attempting to partially dissolve the stone by digging into the layers of cultural sedimentation. Jewish representations become problematic because they have become stoney, reified, hardened, and wedged into historical memory. Moreover, my understanding of what representation means may determine how I interpret what I read and how these readings may affect my very identity.

There is no essential Jew; there is no essential representation of a Jew. There are as many kinds of Jews as there are pebbles on a beach. Like the changeableness of pebbles, Jews are changeable too. If anything, Jewish self-representation and identity are elusive. Suzanne de Castell (1996) tells us that "finally, this place of ambiguity ... must be our destination in all our journeys" (p. 31). Perhaps we do not have a final destination or end place, but the journey is one that is not certain or clear. We take this walk one step at a time. As Paulo Freire (1990b) says, "I am sure that we make the road by walking" (p. 6).

Because the notion of representation is highly complex, I would first like to examine different ways of understanding what representation might mean and the possible effects of representation. More specifically, I will examine how Jews are represented historically by what I term *Jew hating texts*.

UNDERSTANDING THE NOTION OF REPRESENTATION

Recall, object relations theory teaches that self and object representations are co-complex because of unconscious transferences and internalizations of the object. James Grotstein (1994) suggests that

> internal objects whether Kleinian or Fairbairnian are third forms—neither the external person, nor merely split off parts of the self. They are in fact, phantasmically altered, transformed montages. (p. 118)

Internal objects are co-mingled impressions of self and other. Self representations and object representations become difficult to untangle. How the self perceives the other and the other perceives the self depends on a complex, unconscious relationship. Stephen Mitchell (1998) points out that at an unconscious level, individuation of self from other becomes difficult to untangle because primary process thinking knows no division. Mitchell (1998) declares that

> Because on a primary process level minds are permeable, interactions are co-constructed, and time is not linear but simultaneous, separation into the neat categories of secondary process, me/you, then/now ... can never be complete. (p. 56)

Identity formation is always in relation with the other. Unconscious transference may maintain rigid patterns of perception. Significant others who get internalized in early childhood shape the ways in which we perceive others later on in life. Recall, Laplanche (1999) criticizes Freud and others who offer up what he terms a *subjectivist* (p. 73) position around the notion of representation. Laplanche (1999) claims that subjectivist positions

> reduce the other to the subject's perception of the other ... nothing in this approach allows the other any place other than the depths of subjectivity. (p. 73)

Laplanche argues for a "third reality" which is "implanted" (p. 80) by the other into the self. This enables us to speak of the other as other and not subsume her representation under a radical subjectivity which would reduce her to my perception of her. The other is separated from the self. The other's alterity is due to her own internal "alienness" her own "internal alterity" (p. 220). The perception of the other, though, is always already overlayed with transferential relations from the past.

Transference confuses any clear separation or individuation between self and other. Whoever we are in relation to the other, this relation is clouded and co-complexified by the ghosts of internal objects. These co-complex internal objects are dynamic and have a life of their own. The compulsion to repeat old patterns of relations with new others continues throughout life. These ghostly internal objects are guided by primary process thought which knows no time, division, or negation.

Secondary process thinking marks a site of organization, rationality, and categorization. This is what Freud called the *reality principle.* The reality principle suggests that in order to function in reality, the psyche must divide things up or else it will get lost in the flow of time. Dualities and opposites, although constructions, help us function in the real world. However, the primary process hovers right below the secondary process and these processes are in fact co-mingled. Stephen Mitchell (1998) comments that for

> Lowewald [a psychoanalyst] there is a perpetual tension between primary process and secondary process as organization, through which experience is generated. The distinctions between me and you ... now and then are logical distinctions.... All these distinctions, he argues, are not given, but rather are constructions. (p. 56)

The ego must be able to make these distinctions and categorize in order to function in the world. If we were to regress to primary process thinking we could not distinguish between objects, and time would flow seemingly without end; like a dream, life would become hallucinatory, an Alice in Wonderland experience. But because primary process thinking always overlays secondary process thinking, the unconscious guides us. Secondary process thinking separates out thoughts and distinguishes between now and then.

When we talk about *representation* on the secondary process level, what we are talking about are distinctions and separations between things. Philosophical debates, unlike psychoanalytic ones, draw on secondary process thinking to separate this and that. When we talk about images and referents, appearances and reality, signifiers and the signified, we have moved into the realm of secondary process thinking. Let us now move from the psychoanalytic register around mental representations to the philosophic register around the notion of representation. These two kinds of discussions mark different ways of talking about this idea.

Understanding what representation means is no easy task. The classical understanding of representation implies that two things, p and q, are somehow connected. The thing p may represent the thing q. That this represents that usually suggests that an image may represent a corresponding reality. In this sense, then, *representation* clearly and distinctly separates lived experience into two things or two realms. Further, the image p is a mere copy of the real thing q. Since Plato, q has been associated with reality, truth, the given; p, on the other hand, is a mere appearance, a mere copy of the real. The phenomenal (the appearance) realm and the noumenal (the real behind the appearance) are therefore split apart. The trick, then, is to get behind appearance in order to get at truth.

Many modernists since Descartes have appropriated this way of understanding representation. Jan Jagodzinski (1997) tells us that for the modernist, representation collapses onto the term mimesis. Representation means likeness, sameness. In other words, the image may mirror its referent; the image may reflect its referent. More concretely, the image of a cat I conjure up in my mind is simply a copy of a real cat in the world. Therefore, the cat in my mind is a mirror image of the real cat. But the image of the cat in my mind has less value than the real because it is a mere copy (a copy cat). The real cat has more value because it is true; it coincides with the given.

Texts also conjure up images in my mind. A text may discuss, for instance, a cat. The words, then, point to an image of a cat. From the words on the page, I then imagine a picture of a cat in my mind. Thus, texts too can serve as mirrors to the real. Texts about cats, that is, may correspond to real cats in the world. Iser (1989) comments that "semblance, then, appears to be a basic ingredient of representation" (pp. 242–243).

Photographs, like texts, may also be thought of as corresponding to their referent. Realist photographers, who embrace the modernist position of representation, believe that the photographic image can neatly mirror that which is photographed. For instance, Roland Barthes (1981) claims that a photograph of a pipe "is always and intractably a pipe" (p. 87). Further, Barthes declares that "every photograph is somehow co-natural with its referent" (p. 76). Thus, for realists like Barthes, the photographer's frame of reference does not matter, for the photograph simply corresponds to a reality independent of the photographer's cultural frame in which she is situated. The photographer, says Kevin Robins (1995) is a "passive" spectator of the real (p. 30). Realist photographers, then, think of themselves as nothing more than "recorders of reality" (p. 30).

Like realist photographers, writers, such as Christopher Isherwood, describe the process of writing novels in much the same way photographers take pictures. Isherwood describes writing about Berlin during Hitler's rise to power as if he were a realist photographer. He considers himself to be nothing more than a passive spectator of the world waiting to capture images in words, like a photographer who acts as a passive recorder of reality as he shoots pictures, capturing images. Isherwood (1959) says "I am a camera with it shutters open, waiting, quite passive, not thinking.... Someday, all this will have to be developed, carefully printed, fixed" (p. 1). For Isherwood, then, the eye/"I" is like a camera allowing the real to press in on the self, as if the real were completely external to the body. The real is viewed as an independent thing or realm that can be gotten at by fixing it, by catching it, making it still—by stopping time. What my eye/"I" sees can be shot with a camera or recorded in words.

John Bloom (1993) suggests that the "still image [for realist photographers] marks a death ritual driven by an assumed capacity to know the world" (p. 3). Killing images, stilling time, history, capturing truth and boxing it into a frame leads to what I term *massive hysteria*, an overload of anxiety. This anxiety sets in because images keep arriving on the scene, refusing to be stilled. That is, images continually slip through the frame. It is this slippage which leads to nervousness. We can no longer be certain what the image is.

Issues of representation, then, have much to do with how the West has understood what images are. Since Plato, images have had a second-class status because they are considered nothing more than shadow. In fact, these shadows interfere with the quest for truth; they get in the way of understanding ideas. Plato and others have driven a wedge between ideas and images, denigrating images. Western philosophy has been a history of epistemological problems which are caused, in part, because images attempt to creep into what is considered the real. Since Descartes, and even perhaps before the arrival of modern philosophy, which I date near 1659, with the death of Descartes, philosophers focused on problems around how we know ideas, not images. Images lie. Philosophers do not like lies. And because images lie, the West, according to W. J. T. Mitchell (1994), fears image and claims that a fear of images is nothing new:

> The fear of the image, the anxiety that the "power of images" may finally destroy even their creators and manipulators, is as old as image making itself. Idolatry, iconoclasm, iconophilia, and fetishism are not uniquely "postmodern" phenomena. (p. 15)

Many Christians and Jews think that so-called idol worshiping is foolish, or even evil, because images of the godhead are not real. This kind of thinking leads to dangerous, exclusive ways of being in the world. This kind of thinking can lead to religious wars. This Eurocentric way of thinking is what drives missionaries to convert so-called "primitive" people to Christianity. But if Christians and Jews are made in the image of God, does this not mean then that we are not real? Are we mere copies of God? And if we are copies of the real (God) why is it that people like Hitler exist?

Classical understandings of representation are highly problematic. Part of the problem is the eye/"I." Representation as an act of seeing seems, to me, a narrow way of understanding how we move through the world. I approach the world in various ways. I listen. I feel. I smell. I touch. I desire. My being is merged-with-the-world, not separated from it. Merging-with-the-world, thus, makes it difficult for me to get a grip on my surroundings in neat, tidy ways. It is perhaps arrogant to assume that I can know the truth of things, the truth of the world. Classical representation squashes out the mystery of being-in-the-world. It presupposes that I can know things with certainty, and therefore can conquer and control that which I know.

However, lived experience is much more complex and elusive than classical notions of representation allow. I cannot fix time or history in the eye/"I" of my camera. Moreover, there are many problems around the notion of correspondence itself. If I am merged-in-the-world and cannot get a grip on my surroundings, how can I say with certainty that p corresponds to q? As Jean-Paul Sartre (1948) points out "the relationship between the image and its object is very obscure" (p. 21).

The postmodern turn suggests we have arrived at a crisis. The crisis of representation, stated simply, is this: What you see is not what you get. P, in other words, does not correspond to q. Thomas Docherty (1996) points out that "the perception of an image involves us in a specific deception or irony with respect to the status of the real" (p. 23). Thus, this postmodern paradigm shift around the notion of representation points toward obliterating the given, the real, while elevating appearances and images. Plato is turned on his head. Many postmodern thinkers, though, still talk about representation by using visual metaphors. Representation continues to be a discussion, for the most part, around the visible. According to Docherty (1996), Jameson argues that it is not the modern but rather the postmodern which is "essentially a visual culture" (p. 21). Likewise, W. J. T. Mitchell (1994) claims that the postmodern era is a turn toward the "pictorial" (p. 15). But this turn toward the pictorial, according to Mitchell, differs from classical understandings of representation, for pictures do not correspond to the real. Mitchell (1994) comments that the postmodern turn is "rather a postlinguistic, postsemiotic, rediscovery of the picture [image] as a complex interplay between visuality, apparatus, institution, discourse, bodies of figurality" (p. 16).

Culture, then, in all its various manifestations, serves as the intermediary between what we see and what we get. In fact, culture constructs, produces and may even determine what we see in the first place, and it may also determine, in many ways, how we interpret what we see. The always already of culture haunts the whole interpretive process around representation. The crisis of representation is that "the camera portrays something other than what we see" (Bloom, 1993, p. 3). Foucault (1966/1994) reminds us that "it is in vain that we say what we see; what we see never resides in what we say" (p. 9). Or, as Homi Bhabha (1994) declares, "there can be no such immediacy of a visualist perspective, no such face-to-face epiphanies" (p. 50).

Representation is re-configured in postmodern discourse. Representation is a re-presentation of a re-presentation of a re-presentation. What is presented before us is a copy of a copy of a copy. What we see is always already constructed through culture glasses. But these glasses do not help us see better; they convolute and complexify what we see. P represents what? It represents p re-presenting p, while q slips away into oblivion, nothingness. Wolfgang Iser (1989) claims that representation, in this sense, has nothing to do with a pre-given reality, for there is no such thing. Perhaps the given, or pre-given, is just another construction, another phantasy made up to control the viewer's perception of the world.

The crisis of representation becomes disturbing when one attempts to discuss how historical events such as the Holocaust are to be represented. If there is no real, no given, how can we determine whether historians' representations are real or true? How can we even say that real events happen if the real is actually a copy of a copy? Jan Jagodzinski (1997) teaches that

> The crisis of representation ... is to question the accuracy of any representation.... If all representations are artificially and often arbitrarily constructed, the question of what and who to believe can lead to suspicion, skepticism, cynicism, and even paranoia. (p. 39)

By what criteria do we judge the accuracy of a representation? If one representation is as good as the next, how can we tell who is telling the most accurate story? Or is there no truth to tell? The notion of accuracy haunts us especially in the face of the so-called revisionist movement of pseudo-historians who claim, in one way or another, that the Holocaust is a hoax. Does the postmodern crisis of representation allow for this kind of thinking? Does this crisis open the door to any discourse? Petra Munro (1997) asks, "When history is no longer about represention [in the classical sense] what then?" (p. 3) The "what then" is the crisis about which I am most concerned. And the "what then" leads Wolfgang Iser to question "whether one could continue to speak of 'representation' at all" (1989, p. 249). But how can we describe what we see?

A more moderate and convincing position around the re-working of the notion of representation is W. J. T. Mitchell's. Mitchell (1994) suggests, first, that representations are not only visual, but also verbal. He declares that representation is like a "visible language, a form that combines sight and sound, picture and speech" (p. 14). Further, Mitchell argues that images are not separated from words, as Sartre (1948) and others hold, but are rather "already immanent in the words, in the fabric of description" (p. 99). By collapsing images and words, in what Mitchell calls "image-texts" (p. 91), we avoid dualisms that split lived experience up neatly into categories. Image-texts, Mitchell declares, are always already "a site of conflict, a nexus where political, institutional, and social antagonisms play themselves out" (p. 91). Representations, then, are "not a homogeneous field or grid of relationships governed by a single perspective" (p. 419). Stressing that representations are couched in a "cultural field" (p. 57), Mitchell points to the complexities of interpreting how we experience our world. The seer is also hearer and engages in an active way with the text of the world. Martin Lister (1995) calls this engagement "interactivity" (pp. 19–20). No longer am I a passive eye/"I," a spectator who allows the world to pass by, but rather I am an active being who is merged with the woof and web of the world. I am an active being who is interconnected in elusive ways to cultural texts. Mitchell (1994) also suggests that we ought to think of representation as a "set of relationships" (p. 47) and not as a "kind of object" (p. 420). Representation is a "process in which the thing is a participant" (p. 470). Although Mitchell's position is perhaps the most useful way I have found to talk about the notion of representation, I still think that as long as our discourse uses the word representation to describe the way we experience the world, it will always conjure up subject–object dualisms. The "thing" Mitchell talks about as being a participant in the process of representation is still something which resides outside of the person who experiences it. Further, representation still conjures up the appearance/reality split postmoderns have tried to overturn. Thus, the crisis of representation is also a crisis of language.

Jagodzinski (1997) suggests that what is important for scholars to think about are the possible "effects" (p. 90) of representation. I argue that one of these effects that tends to get overlooked in the debate over representation is the emotional response we have to textual representation. Of course, the emotional response is not separated from the intellectual one and, in fact, they are interconnected in highly complex ways.

But I think scholars need to pay more attention to how they feel when trying to understand what a particular representation means. Emotional responses to texts emerge with all sorts of complexities and ambiguities associated with reading and interpreting. Interpreting texts, though, cannot become a productive or generative act if I have not sorted out my emotional response to the text with which I am working. If I feel outraged by the way in which subjects are represented in texts, what am I to do?

HISTORICAL OVERVIEW OF ANTI-SEMITISM

Here, I would like to examine what I term *Jew hating texts*, and I would like to suggest that unexamined emotional responses to these texts, these representations, lead to internalizing hate. Internalization leads to self-hatred. Self-hatred damages. What is disturbing to me is that, as Linda Nochlin (1995) points out, Jews and anti-Semites have "the same representational trajectory" (p. 10). Therefore, it becomes crucial to examine Jew hating texts in order to understand how the Jew has been created. Once we grapple with this, it becomes possible to break the inscription of Jew hatred by re-imagining who we are. I will also argue that my understanding of the notion of representation may determine how I interpret and interact with these texts, and this ultimately affects how I construct my own image of who I am. If I understand representation to mean that images in the text correspond to real people in the world, then my interpretation of this text may collude with Jew hatred. However, if I understand representation to mean that images in the text do not correspond to real people in the world, then I may resist the image in the text, not appropriate it, and perhaps avoid taking up self-hatred. But if the images in these texts do not correspond to real people in the world the question might arise as to why I should take these texts seriously in the first place. If these images are bizarre phantasies of anti-Semites why should I bother reading them at all? I will argue, indeed, that these representations of Jews by Jew haters are utter phantasy and do not have anything to do with real Jews. These representations spring from paranoia and hatred. If I am concerned about the emotional effects of representation and examine these texts as events that co-arise with my own identity formation, I might take them very seriously because I understand that texts are co-textual with my very being. No matter what I think of these texts, they will impact my own self-formation.

Who is the anti-Semite? Perhaps to ask the question is immediately problematic because anti-Semites are produced out of many cloths.

Jean-Paul Sartre (1946) argues that there is an essential anti-Semite. Sartre declares that the anti-Semite "has chosen hate" (p. 18). And hatred is a "passion" (p. 17) that "involves the entire personality of the anti-Semite" (p. 33). Sartre argues that anti-Semitism is not just an "opinion" (p. 33) but a way of being in the world. Furthermore, anti-Semitism is "a basic sadism" (p. 46) and thus the anti-Semite has a "profound sexual attraction toward Jews" (p. 46). But perhaps there is no essential anti-Semite, just as there is no essential Jew. Paul Rose (1990) points out, as against Sartre, that when one examines many German anti-Semites, their profiles are quite contradictory. German anti-Semites, says Rose, are often "simultaneously revolutionary and national, "left" and "right"" (p. xvi). Rose tries to suggest that within the character of a single individual, all of these contradictory stances around Jew hating emerge. Martin Luther and St. Paul are good examples of these contradictions. They both despised and felt at certain times in their lives benevolence toward Jews.

Ernst Rappaport (1975) argues that the anti-Semite has introjected his hatreds during early childhood. Both parents and teachers, says Rappaport, are responsible for cultivating Jew hatred. Ackerman and Jahoda (1950) argue that introjection, imitation, and conformity shape the anti-Semite. Freud (1920–1922) suggested that imitation is key when looking at the formation of aggression within groups. The horde mentality allows defense mechanisms to vanish, unleashing all sorts of hatreds. Freud suggests that group ties are bound by thanatos and eros. Freud claims that, at bottom, group ties are sexual. Is there something sadistic about the anti-Semite, as Sartre (1946) claimed? Ackerman and Jahoda (1950) argue that the anti-Semite suffers from ""paranoia," "character disorders," "sado-masochism" and other "psychotic" personality types" (p. 25). Adorno (1950), Fromm (1941/1969), and Horkheimer (1950) also argued that anti-Semites are sadistic.

However, recent Holocaust scholarship questions these earlier positions around the nature of the anti-Semite. Lifton (1986), Browning (1998), Goldhagen (1997) and Langer (1998) argue that German anti-Semites, for the most part, were not sadistic. Even if some were, Langer (1998) argues that "sadism and psychotic rage" cannot explain mass murder (p. xii). These scholars contend that anti-Semites were "ordinary Germans," not sadistic psychopaths.

When scholars suggest that hatred is caused primarily by introjection, they are suggesting that hatred is internalized from without. This internalization is then projected back out onto scapegoats. As I mentioned earlier, this is most fundamentally a Fairbairnian or Kohutian position. People are not natural born killers, these analysts would argue; they become killers because the environment encourages this. Fairbairn and

Kohut would argue that when young children are abused by significant others, this early introjection of the bad object permanently ruins the child. The child becomes self-hating and then projects this hatred onto the world and onto the other. But what is it that he projects? The anti-Semite projects that shadow side of himself which he cannot integrate; he projects his heart of darkness onto the other, he rids himself of negativities. Peter Loewenberg (1995) explains this complicated move of projection as follows:

> The delusional position of Jew haters is that they must persecute the Jew because they themselves are persecuted by the Jews because of the projective quality of the fantasies of persecution.... Jews are always demagogically accused of the very crimes that are about to be committed against them.... Those who martyr and kill Jews actually are expunging the asocial anti-religious, ambivalent part of themselves. (p. 188)

The cycle of introjection and projection continues throughout life, as Melanie Klein teaches. But ultimately, it is projection that marks the anti-Semite. As Ackerman and Jahoda (1950) remark, it is "the mechanism of projection [which] permeates the entire personality of the anti-Semite" (p. 56). A Kleinian interpretation of the anti-Semite might suggest that he is stuck in the paranoid–schizoid position. Recall, here human subjectivity is guided by bizarre phantasies of the mother as bad breast. She is the persecutor. These phantasies have no basis in reality; the badness comes not from the mother but from the child's phantasies that the mother is bad. The implication is that original sin lies within. Hatred is not brought about by external factors, but it is born actually within the heart of humanity. Klein would argue that human beings are natural born killers. Aggression is innate. And Freud would agree.

Who is the anti-Semite? Who knows. What makes him hate remains a mystery. Anti-Semites are everywhere and are every type of person imaginable. They are American, German, Austrian; they are Christian, Muslim, and athiest. There is no essential anti-Semite as Sartre would have us believe. But some scholars feel that the basic characteristics of anti-Semitism are "uniform" (Yardeni, 1990; Rose, 1990; Carmichael, 1992; Nicholls, 1993). These scholars suggest that there is a certain continuity about anti-Semitism because of its long and intense presence. However, Wistrich (1990/1991) argues that anti-Semitism, in spite of this continuity, continually changes form. Although Jew hating texts have been a continuous phenomena throughout Western history, specific images and representations of Jews have changed over time, to fit the times.

There is much debate in the literature around the term *anti-Semitism*. The term did not appear until 1879 when it was coined by Wilhelm Marr. Therefore, some historians and theologians insist that when we are talking about Jew hatred we need to draw a distinction between what many theologians term *anti-Judaism* and *anti-Semitism*. There is little consensus here, though. When exactly anti-Semitism begins is debated. Some argue that we can draw a distinction between these terms even before the arrival of the 19th century. For example, Gavin Langmuir (1990) suggests that we can begin to call Jew hatred anti-Semitic with the appearance of irrational phantasies Christians had about Jews in the medieval era. It is this irrationality that makes them anti-Semitic. Langmuir (1990) names four such irrational phantasies:

> that Jews ritually crucified Christian children, used human blood and flesh in their rituals, tortured the wafers of the Eucharist, and sought to destroy Christendom by sowing the Black Death. (p. 302)

If we want to discuss irrational phantasies Christians had of Jews, we can trace these even farther back in history to perhaps the biblical John who called Jews devils (Lazar, 1991). Why does Langmuir draw the distinction between anti-Judaism and anti-Semitism where he does historically? Is he trying to exonerate the early church by suggesting that anti-Judaism, because it was not irrational, was not as bad or as morally reprehensible as medieval Jew hatred? Heiko Oberman (1984) warns that "The search for the root [of anti-Semitism] conceals the dangers of wishing to absolve Christianity entirely in every period" (p. xi).

Anti-Semitism and anti-Judaism basically underscore the same agenda: Jew hatred. When scholars attempt to drive a wedge between these two terms, John Weiss (1996) tells us that they tend to miss the "strong influence of Christian anti-Judaism on modern secular racism" (p. x). Thus, the terms *anti-Judaism* and *anti-Semitism* conceal more than they reveal. One of the things that they conceal is that both, in many ways, are forms of hatred. It is one thing to be against Judaism as a system of ideas, but it is another thing to hate the followers of this religious movement and persecute and kill them for their beliefs. Anti-Judaism and anti-Semitism are nothing more than euphemisms for Jew hatred. Thus, I suggest we call this thing what it is: Jew hatred.

Nicolas de Lange (1991) claims that the word anti-Semitism is "itself anti-Semitic in that it assumes the existence of a semitic (i.e. Jewish) race" (pp. 21–22). *Semitic*, Robert Wistrich (1991) explains, was a term that described, first, language groupings "including Hebrew, Arabic, Aramic, Babylonian, Assyrian, and Ethiopian" (p. xvi). So-called Aryan languages were associated with Sanskrit, Greek, Latin, Celtic, and Gothic (Poliakov, 1975). Leon Poliakov (1975) suggests that in the 19th century, William Jones attempted to show that Sanskrit, Greek, Latin, Celtic and Gothic had similar linguistic structures. Poliakov argues that the point of this assumption was to "attribute preeminence to the Indian language" (p. 311). August Wilhelm Schlegel, according to Poliakov, also claimed the "superiority" (p. 312) of the Indian language. These languages were considered to be Ayran.

According to Lewis Hopfe (1991) the word *Aryan* means noble and was used in the 19th century to describe people who lived in Iran prior to about 1750 B.C.E. and spoke an early version of Sanskrit. Some of these Iranians or Aryans are said, by some scholars, to have conquered the Dravidians or pre-Aryan natives of India. Other scholars are not so sure. The Dravidians could have perished from some natural disaster before the Aryans arrived on the scene. However, it is more likely that the Aryans slaughtered many of the Dravidians. The Aryans were responsible for developing both Zoroastrianism in Persia, which is present day Iran, and Hinduism in India. Poliakov (1975) declares that the word Aryan was coined by Johann Gottfried Rhode and was made respectable among academicians by Oxford scholar Max Müller.

Poliakov (1975) suggests that the trouble for Jews started when the "West decided to establish a new genealogy for itself" (p. 321). When people such as Rhodes and Müller legitimated the supposed superiority of a so-called Aryan race, they invented a new way to think about themselves, a way that denigrated the Jews. Christians wanted to detach themselves from their historical relatedness to Jews. Still, Poliakov (1975) points out that "the Ayran myth ... was modeled on the biblical myth while trying to free itself from it" (p. 312). Once Christians "discovered" their new roots, their relatedness to Indo-European Iranians or Aryans, they could boast of their supposed superiority over the Semites or the Jews. This new-found genealogy served, in effect, as a justification for oppressing the other, the Jew.

It is no accident that the term anti-Semitism arrived on the scene when it did. In 1879, when Wilhelm Marr coined this term, Jews had already been under fierce pressure to assimilate into European culture. Many Jews did assimilate, perhaps following the lead of Moses Mendelssohn. Those who assimilated, and dropped the old style of dress and the use of Yiddish, began to blend into European culture. However, Poliakov (1975) declares that "the more like Christians they became, the more mysterious, elusive and frightening they appeared" (p. 460). Thus, naming Jews "Semites" was a way to define the other, supposedly in a clear and distinct term, precisely at the moment when Jews began to look and sound like everyone else. In addition, the notion of a Jewish race, or a "semitic" race, then, served to drive the wedge between Christians and Jews even deeper. The notion of race served to oppress. Robert Wistrich (1991) points out that Ernest Renan and Christian Lassen (1991) "popularized the racial concept of 'Semites'" (p. 47). Today, much of our discourse take these notions of the semite and anti-Semite for granted. These terms, however, are social constructions which now have become very difficult to untangle.

Anti-Semitism as a political movement emerged, according to Nicholas de Lange (1991), "between the Franco-Prussian war and the Second World War" (p. 21). Robert Wistrich (1990) traces the anti-Semitic political movement to the 1890s. Wistrich and Rose (1990) agree that anti-Semites politically were both leftists and rightists, and sometimes were both, simultaneously. Disturbingly, Wistrich (1991) points out that it was historian Heinrich von Treitschke who "gave academic legitimacy and respectability" to the first anti-Semitic movement in Berlin, led by Adolf Stoecker (p. 59).

However we choose to define anti-Semitism, its premises can be traced, without a doubt, to early Christianity. It can be traced as far back as Paul who lived around 50 C.E. Poliakov (1975) insists that "a history of anti-Semitism is first and foremost a theological history" (p. 397). Thus, at this juncture I briefly trace this theological history to show how pervasive Jew hatred is in Christian doctrine.

Robert Wistrich (1991) says of the biblical Paul that it was he who was "most responsible for the detaching of Jesus from his Jewish background, for the shifting of guilt for the crucifixion from the Romans to the Jews" (pp. 14–15). It was not until Vatican II, in 1962, that the Roman Catholic Church formally retracted this position. Jew hatred, thus, stems primarily from the belief that Jews are nothing more than Christ-killers.

Unlike Paul, the biblical figure John talked about Jews in language that was much more vitriolic. Mosche Lazar (1991) relates that John was the first Christian writer "to transform the Jews from human beings into a mythical and monstrous race" (p. 44). John is the first Christian writer, said Lazar, to "identify the Jews with the devil" (p. 44). Some theologians attribute the book of Revelation to John, others attribute it to John's disciples. Nonetheless, John's teachings about the Jews, and the end time, or the eschaton instigated, in part, the actual apocalypse which occurred between 1933 and 1945 for European Jews. Of course, Christian teachings cannot be blamed for the Holocaust. Certainly there were many other factors leading up the that event. Still, Christian theological doctrine against Jews had much to do with fostering Jew hatred.

Unlike the biblical writers, church fathers, or patristic writers codified Jew hatred in what was called "the *adversos Judaeos* tradition" (Ruether, 1974, p. 137). Rosemary Radford Ruether (1974) explains that the church fathers defined Christianity by what it was not. These writings against the Jews became webbed into the very definition of what it meant to be a Christian. In order to be considered a "real" Christian, then, you had to hate the Jews. If not, you were thought to be a heretic.

Ruether claims that the church fathers all wrote tracts against the Jews. Cyprian, Tertullian, Augustine, Origen, Eusebius, and Chrysostom all engaged in Jew hating dogma. Along with these, Robert Wistrich (1991) adds more names to Ruether's list. He tells us that Gregory of Nyssa, St. Jerome and St. Ambrose wrote Jew hating tracts too. Jews were imaged by Chrysostom as "thieves, grave robbers, and sorcerers" (Ruether, 1974, p. 143). Jews "sacrificed their children to demons" (p. 128). Whatever the Jews were charged with, Ruether points out that it was "axiomatic in the *adversos Judaeos* tradition that Jewish reprobation is permanent and irrevocable" (p. 144).

Although the patristics were filled with Jew hatred, they felt, at least until the Inquisition, that Jews had a place in God's world. Jeremy Cohen (1982) suggests that it was Augustine "who had ordained the survival of the Jews ... so that they would convert at the end of days" (p. 14). Changes, though, toward the Jews could be seen after the death of St. Anselm around 1104 C.E. Cohen (1982) claims that, according to Amos Funkenstein, Anselm's followers justified killing Jews because it seemed the 'reasonable' thing to do. The real changes in attitude toward Jews, however, came during the Inquisition. Franciscans and Dominicans were responsible for the move from tolerance to murder. Cohen (1982) wrote "It was they who developed the papal Inquisition ... [the Franciscans and Dominicans] directed the burnings of the Talmud" (p. 13).

Along with the Inquisitors, Martin Luther, an early reformer and initiator of what later became known as *Protestantism*, raged against the Jews. Luther's three writings against the Jews, *That Jesus Christ was Born a Jew* (1523/1962); *Against the Sabbatarians: Letter to a Good Friend* (1538/1971); and *The Jews and their Lies* (1543/1971), became deeply etched in the hearts and minds of Germans for centuries to come. Paul Rose notes that "Luther legitimated hysteria and paranoia in a major European culture" (1990, p. 8). Luther was not alone in advocating this. There were others like Johannes Pfefferkorn who, according to Heiko Oberman (1984), distributed the highest number of pamphlets against the Jews during the early Reformation. However, Pfefferkorn was relatively unknown. Luther was not unknown, especially after 1517 when he nailed his *Ninety Five Theses* on the door of the Wittenberg Church in Germany.

When we trace Luther's writings, it becomes apparent that he changes his position around Jews as he grows older. By 1538 Luther grows more and more angry toward Jews. By 1543 he is a fierce Jew hater. Paul Rose suggests that scholars who support the thesis that there was a "young pro-Jewish," but an "old anti-Jewish" Luther are nothing more than "apologists" (1990, p. 7). Rose claims that Luther was always an anti-Semite and "throughout his life Luther longed for the destruction of Judaism" (p. 7). I would like to make two comments about Rose's claims. First, I do not consider myself, in any way, an apologist for Luther because I argue that it was not until 1538 that we can say that Luther was a Jew hater. I do not hold, however, that Luther was ever pro-Jewish. He was tolerant of Jews in his early days. But tolerance does not mean pro-Jewish. Secondly it is impossible to determine Rose's claim that Luther always longed for the destruction of Judaism. We do not see this kind of language until 1538. If Luther did long to destroy the Jews, he does not say it until 1538. It is hard to say what Luther wished for all along. Thus, Rose's claim, I think, is exaggerated.

Here, I want to show how Luther's attitudes toward Jews evolved between 1523 and 1543. I first turn to Luther's 1523 work *That Jesus Christ was born a Jew.* Luther (1523/1962) wishes to persuade Jews to convert to Christianity. "I hope that if one deals in a kindly way with the Jews and instructs them carefully from Holy Scriptures many of them will become genuine Christians" (p. 200). I suppose conversion of Jews could be interpreted broadly to mean "destruction of Judaism" (Rose, 1990, p. 7). But I take "destruction" to mean something much more radical, like burning down synagogues. Luther argues in this early work that Jews are, in a way, important for Gentiles because "Jews are of the lineage of Christ" (p. 201). We hear echoes of St. Paul, who in a Letter to the Romans suggests that Christians are like branches and Jews are like roots of the same tree; thus, Jews should be respected because they are historically related to Christians, and Judaism serves as the foundation for Christianity. It is clear that both St. Paul and Luther felt torn by the presence of Jews; both expressed benevolence and hostility toward them. Luther wants to "help" (p. 229) Jews "by the law of Christian love" (p. 229). He declares "we must receive them cordially, and permit them to trade and work with us" (p. 229). But Luther does not remain friendly toward Jews.

In 1538, Luther's tone begins to change toward the Jews. In *Against the Sabbatarians: Letter to a good Friend,* Luther has grown frustrated, it seems, because his mission to convert Jews has not been successful. Luther (1538/1971) comments, "the Jewish people have become very stubborn because of their rabbis. As a result they are very difficult to win over" (p. 65). In this piece, Luther talks much about the "terrible sins" (p. 67) of the Jews. The worst sin, according to Luther, is that the Jews killed Christ. The Jews "must have committed gruesome and terrible sins previously unheard of on earth" (p. 67). And for these "gruesome" sins the Jews "deserved complete destruction" (p. 71). That is the passage to which Paul Rose (1990) probably refers.

It is not entirely clear why Luther turned against the Jews in his later years, but he did, and by 1543 Luther's words become scandalous and almost unbearable to read, especially for Jews. In *On the Jews and their Lies*, Luther sets the stage for what is to happen in Europe. It is here that some might begin to draw connections between Luther and Hitler. Others might contend that this connection is inappropriate because, for one thing, the two men lived centuries apart. It must seem almost blasphemous for Lutherans to even think that this connection might be possible. Nevertheless, Rose (1990) suggests that Luther and Hitler "remain uniquely charismatically German figures. They were both charismatics in whom revolutionary and reactionary impulses flowed together.... It will not do to dismiss these parallels as pure accidents" (p. 8).

Like Paul Rose, Erik Erikson (1962), in a psychobiography entitled *Young Man Luther*, suggests that there is a connection between Luther and Hitler. Erikson (1962) declares that "Hitler was a totalitarian leader. Luther became the leader of a rebellion too ... trends in him [in Luther] may have prepared his nation for the acceptance of a leader like Hitler" (p. 109). Erikson claims that Luther, like Hitler, suffered from borderline personality disorder. Robert Waite (1977), who also suggests that Hitler suffered from borderline personality disorder, tells us that "borderline patients characteristically show paranoid tendencies. They ... fantasize about their 'magical omnipotence' ... [they have] an impulse to self destruction ... [they are] oral-aggressive ... narcissistic ... [they have] phobias about dirt, feces" (p. 357). Luther, Erikson (1962) claims, matches the borderline personality profile: He suffered from "suspiciousness, obsessive scrupulosity, moral sadism, and a preoccupation with dirtying infectious thoughts" (p. 60). Luther also suffered from occasional psychotic episodes. The most famous episode that has been described to us from chroniclers of Luther's life concerns the devil. Luther hallucinated that "the devil [was] sitting on a rainpipe outside his window, exposing his behind to him" (pp. 58–59). Erikson remarks that Luther was "compulsively retentive" (p. 176).

On analyzing Hitler's mental topography, many scholars point out that his behavior was, in many ways, very much like Luther's. In later chapters, I tease out what it is that some psychobiographers of Hitler have to say. However, for now I will raise a few questions. Erikson offers an interesting psychological portrait of Luther. But I believe making comparisons between Luther and Hitler is problematic. Whenever we compare two individuals we tend to oversimplify. Diagnosing Hitler and Luther as borderline personalities, labeling both as having the same character type, reduces them to the same. One of the dangerous implications here is that these characterological portraits suggest that there is some innate thing or essence lurking in the psyche of all Germans. There is no essential Germanness. Even if Luther and Hitler were borderline personality types, they were still radically different men who lived in different eras. Both, however, were products of culture, of a Christian culture which has always perpetuated anti-Semitism. Still, Erikson's psychobiography is important and it does give us some insight into Luther's ravings. However, I caution that psychobiographies that claim to get into the mind of their subject are suspect because it is impossible to know what it was that really motivated Luther.

In *On the Jews and their Lies* (1543/1971) Luther gave "advice" to Christians about what they should do with Jews. It is this so-called advice that is really frightening, especially for post-Holocaust readers. Luther declares, "First ... set fire to their synagogues or schools and ... bury and cover with dirt whatever will not burn" (p. 268). Luther goes on to say that if Moses "were alive today [he] would be the first to set fire to the synagogues and house of the Jews" (p. 269). Luther's advice continues:

> I advise that all their prayer books and Talmudic writings be taken from them.... I advise that their rabbis be forbidden to teach ... I advise that safe conduct on the highway be abolished completely ... I advise that usury be prohibited to them, and that all cash and treasure of silver and gold be taken from them and put aside for safe keeping. (pp. 269–270)

Luther also says in this piece that the Jews are "base, whoring people" (p. 167). Their "law must be accounted as filth" (p. 167). Jews are like a "defiled bride ... an incorrigible whore and evil slut" (p. 166). Thus, Luther put the nail in the coffin for European Jews. What gives these rantings legitimacy is that Luther was basically the founder of Protestantism. Yet, unlike Luther, other Protestant reformers did not feel this way toward Jews. John Weiss (1996) points out that Luther "was the only important Protestant leader who believed in the irredeemable corruption of Jewry. John Calvin and Ulrich Zwingly ... were not obsessed with the Jewish refusal of Christ" (p. 25).

Along with Luther, many Catholics during the Counter Reformation argued that Jews were evil and must be dealt with. Pope Paul IV, according to John Weiss (1996), decreed that the Reformation "was a Jewish-inspired plot to destroy the Vatican" (p. 30). Robert Wistrich (1991) recounts that the Counter Reformation brought with it the "introduction of ghettos in the second half of the 16th century, first in Italy and then in the Hapsburg Empire" (p. 37). Thus, Catholics were no friend to Jews either.

Ironically, when the church lost its grip on the West and secular culture gained a foothold, especially during the rise of scientism, Jewish oppression increasingly worsened, although in some regions Jew hatred seemed to fade. However, in Austria and Germany it did not fade; It got worse. John Weiss (1996) declares that it was during the Napoleonic era that Jew hatred began to grow. Moreover, Robert Wistrich (1990) claims that it was not difficult for secular culture to embrace Jew hatred. In fact, Wistrich (1990) comments that "the task of integrating anti-Semitism into the mainstream of central European culture was greatly facilitated by ... Luther, Kant, Goethe, and Fichte ... Hegel, Feuerbach, Schopenhauer, Richard Wagner" (p. 39). Interestingly enough, Leon Poliakov (1985) declares that Germans were far surpassed in the intensity of their Jew hatred by the French, especially during the Dreyfus Affair (1898–1900).

European Jew hatred, no doubt, was much more dangerous than it ever has been in the United States. However, David Gerber (1986) contends that "European images [of Jews] were embedded in the American consciousness in the first half of the 19th century" (pp. 22–23). In spite of the fact that European images—stereotypes—of Jews crept into American culture, many historians agree that America has always been an exceptional place for Jews. Americans seem to tolerate Jews more so than do Europeans. This toleration is termed *American exceptionalism* (Gerber, 1986, pp. 9–10). The idea that America is an exceptional place for Jews has gone basically unchallenged until around the 1970s. Since the 1970s, many argue that the description of America as an exceptional place for Jews is not entirely accurate (Gerber, 1986; Dinnerstein, 1994; Learner, 1986). This position presupposes that Jew hatred is virtually absent in America. But Gerber (1986) claims that the "lack of anti-Semitism in the American past" has more to do with "the concerns of historians" (p. 9) than with the experiences of Jews living in America.

It seems that historians have been so concerned to show how Jews have helped build America as a nation that they omitted the story about Jew hatred because they felt it would make things worse for Jews (Gerber, 1986). So historians sanitized and erased Jew hatred in America. Historians, keepers of memory, altered the ways in which Jews talk about living in the United States. Jew hatred is here, and has been here, since the Puritans arrived. But why Jew hatred in America did not lead to the brutalities it did in Europe is difficult to answer. Lucy Dawidowicz (1982) suggests that America's history of nonviolence against Jews has to do with Puritan doctrine. Puritans embraced a "philo-Hebraic strain" (p. 29) and "encouraged a neutral interest in Judaism [and] at times even a favorable one" (p. 29). Perhaps, in part, Puritan philo-Semitism kept back the tide of hatred. But philo-Semitism is merely the flip side of anti-Semitism and one wonders why these extremes did not lead to overt violence.

It was not until 1994 that American Jew hatred was grappled with in an extensive way. Leonard Dinnerstein (1994) compiled the first "comprehensive survey" (p. vii) of anti-Semitism in the United States. Another alarming facet of Jew hatred in America is the way in which university and school officials handled Jewish presence in their institutions. Many universities developed policies to keep Jews out. Dinnerstein (1994) claims that Harvard, Princeton, Williams, Yale, the University of Pennsylvania, Columbia, and a host of others limited the number of Jewish students and faculty allowed in their institutions. Dinnerstein declares that

> before the 1920s few Jews had earned doctorates.... This was especially true in the disciplines of English and History where it was thought inconceivable for a Jew to transmit or comprehend the culture or traditions of an American Christian society. (p. 87)

Universities were not alone in discriminating against Jews. David Gerber (1986) says that between 1920 and 1945 "Jews in Minneapolis ... were never employed in public schools" (p. 28). Of course, this was no accident.

Times have changed, and Jews in America certainly have it better today than in the past. But Jew hatred still thrives. Under every unturned stone, hatred is getting ready to be born. In Europe, notably in Germany, Jack Zipes (1991) warns that Jew hatred is on the rise again. Recently, in Austria the far right has gained a foothold in government. Nazi sympathizers are in positions of power and the world looks on in horror. The message here is that Jews must never become complacent. Mortimer Ostow (1996) wisely points out that he is not

> reassured by the fact that for American Jewry, this might be called a golden age.... Jews have enjoyed similar golden ages in the past, in Babylonia, in Spain, in Italy, in Poland ... and yet changes in the political, economic, or military situations have brought each golden age to an end whereupon anti-Semitism revived. (pp. 1–2)

Thus, historical memory teaches that hatreds brew around every corner, and it is crucial to keep awake and sniff out odors of hatred. Hatred must be undone.

EFFECTS OF ANTI-SEMITIC REPRESENTATIONS

Throughout the long history of Jew hatred, troubling images and representations of Jews have appeared in almost every country in the West. What is interesting about these representations is how varied they are. In fact, Linda Nochlin (1995) comments that "only mutually exclusive categories would seem large enough to encompass the totality of our iniquity" (p. 7). At this juncture, I would like to 'paint' a montage of these hideous images. The question I ask here is, How do these representations affect Jewish subjects?

Let us begin with Peter the Venerable (1092–1156). Peter the Venerable called the Jews "beasts" (Cohen, 1982, p. 28). During the 13th century, Jewish males were thought to be sexually "damaged" (Gilman, 1995, p. 75) because of circumcision. Not only this, Gilman explains that some 13th century Christians believed in "Jewish male menstruation. Thomas de Cantimpre ... presented the first 'scientific' statement of the phenomenon" (pp. 74–75). Near 1350, Jews were imaged as "bribers, secret killers, sorcerers, magicians" (Wistrich, 1991, p. 29). Further, in medieval art, "Jews were portrayed as agents of Satan, with evil faces, horns and a tail.... Sometimes the Devil might be seen in a painting or sculpture as riding on the back of a Jew" (p. 29). Weiss (1996) claims that during the 14th century, Jews were imaged on "the sides of cathedrals ... as scorpions or pigs" (p. 19). During the Reformation, it was believed that Jews could "transform themselves into demons and serpents" (p. 24). Napoleon called the Jews caterpillars who attempted to "ravage the countryside" (Poliakov, 1975, p. 226). Poliakov (1985) says that Schopenhauer "vented against the ubiquitous Jewish foul odor" (p. 7). Schopenhauer was not the only one to think that Jews had a foul odor. Sander Gilman (1986) explains that this supposed foul odor of Jews could be traced back to the medieval era. Gilman (1986) explains that this odor was connected with a mythology connected with the goat and the devil.

> The smell of Jews, the *foetor Judaicus*, is always associated with the Other. For Jews it is a quality ascribed to them by the medieval anti-Semitism that is linked with the sexualized image of the goat. For Jews, like the devil, are horned and have a goat's tale and a goat's beard. (p. 174)

Paul Brienes (1990) comments that all of these types of representations of Jews are ultimately "overshadowed by Nazism's dead Jewish bodies" (p. 17). Next, I turn to 20th century images of dead Jewish bodies that are displayed on the Internet by the Holocaust Museum in Washington (1997). Questions around representation become particularly difficult for many reasons I hope to explore.

First, I would like to examine different ways of understanding these photographs. Understanding these images as a source of evidence that the Holocaust happened is the most obvious reason the Holocaust Museum has such an exhibit on the Internet. As against the rising tide of Holocaust deniers, these computerized images prove that, indeed, the Holocaust happened. Thus, the displays are important in a crude way. Here it is easy to be more sympathetic with the realist view that photographs reflect their referent. As Roland Barthes (1981) suggests, "the photograph [or the computer image] is indifferent to all intermediaries: it does not invent" (p. 87).

If we understand these images from a constructivist stance, whereby the image is constructed by the photographer looking through the grids of culture, we might think that "photographs are as much an interpretation of the world as paintings" (Sontag, 1977, pp. 6–7). Some scholars, like W. J. T. Mitchell (1994) might argue that these images are no less 'real' because they are constructed through cultural grids. Mitchell does not reduce everything to imagination or phantasy; he complexifies how we understand the ways in which representations or images are produced. However, when we begin to question how these images were produced troubling questions enter the picture. Jan Jagodzinski (1997) insists that we must ask the question: "Whose images are they?" (p. 139). According to Daniel Goldhagen (1997), most of the photographs of Holocaust victims were taken by Nazi SS. The reason, Goldhagen says, that we have so many photographs is that the Germans insisted on taking them, even against the wishes of their commanders. Goldhagen tells us that these photographs were distributed among Germans and even placed in family albums. If someone wanted copies of the photos, these too, were available.

Most of the photos we find on the Internet at the Holocaust Museum Web site were taken by Germans. Knowing that many of these photos were displayed in family albums and were considered trophies by German police and Nazi SS may undermine the viewer's willingness to continue viewing this Internet site. Goldhagen (1997) comments that these photographs make certain that "the victim's shame would be displayed for years to come" (p. 296). There is something almost obscene about viewing these images. In fact, some might even argue that viewing pictures like these is not dissimilar to the viewing of pornography. W. J. T. Mitchell (1994) argues that the "taking of human subjects by a photographer ... is a concrete social encounter, often between a damaged, victimized, and powerless individual and a relatively privileged observer, often acting as the 'eye of power'" (p. 288).

The power relations between photographer and that which is photographed certainly demand interrogation. In the case of the Holocaust photos, we can see a clear power relation, with the victim losing every time. These photo-images affect both emotional and intellectual registers more intensely than, say, images we read about during the medieval era. The images produced out of the medieval era seem so remote and bizarre that the reader may simply shake her head. But when viewing photos that are not so far off in the distant past, we begin to understand the emotional impact images can have on viewers. Further, we begin to see just how tangled the emotional and intellectual registers are when attempting to sort out what is going on between image, viewer, computer, and photographer.

Intellectually, I can understand why these images are on the Internet. At one level people need to know that this event happened. We need to squash revisionists' myths at every turn. The Internet is a good opportunity to get this message across because it is global. However, emotionally, I think these images are potentially damaging to both the memory of the victims and to their living relatives. In a way the victims' memories are desecrated. There is something really awful about this Web site, but exactly what it is I do not know. As Mitchell (1994) points out, "We still do not know exactly what pictures are, what their relationship to language is, how they operate on observers" (p. 13). I worry about how these images operate on me and on others because their potential effects could be damaging to one's psyche. Images and representations are interdependent events with the eye/"I" of both my intellect, my emotions, and my very process of self formation. But I am uncertain about the impact of such an encounter. Homi Bhabha (1994) tells us that

> the image—a point of identification—marks the site of an ambivalence. As representation is always spatially split—it makes present something that is absent—and temporally deferred: it is the representation of a time that is always elsewhere a repetition. (p. 51)

The site of ambivalence confuses my sense of identification with these images. The distance I put between myself and the images, in some ways, contributes to the sense of guilt that I feel, because I was graced by being born later and being born in America and not in Europe. What makes me feel bad, though, is that I think this Web site is cheap. Susan Sontag (1977) reminds us that "the main effects [of viewing photographs are] to convert the world into a department store ... every subject is depreciated into an article of consumption" (p. 110). The visual consumption of corpses, or of dead bodies or near-dead bodies, can be had on this Web site. Simply click on the word 'corpses' and a series of images appear on your computer. The viewer can consume thousands of images of corpses if she wishes. Photograph #11472 reads "A wagon loaded with corpses intended for burial at Buchenwald." Photograph #74819 reads "Corpses in the Woebbelin concentration camps." Click on the word 'women' and you can see many photographs of women about to be executed. Photograph #76461 reads "A woman about to be executed in Belzec concentration camp." Photograph #43195 reads "German police and Ukrainian collaborators in civilian clothes look as Jewish women are forced to undress before their execution."

After clicking on various places on this Web site, after viewing hundreds of photos like these, one simply becomes numb to them. Sontag (1977) explains that "After repeated exposure to the image, it ... becomes less real" (p. 20). She comments that "images anesthetize" (p. 20). This is the crime. The effects of viewing these photographs on the Jewish subject are not clear. The effects of reading anti-Semitic texts are not clear either. It becomes difficult to avoid internalizing hatred. But we must continually try to undo the hate. Self-hatred is destructive. Keeping psychological distance intact when encountering anti-Semitic texts is crucial. But I do not think that it is possible to completely break the inscription. Texts get introjected into readers in strange ways that we do not understand. Perhaps trying to articulate feelings and responses to these texts is a start.

FOUR

Memory and History

> Asked by a reporter if he had forgiven the Nazis, Wiesel answered: "I didn't speak about forgiving.... Nobody asked me to forgive, nobody authorized me to forgive. I speak on behalf of memory without hatred, and I think memory, in my case, is a shield against hatred" (Kemptser & Chen, 1999, p. 22).

Elie Wiesel tells us that remembering the Holocaust does not mean forgiving the perpetrators. Remembering the Holocaust does not mean making "meaning" out of it either. Lawrence Langer (1998) comments that "When asked if there were any meaning in the Holocaust, historian Raul Hilberg is said to have replied "I hope not."" (p. xvi). The Holocaust and its remembrance is difficult and yields difficult memories devoid of meaning. But this lack, this void, this meaninglessness does not necessarily slide into nihilism because memory work, as I see it, is a form of justice. As Edith Wyschogrod (1998) points out, the memory worker makes "a promise to the dead to tell the truth about the past" (p. xi). Of course, this "truth" is not absolute but rather yields "truths" which reflect differing perspectives and interpretations. Some truths are more adequate than others. A radical relativism will not do.

Memory and history are complex notions. Their intersections are also co-complex. In this chapter my aim is to unpack these notions philosophically and psychoanalytically so that we might begin to understand competing interpretations of these ideas. Traditionally, *memory* has been seen by historians as a negative term. Memory has been relegated to the realm of unreliability. This maneuver has served to erase victims' narratives from texts. I argue that this erasure demands interrogation.

The notions of memory and history need to be deconstructed before turning to Holocaust historiography itself. I think it is important to begin thinking about what these terms might mean and the complex ways in which these ideas have been traditionally understood. Raising questions about what memory is, and about what it means to think historically are crucial. Without thinking through these notions, one cannot approach Holocaust historiography with depth.

The construction of memory, as Freud (1937–1939) explains, is also a reconstruction of the past. With the understanding that the task of interpretive work is difficult emotionally and intellectually, memory should attempt to get at that "kernal of truth" (pp. 267–268) we call the Holocaust. But that kernal of truth is not exactly a construction or a reconstruction, but a third thing; it is a translation. And that translation is always already other. The text of the Holocaust is always a stranger to us and must remain so if we want to avoid the trap of arrogance and domestication. Translations of this event must always be tentative. Response to the call of doing interpretive work beckons. So we listen with caution and care.

Psychoanalytic memory work with Holocaust survivors is both a process of construction and reconstruction. As analyst Dori Laub (1992) explains,

> Indeed, historical reality [of the survivor's memory] has to be reconstructed before any other work can start.... [Once the memory is reconstructed] the therapeutic process of constructing a narrative ... [and] the re-externalization of the event—has to be set in motion. (p. 69)

Freud (1937–1939) compares the process of memory work to archaeological excavation. He contends that the "work of constructing [memory], or, if it is preferred, of reconstructing, resembles to a great extent an archaeologist's excavation of some dwelling place that has been destroyed and buried" (p. 259). The old sites of memory exist alongside the new ones; the ruins remain even if they are buried. Holocaust survivors live alongside their memories and it is unlikely that the memories fade. Ironically, Holocaust memories may intensify as the survivor ages.

Paul Ricoeur (1990) suggests that memory workers "owe a debt to the past, a dept of recognition to the dead" (pp. 142–143). Remembering the dead, remembering the victims and survivors of the Holocaust, is clearly an ethical imperative. Not only is memory work an ethical imperative, it is also a religious one. For Jews, Yerushalmi (1982) contends that memory is "felt as a religious and ethical imperative" (p. 10).

Yerushalmi explains that "Altogether the verb *Zakhar* [to remember] appears in its various declensions in the bible no less than one hundred and sixty nine times" (p. 5).

Memory work is tied to loss, especially for Jews. When we examine the etymology of the word memory, Edward Casey (1987) reminds us that *"MEMOR"* the Latin root means "to grieve" and the Greek *"MERIMNA"* means "sorrow"" (pp. 273–264). Yet, how can we remember an event that is so hideous as to seem beyond representation, beyond thinkability, beyond understanding? How can a third generation Jew like myself remember this event? How can I do justice to a memory that is three generations removed from me? With caution and care.

We must be cautious never to domesticate the memory of the Holocaust by making it more comfortable. This memory is difficult and unbearable, too difficult to take in psychologically at times. We must never assimilate the memory into our own lifeworld, but perhaps live alongside it: to remain a stranger to it. We must never make the strange familiar. As Richard Stammelman (1995) stresses

> The extremity of the genocidal condition, its unimaginability and horror, generate a difference, a strangeness, an alterity lying beyond the powers of thought, language, and memory. (p. 267)

This memory refuses to be made into the same, the sameness of other atrocities. This is a uniquely Jewish tragedy, not simply a humanitarian one. Researchers must remain strangers to the event of the Holocaust, especially if they did not actually live through this event. To say that research around the Holocaust grants more or better understanding may be a trap, a trap of arrogance. What we understand is very little indeed. The complexities of remembering the Holocaust are overlaid by the difficulties of psychologically dealing with loss. Difficulties also abound because of the ways in which memory comes to be inscribed in one's individual consciousness and memory traces. Difficulties also abound because memory of the Holocaust may be silenced within Jewish and German families. Silence haunts. Silence hovers.

COLLECTIVE AND PERSONAL MEMORY

Memory is not monolithic. Different kinds of collective memories abound. Historical representations, oral histories passed down through generations, literary representations, film, artwork, museums, and other kinds of memorials all point to our collective memory of this event. Iwona Irwin Zarecka (1994) remarks that "A collective memory—as a set of ideas, images, feelings, about the past—is best located not in the minds of individuals but in the resources they share" (p. 41). Memory inscribed in individual consciousness tends to be blurred with the collective because we are always already born into a collective social setting. The point here is that memory is never solipsistic, although it is individually formed; yet it is always already culturally produced. There is a blurring between my own personal memory and the memory that is handed down to me by my family, school, and other cultural institutions.

George Herbert Mead (1913/1964) claimed that the self is social; therefore, selfhood does not arise in a vacuum. Like Mead, Maurice Halbwachs (1992) agrees that memory is not private or personal but rather it is primarily social. "Yet it is in society that people normally acquire their memories" (p. 38). Against these positions, I will contend that memory is not primarily social, nor is it primarily personal; rather, it is a complex combination of both.

Collective memories arise for all sorts of political, ideological, and psychological reasons. Collective memory has everything to do with the politics of national identity. Collective memory "defines such key ingredients as pride, shame, fear, revenge.... It is central to an understanding of nationalisms" (Markovits & Reich, 1997, p. 9). The collective memories of heroes and resisters, rhetoric that is robed in anti-Fascist myth, overlays former East Germany. These myths of Communist resisters of Fascism served to erase East German complicity in the perpetuation of crimes against Jews during the Holocaust. Shameful national memories may tend to be repressed for decades. Vichy, and the relatively late acknowledgment of France's complicity with the Holocaust, signals repressed memory. Maurice Halbwachs (1997) insists that we only remember events in what he calls *collective frameworks* (1992, p. 40) which are shaped by culture. According to Markovits and Reich, "Collective memory is invoked to heal, to blame, to legitimate. It has become a major idiom in the construction of identity, both individual and collective" (p. 9). These collective frameworks function as frames which actually limit what it is we are able to remember. For example, an American collective framework might be limited by the mere fact that we were bystanders during the Holocaust. Bystander perspectives, which are not monolithic, differ radically from victim or perpetrator perspectives. Furthermore, American culture might be limited in its collective framework by its Puritanical character, and by its difficulty dealing with race, ethnicity, and violence. The American collective framework still may be limited in its refusal to see Jews as Jews, Jews as other. Jewish Americans who do not assimilate are still marginalized and are considered 'too Jewish.' But the American collective framework is highly complex and elusive. The notion of a collective framework becomes problematic because it suggests that there is, in this case, an American character, an essential Americanness. But America is made up of so many different kinds of people that it becomes difficult to say what a collective framework is after all.

Memory is not only collective, it is also intensely personal. As Susanne Langer (1953) tells us "memory is the great organizer of consciousness. It simplifies and composes our perceptions into units of personal knowledge. It is the real maker of history" (p. 263). And of course, memory is not one thing, nor is it even "one faculty" (Warnock, 1987, p. 14). Memory is dense and scaffolded, horizontally and vertically, over time and place. Some memory traces haunt while others vanish. Mary Warnock (1987) remarks that "memory images are like guests. Some are invited, even sought after, others invite themselves, they are welcome or unwelcome" (p. 16).

Recalling personal memory, especially of the Holocaust, becomes complex because as Ruth Linden (1993) points out that "As we fashion the stories of our lives, memories naturally blur with subsequent interpretations of remembered events" (p. x). Memories seem to come from deep recesses in the psyche, arriving on the scene in their own time. Memories seem to have a life of their own. Patricia Hampl (1997) suggests that "there's precious little order to the slides [of memory] in the rotating carousel [of the mind]. Beyond that confusion, who knows who is running the projector?" (p. 66). The otherness of memory leaves unconscious inscriptions, traces deposited in the sites of the body. Memory is embodied and memories pain and course through the body. At the end of the day, memory is fuzzy.

Not only is memory fuzzy, its relation to history is fuzzy too. Saul Friedländer (1993) and Eric Hobsbawm (cited in Friedländer, 1993) suggest that memory and history have a fuzzy relation. In fact, Hobsbawm declares that

> there is a twilight zone between history and memory between the past as a generalized record which is open to relatively dispassionate inspection and the past as part of, or background to, one's own life. (p. viii)

This fuzziness between memory and history is also due, in part, to the fact that "Memory is the raw material of history, whether mental, oral, or written, it is the living source from which historians draw" (LeGoff, 1992, p. xi). As Carl Becker (1935) declares, history is, in fact "the artificial extension of social memory" (p. 248). However, Halbwachs argues that social memory differs from the notion of history. For Halbwachs, collective memory is completely antithetical to history. Markovits and Reich (1997) point out that for Halbwachs, "history is universalistic, [whereas] collective memory is particularistic ... history is timeless, collective memory is an expression of feeling" (p. 14). But bifurcations such as these make little sense. History is the systematization of memory. History is about the particular, and may have universal significance even if it does not explain universal laws or a priori principles. Doing history involves both cognition and emotion. History is both time-bound and subjective. Historians work out of their own memories and the memories of their subjects. And historians' renderings of the past are clearly affected by the ways in which they remember the event, if, that is, they are writing about recent history. If historians repress their own memories around the event that they are working on, their interpretations will reflect this repression. Memory, however, is not the same thing as history and I argue that history should not be collapsed onto memory. As Jacques LeGoff (1992) stresses, this move would be "naive" (p. xi).

Collapsing memory onto history, or conversely, polarizing memory and history, reduces the complexities of the past. Both of these ways of explaining memory suffer from the disease of a Cartesian logic—an infantile wish phantasy to move toward simpler and simpler ideas. Should not explanations of the past be complexified?

Polarizing memory and history also results, usually, in valorizing history at the expense of memory. Halbwach's position clearly valorizes history at the expense of memory. Memory is reduced to emotion and feeling, fragility, and unreliability. Early Holocaust scholarship appropriated this kind of position. One of the unfortunate consequences of such a position is the exclusion of voices of the victims. Holocaust victims have been othered from their own history.

It is important to note that historians do not simply remember historical events, they systematize events by relying on documents. Although documents are forms of memory, because they are constructed by human beings who remember, doing history is still different from remembering it. But historians, if writing about recent history, do remember, and the ways in which they remember ultimately shape their constructions of the past. Thus, history and memory overlap in uncanny ways.

I think that memory, because it is the very stream out of which we operate as human beings, is the larger category under which history is subsumed. Therefore, I want to privilege memory, because it shapes consciousness, perception, and lived experience in general. If anything, privileging memory complexifies our notion of history because it risks getting lost in "the unconquerable flow of time" (LeGoff, 1992, p. vii). History is a form of memory of course, but it is not the same as memory. To signify this co-complex interrelation, I term history a memory text. I emphasize that memory and history are overlapping categories, yet they are not the same.

Whatever history is, it is ultimately ambiguous. Paul Thompson (1988) points out, though, that "All history depends ultimately on its social purpose" (p. 1). History may serve as a "justification of war," as an "escape," or as a form of what Thompson calls "Bland contemporary tourism which exploits the past as if it were another foreign country to escape to ... purged of social suffering, cruelty and conflict" (1988, p. 1). Or, some may feel that the purpose of history may be to master and control the past. To write about history, in other words, is a way of feeling that one is in control of the past. As LaCapra (1985) suggests:

> The dream of a "total history" corroborating the historian's own desire for mastery of a documentary repertoire and furnishing the reader with a vicarious sense of ... control in a world out of joint has of course been the lodestar of historiography from Hegel to the Annales School. (p. 25)

But the past is forever slipping.

Before the discipline of history separated from philosophy of history in the 19th century, philosophy of history, especially as instantiated in Hegel and Marx, embraced a passion for control and mastery by offering up total systems, or grand metanarratives, and a priori principles to which history might adhere. Historical idealism was outstripped by historical empiricism and like historical idealism, empirical studies, like Ranke's and Bury's, attempted to match "facts" with reality in a correspondence-like fashion. But already in 1752

> The epistemological basis of [history's] ... ideal of impartially copying or representing the real was put into question ... the German theologian Johann Martin Chaldenius, elaborating a position outlined by Leibniz and Bayle, made the concept of point of view fundamental. (Grossman, 1990, p. 230)

Point of view, or interpretation, undermines the historian's quest to master and control the past, because interpretation and translation admit of slippage between the signifier and the signified.

Some feel that the purpose of history serves to bolster national pride and national identity, especially when a nation suffers from an embarrassing past. History, accordingly, is rewritten to suit national and political agendas and ideologies. For others, the purpose of history may revolve around the notion of "conversation" (LaCapra, 1985, p. 36) with the past. LaCapra (1985) contends that "historiography is dialogical in that, through it, the historian enters into a "conversational" exchange with the past.... The problem is the nature of the conversation" (p. 36).

For me, though, the purpose of history is ethical. Edith Wyschogrod (1998) remarks that the historian who embraces an ethics of remembering, "the historian when bound by a responsibility toward the dead for whom she claims to speak becomes ... the heterological historian" (p. 3). The heterological historian "feels the pressure of an ethics that is prior to historical judgment" (p. 3). This "ethics of an ethics ... would bring the dead to life" (p. 3). The call of the other beckons.

Constructing historical narratives opens questions around the ways in which historians rely on imagination. It opens questions around whether or not history and fiction overlap. Georg Iggers (1997) suggests that history and fiction are overlapping categories because the historian must rely on imagination. But he stresses that history is not fiction. Iggers tells us that,

> The panel on 'Fictionality, Narrativity, Objectivity' at the International Congress of Historical Sciences in Montreal in 1995, was to occupy a middle position, to recognize, as Roger Chartier formulated it, that while "one among many forms of narration, history is nevertheless singular in that it maintains a special relation to truth. More precisely its narrative constructions aim at reconstructing a past that really was" (pp. 1–2).

I will argue that history, or what I term, the *memory text of history*, occupies this middle position between construction and reconstruction and takes up a place where a third thing resides. This is the third thing of translation (Edgerton, 1996). Translation is not exactly a correspondence and not exactly a fiction, but something else, something complex, a translation of the other, the other of history and the other of memory. And I argue that although history is "subject to fiction" (Munro, 1998), it is not the same as fiction. Although historians draw on imagination to construct narratives, history making is constrained by the discipline of history, and is constrained in its attempts to make truth claims. Thus, history and fiction, although overlapping, are not the same. As Paul Ricoeur (1990) suggests, history and fiction are two different things although both draw on narrative and imagination. Historians attempt to get at the reality of the past. Fiction writers do not necessarily do this. Ricoeur (1990) remarks that

> Whatever may be said about the selective aspect of gathering, conserving, and consulting documents or about their relationship to the questions historians put to them, or even about the ideological implications of all these maneuvers, the recourse to documents does indicate a dividing line between history and fiction. Unlike novels, historians' constructions do aim at being reconstructions of the past. (pp. 142–143)

APORIAS OF MEMORY: THE UNCONSCIOUS AND THE HOLOCAUST

There is always already a tension between what has actually happened in the past and our present interpretation of that event. There is a co-complex interrelation between knowing what we remember yet not fully understanding what memory is in the first place. Part of the problem is that memory is shot through with unconscious traces which may become manifest as reversals, projections, resistances, and transferences. The strangeness of the unconscious, or the otherness of the unconscious, shapes memory in uncanny ways. Memory is subject to many uncanny aporias. I would like to examine what I consider to be difficulties in understanding memory. Following, I highlight some aporias of memory and of doing memory work around the Holocaust. I will argue that the memory text of lived experience becomes complexified because of unconscious traces. Memory and the unconscious are inextricably tied. Memory of the Holocaust is subject to our own unconscious operations.

Edward Casey (1987) remarks that memory is "thick" (p. 265). Memory has a "depth not easily penetrable by the direct light of consciousness ... [and it is] resistant to conceptual understanding [because it is] sedimented in layers" (p. 265). Casey further declares that memory is "gappy" (p. 72) and this gappiness results in "undefined and unlocalized particles of space" (p. 72). Thus, memory's gappiness can never fully recapture exact representations of the past, but only "pastiches" (p. 72). These pastiches come to us in what Casey terms a "quasi-narrative" (p. 44) form primarily because "what is lacking in memory is a proper narrative voice, the voice of an authoritative narrator who spins out the tale" (p. 44). These quasi-narratives are situated first in what Casey calls primary memory, but are more properly located in secondary memory or recollection proper. In order to remember at all, an event must have some "persistence" (p. 39). The "just-lapsed" (p. 39) memory traces must have "prolongation" (p. 39) to be remembered at all. But unless the memory is an "ex-perience" (p. 41), that is, unless the memory jolts us in some way as being different from the perception of the just-passing-by, recall will not happen later. Primary memory, then, "occurs so continually and often so imperceptibly that we rarely notice it at all" (p. 49).

The operation of actually recalling memory traces belongs to the realm of secondary memory. For Casey (1987), secondary memory is a form of "remembering again or re-remembering" (p. 51). The function of secondary memory is "that of rescuing former experiences from oblivion" (p. 50). These recollections are embodied and "emplaced" (p. 182). The body serves as an "intra-place" (p. 196) or interior site which "opens out onto place" (p. 182) as an exterior site. In other words, memory, for Casey, occurs in the interior place of the body but also flows outwards toward the world. Thus, memory has a kind of elastic quality that stretches over places and bodies.

I draw on Casey's work because he stresses that memory is embodied. And it is an embodied memory that pains Holocaust survivors. Memory literally pains in the body. Because of the workings of the unconscious, memory is subject to displacements and these displacements are embodied. *Psychological displacement* is marked, as John Fletcher (1999) explains, by

> Affective reactions that separate from and appear to forget their circumstances of their genesis, becoming bound to very different representations; the somatization of hysteria ... free-floating anxiety ... transference [are embodied memories that have been displaced]. (p. 29)

Somatizations may manifest bodily traces such as sweaty palms, quickened heartbeat, numbness, headaches, anxiety, panic attacks, nightmares, depression, dissociation, phobias, paranoia, manic speech, defensive reactions, psychosis, and hallucinations. Memories that get repressed manifest in displaced forms which get acted out in sites in the body. Displacements mark a site that is out of joint with current lived experience. It would seem that nothing in the present situation would warrant these somatizations. Memory traces leave residues if they do not get worked through, at least partially.

These psychological interruptions of memory become sedimented over time, especially for Holocaust survivors. When memory is repressed and pushed down into the registers of the unconscious, the repressed returns and haunts. Aaron Hass (1996) explains that it was William Niederland, who in 1964 coined the term *survivor syndrome* (p. 1), a term that signifies many kinds of displacements of memory from which Holocaust survivors often suffer. Some of the symptoms of displaced memory, according to Niederland include "chronic anxiety, fear of renewed persecution, depression, recurring nightmares ... anhedonia ... social withdrawal, fatigue ... hallucinations, and depersonalization" (cited in Hass, p. 8). However, diagnoses such survivor syndrome are problematic when they reduce suffering to stable categories which serve to simplify what it means to suffer.

Pathologizing and categorizing reduces suffering to sameness and squashes out the "alien-ness" (Laplanche, 1999, p. 67) of suffering. The suffering caused by the Holocaust is nothing strangers to the event can imagine. Diagnoses presuppose that we can understand this kind of suffering. These diagnoses, therefore, tend to domesticate and trivialize. Paula Salvio (1999) remarks, "We might ask ourselves what we use these diagnoses to keep ourselves from thinking about" (p. 186). Diagnosing Holocaust survivors keeps us from thinking about the unintelligibility of what it is survivors must endure over a lifetime. The pain that memory brings is not something that can be reduced to a this or a that. Suffering is personal and idiosyncratic, strange and alien.

Like Casey, William James's (1890/1950) work on memory helps to raise questions relevant to Holocaust survivors. James argues with Casey that, basically, there are two kinds of memory, "elementary memory" (p. 646) and "secondary memory" (p. 648) or "recollection" (p. 646). Primary memory, if it is to exist at all, must have a certain "endurance" (p. 643), what James terms a "substantive state" (p. 643). This substantive state results in an "after-consciousness" or "after-image" (p. 645) of the event. The difficulty of grasping this after-image is that it "blends in" (p. 645) with subsequent after-images. "The just-past" (p. 646) blends in with fresh impressions. If this primary memory is recollected later, it is not recollected in an originary form, but is remembered, rather, through the lenses of the present. Primary memory is recollected or re-presented in "the nearward portion of the present space of time and [is not a representation of] the genuine past" (pp. 646–647). The genuine past, says James, is always already gone and what we recall is the "belief" that we remember the event. James declares that "Memory is the feeling of belief in a peculiar complex object" (p. 652). The genuine past is remembered in highly imaginative ways because we cannot capture the "genuine past" or the "just past" any longer. Secondary memory, or recollection, is not located around a singular event, but rather it is layered over by "associations" (p. 650). James (1890/1950) explains that

> the more facts a fact is associated with in the mind, the better possession of it our memory retains. Each of its associates becomes a hook to which it hangs when sunk beneath the surface. Together they form a network of attachment by which is woven into the entire tissue of our thought. (p. 662)

But we generally do not recollect all of these associations, James claims. Rather, we select this and that. In fact, James argues that "selection is the very keel on which our mental ship is built" (p. 680).

Does James focus too much on the conscious activity of memory? Is it the case that most of our memory is selected consciously? Or does the unconscious operate in uncanny ways shaping what is remembered and what is forgotten? Unwanted and repressed memories arrive in their own time, arising out of the unconscious. Certainly, Holocaust survivors' nightmares attest to this. These are unconscious memories that survivors do not consciously select. It seems that repressed memories select themselves as the unconscious pushes them upward, unwanted. Freud suggests that most of our so-called conscious lives, which includes our memories, are covered-over in unconscious traces.

James (1890/1950) declares that the more associations one has with an event the more likely one is "in possession of it" (p. 662). This may be the case sometimes. But when memory is horrific, the rememberer, in many instances, is not in possession of the memory; rather, the reverse is true. The memory is in possession of the rememberer. The rememberer, that is, seems possessed. Freud and Breuer certainly would adhere to this. Before the advent of psychoanalysis proper, Freud and Breuer engaged in the hypnotic method to release their patients from buried memories. These patients seemed to be possessed by their memory.

Charlotte Delbo (1990), a Holocaust survivor, remarks about the "alien-ness" (Laplanche, 1999, p. 67) of her own memory. Delbo says she feels possessed by memory's strangeness. "I live in a twofold being" (p. 3). This twofold being lives in the everyday postwar world and in Auschwitz, simultaneously. Delbo comments that it is not that she lives "with Auschwitz ... [but she] lives next to it" (p. 5). Possessed by the memory of Auschwitz, Delbo becomes dissociated from herself and often talks in the third person.

> For all these years she has done little things, gone through the little motions of everyday life, she listens to the sounds of life moving around her. She hears only the wind blowing across the icy plain, the shouts of the female guards.... She smells only the smell of the crematoriums. She hears only the voices of her friends who tear her away from her dead sister's body. (p. 6)

Clearly unwanted memories kept Delbo a prisoner during her life.

Memory disturbs and interferes with everyday life. Disturbances of memory are due to unconscious traces. These kinds of disturbances and interferences suffered by trauma seem to undermine the neat and tidy epistemological schematization that both James and Casey offer. What does it mean to have a primary and secondary memory? Why do these distinctions even matter? What is significant about them? For Holocaust survivors, memory does not seem to follow a clear chronology, and it does not seem to break down into tidy distinctions between the here and now, the first and the second, the there and then. Memory lacks coherence. Memory interrupts and breaks into the everyday. Memory brings nightmares. Perhaps the more associations one has with an event, if that event is traumatizing, the more it gets repressed. But repressed memory returns. When repressed memory returns, it takes its own idiosyncratic path, a path that is marked by displacements and reversals. Fletcher (1999) says the memory and its

> unconscious inscription, however, behaves quite differently from a single memory or copy [what James would call the genuine past] of what was once conscious: for making conscious the representation does not automatically abolish the unconscious inscription and its effects. (p. 36)

Memory traces have a life of their own, traveling across an unconscious trajectory that offers up strangeness.

In spite of my criticisms of James, I think his work is important for several reasons. The notion of associations, one that would become very important to Freud, is crucial when doing memory work. To freely associate opens the doors to the unconscious. This is the goal in analysis. But free association does not come easily, for it is blocked by secondary process thinking. This is why dream work, for Freud, became key to opening the doors to the unconscious. To freely associate around dreams opens the doors to blocked memories. Consciously trying to remember traumatic events is made difficult by the psyche's own censorship and resistances. Whether associations help us remember more of the past, or the genuine past, as James would put it, is really not as important as are the latent thoughts and state of mind that these repressed memories currently create. And the associations are not peripheral. They tell us much about the ways in which the rememberer gathers and collects remnants from her past. The gathering and collecting of remnants are just as important as the actual event itself.

James's notion of belief and the way in which belief is inextricably tied to memory is crucial. I think he is onto something when he asserts that memory is shot through with belief. To have believed something to have been true does not make the memory of the event less real. Even if memory is covered over with belief and imagination, it still clues into something important about the rememberer's complex relation with her past. Paul Thompson (1988) remarks that

> History [or memory], in short, is not just about events, or structures, or patterns of behavior, but also how these are experienced and remembered in the imagination. And one part of history, what people imagined happened, and also what they believe might have happened ... may be as crucial as what did happen. (p. 139)

Belief, associations, and imagination are all important because they tell us about the ways in which memory gets inscribed in all kinds of different emotional registers. All of these seemingly peripheral and unimportant feelings that surround the actual memory become clues to the ways in which unconscious traces shape memory. Thus, belief, associations, and imagination are not peripheral at all; in fact, they become central when thinking about the complexities of memory.

Unlike Casey and James, Henri Bergson (1988) complexifies memory through the notion of "duration" (p. 83). Bergson seems to emphasize more than Casey or James that memory, as a function of time, rather than of place, is, as Patrick Slattery (1999) might suggest, *proleptic* (p. 30). A proleptic sense of time is without rigid boundaries. Past, present, and future blend together. The categories of past, present and future, which are, of course, constructions, may be a function of the ego and secondary process thinking. Time experienced in a more regressive way has no boundaries; it is free-flowing. It is this sense of time and memory that Bergson offers to us. For Bergson (1988), sometimes the past overtakes and blurs with the present. "Our consciousness of the present is already memory" (p. 151). No sharp distinctions exist between that which is remembered and that which is experienced in the here and now. Experience is always already beginning to be remembered as it is happening.

Bergson does not draw a distinction between the categories of perception and memory. He seems to blur these to suggest their co-complexity and interrelation. Bergson (1988) declares, "Your perception, however instantaneous, consists then in an incalculable multitude of remembered elements, in truth, every perception is already memory" (p. 150). Memory, if it is to "survive" (p. 66), "must constantly mingle with our perception of the present and may even take its place" (p. 66). For Holocaust survivor Charlotte Delbo, past and present overlap. Recall, she remarks that she lives in two worlds simultaneously. She lives in the postwar world doing everyday things, and at the same time, she lives alongside Auschwitz. Auschwitz is there with her always and overtakes the present. Bergson (1988) claims that "successive perceptions ... extend over a certain depth of duration" (p. 70). "Memory condenses ... appears to us all at once, although [it happens in moments that are] successive" (p. 70). But for Holocaust survivors, successive moments of time seem to stop. Memory condenses, becomes displaced and takes on a life of its own. Memory has its own uncanny pattern. But this pattern seems to be jagged and haphazard.

Bergson's notion of duration may not be incompatible with loss. Jean Laplanche (1999) explains that "loss is probably co-extensive with temporalization itself ... [mourning is] an affect with a duration ... it occupies a lapse of time" (p. 242). Traumatic memories get lodged in voids and lapses and they seem to return in their own time and have their own "depth of duration" (Bergson, 1988, p. 70). For Holocaust survivors, time may be experienced differently than, say, third-generation Jews after Auschwitz. Memory may overlap with the present, remaining unintegrated. Memory may lack coherence, yielding up, as Casey (1987) would say, only "gappiness" (p. 72).

Bergson does not deny that memory and the unconscious are related. However, he does not discuss the unconscious much at all. It is Freud who takes up the notion of the unconscious and its complex relation to memory in a systematic way. Unlike Bergson, Freud (1900b) draws a distinction between perceptions and memory traces, making the former less complex than the latter. "A trace is left in our psychical apparatus of the perceptions which impinge upon it. This we may describe as a memory trace; and to the function relating to it we give the name memory" (p. 538). Perceptions, Freud tells us, form "associations" (p. 539) when connected. But many of our memories and their associations are unconscious. Freud (1900a) declares that we only realize this through the study of dreams. "It may happen that a piece of material occurs in the context of a dream which in the waking state we do not recognize as forming a part of our knowledge" (p. 11) Yet it is not a literal dream that yields up the memory but the associations that the dream yield that are crucial for "recovering memory" (Pinar, 1991, pp. 173–174). What becomes difficult, though, is that the psychic apparatus shields itself through "resistance" and "censorship" (Freud, 1900a, pp. 143–144). Thus, it is what is not said and not remembered that becomes key to doing dream work. What is repressed is forgotten but still remains in the ruins, buried. Freud (1893/1899) claims that "Both memory and trace and the affect which is attached to the idea are there once and for all" (p. 42). What we remember we never really forget; the contents of memory become repressed and are pushed down into the unconscious.

When we try to recollect our memories, repressed memories are censored by what Freud terms *screen memory*. Freud (1899/1989) remarks that "Recollections ... whose value lies in the fact that it represents in the memory impressions and thoughts of a later date whose content is connected with its own by symbolic or similar links, may appropriately be called screen memories" (p. 126). In other words, *screen memories* serve the function of screening difficult memories by producing other memories that are closely connected and associated with that actual event, but are not the original memory. The originary memory is screened because it is too painful. Freud (1911–1913) believed that what is unconscious and repressed could be made conscious through analysis and dream work. But until unconscious memory traces are made conscious "acting out" (p. 150) wins the day. Acting out is a way of not remembering. Freud terms this *repetition compulsion*. He declares that with repetition compulsion,

> the patient does not remember anything of what he has forgotten and repressed, but acts it out. He reproduces it not as a memory but as action; he repeats it, without of course knowing that he is repeating it. (p. 150)

And it is this acting out or repetition compulsion that lies at the heart of transference. In order to undo transferential relations, which Freud (1900a) thought inappropriate to the current situation, it would become necessary to trace back through the ruins on the path toward repressed memory. Freud comments that through analysis one could be able to make the unconscious conscious through what he called *intentional recollection* (p. 54). This *intentional recollection* attempts to lift memory traces that block recollections. The "reconstruction" of memory would be possible through the patient's "construction" of narrative and dream work (Freud, 1937–1939, pp. 267–268). Memories are repressed and pushed into the unconscious because they are too overwhelming.

Freud's earliest work on repressed memory was tied to incest. Freud's seduction theory turned on the idea that all repressions were due to incest. But in 1897, he abandoned this theory. As John Fletcher points out, although Freud abandoned this theory, Laplanche argues that traces of it can be found throughout Freud's work. Fletcher (1999) says

> As Laplanche has argued, the 'turning point' of 1897, the abandonment of the seduction theory, does not represent a clean or absolute break. Elements of the theory persist in different forms ... the acknowledgment of the traumatic power of actual events, infantile sexuality and the dominance of two theories of the drives. (p. 9)

Laplanche (1999) suggests that Freud actually "domesticates" (p. 67) the notion of the unconscious. He domesticates it by "reducing it" (p. 66), by taking the "alien-ness" (p. 67) out of it. Recall, Freud claims that what is unconscious can be made conscious again and transference can be resolved at the end of analysis. Yet Laplanche (1999) argues that these clean resolutions serve only to domesticate by making the strange familiar. Laplanche reappropriates Freud's seduction theory by claiming that we are always already seduced by significant others. We are seduced by "enigmatic messages" (p. 80) that get "implanted" (p. 258) in our psyche. These messages are, for the most part, beyond translation. Laplanche argues that Freud went astray when he abandoned the seduction theory because all of life, for Laplanche, is about seduction.

One reading of Freud might suggest that if repressed memory, in the case of Holocaust survivors, were made conscious, the sufferer of memory would be "cured" because the repressed would stop returning in unhealthy and bizarre ways. This reading also suggests that transference and acting out, the compulsion to repeat, will just go away after the Holocaust survivor endures analysis and works through her nightmares, depression, anxiety, or depersonalizations. However, this reading of Freud tends to simplify what it means to be a Holocaust survivor.

We must keep in mind, though, that toward the end of Freud's life he became more and more skeptical about the prospects of psychoanalysis (1937/1991). He was well aware that going through analysis guaranteed little. In fact, he argued that psychotics were untreatable. It was Jung's work with schizophrenics that changed the minds of those in the psychoanalytic community who were weary about the prognoses of psychotics. Nevertheless, Freud, at least early Freud, seemed confident that analysis could offer up a cure. Paula Salvio (1999) terms this kind of thinking an *epistemology of cure* (p. 186) and she suggests that it "invoke[s] a cultural desire for an imaginary 'ending'" (p. 185) to suffering. Salvio argues that we must move beyond this epistemology of cure to admit that suffering does not just go away through analysis. There is no way to work completely through Holocaust memories. This implies a getting better when there was no illness to begin with. Laplanche's (1999) post-Freudian turn, his post-Freudian reading of Freud, moves beyond what Salvio (1999) terms *a narrative of closure* (p. 185). Again, Laplanche suggests that if we remain open to our own otherness in relation to the other's otherness, and if we understand the aporias and complexities of the strangeness of the unconscious, the task of recovering memory becomes much more difficult. There is no cure for repressed memory because it was never pathological to begin with.

THE MEMORY TEXT OF HISTORY: THE UNCONSCIOUS AND THE HOLOCAUST

At this juncture, I turn to what I call *the memory text of history*. Here I will examine different positions on what it is that historiography might be. What is it that allows us to think historically in the first place? What are some connections between philosophy of history and the work of current historiography? Have Hegelian and Marxist interpretations of history marked current trends in thinking about the Holocaust? Does history produce subjects or do subjects produce history? Or, is there a dialectic that moves between these two positions? In what ways do historians' unconscious inscriptions shape history? In what ways do historians' own pasts mark their texts? Here, I am interested in the aporias of historical understanding because these have implications for reading Holocaust texts. First, let us turn to Hegel.

Hegel's (1837/1987) work around the philosophy of history is scandalous, for it serves as a justification of evil, what theologian John Hick (1978) calls *dysteleological evil* (p. 362). *Dysteleological evil* is massive evil. Hegel contends that all historical events, whether evil or not, have a final purpose: a telos, a justification. This final purpose or justification is the self-consciousness of God. God comes to himself (Hegel's God is male) through history. Ultimately, for Hegel, history is the story of divine providence. Hegel (1837/1987) explains that "divine providence is wisdom endowed with infinite power which realizes its own aim, that is, the absolute, rational, final purpose of the world" (p. 15). Hegel's God is all knowing and all powerful. But is this God good? How could a good God allow the Holocaust to happen? How could this event be part of God's divine plan? A Holocaust survivor, Primo Levi (1996) writes "Today I think that if for no other reason than that an Auschwitz existed, no one in our age should speak of providence" (p. 158).

Theodicists and theologians attempt to exonerate God from crimes like these by redefining the notion "God." The formula that God is all knowing, all powerful, and all good gets redone to save God from accusations of evil. For some, especially process theologians like John Cobb (1975) and David Griffin (1973), God is all knowing and all good, but not all powerful. Because God is not all powerful, he could not prevent the Holocaust. God gets off the hook. I do not find this maneuver to be convincing.

Another argument some offer, like John Hick's (1978), is what is called the *free-will defense*. Here, Hick contends that God endows human beings with free will, so human beings are free to do as they please. Thus, human beings get blamed for bad events because they are free to choose evil or good. God gets off the hook again.

If evil gets injected into God, then we might do away with the notion of God altogether, for who needs an evil God? But is the problem of evil this simple? Theodicies tend to split evil and good into neat and tidy categories. The problem with theodicies is that they tend to suggest that evil is an absolute category. But on examining the Holocaust, it seems to me that this notion of evil gets complexified by the very fact that perpetrators were not demons; they were human beings, ordinary, everyday Germans. I am not exonerating or excusing Germans who were complicit in crimes against Jews; I am suggesting, rather, that individuals are neither good nor evil; they are complicated. These absolute categories, I think, serve to simplify. Marion Kaplan (1998) points out that it was only after *Kristallnacht*, in 1938, that Jews began to realize that they were in real danger. And what made it hard for Jews to leave Germany, according to Kaplan, is the fact that many Germans remained friendly to Jews. This became confusing because Germans were giving Jews mixed messages. How could anyone believe what the future would bring? Human relatedness is much more nuanced and complicated than the splitting of good and evil.

Theologians and theodicists, at the end of the day, continue to exonerate God by redefining him. Perhaps they need to think again. Perhaps theologians should listen to Elie Wiesel (1986), who put God on trial in his novel *The Trial of God*. Rabbis put God on trial but continued to pray. The question that some might raise is how Jews could keep their faith after Auschwitz. The black sun of Auschwitz has made many Jews more religious. I think my turn back to Judaism is partially a result of my work on the Holocaust. But still, many Jews of my parents' generation are secular and not religious. Is this a result of the Holocaust? Or perhaps it is a result of the pressures of assimilation? I leave these as open questions. Jews respond to life after Auschwitz differently. Hillesum (1983) wrote:

> More arrests, more terror, concentration camps, the arbitrary dragging off of fathers, sisters, brothers. We seek the meaning of life, wondering whether any meaning can be left. We are but hollow vessels, washed through by history. (pp. 28–29)

These are the words of Etty Hillesum. She died in Auschwitz at the age of 29. It is through her words that I hear the echoes not only of Wiesel, but of Hegel. The specters of Hegel can be heard in her words as she says, "We are but hollow vessels, washed through by history." Hayden White (1987) comments that Hegel's philosophy of history "wears such a face of regularity, order and coherence that it leaves no room for human agency" (p. 21).

"We are but hollow vesels" throughout which spirit runs. Hegel's (1837/1987) philosophy of history is the adventure of spirit as it makes its way through the world. Anything or anyone in the way of spirit is destroyed. We are but hollow vessels. "World history goes on within the realm of spirit" (p. 30). The spirit of which Hegel speaks is derivative of the Christian notion of spirit, or the Holy Ghost. But spirit, for Hegel, differs from the Christian notion, because it is divided into an objective and subjective side. The subjective side of spirit is nature, matter, and human life. But this subjective side that moves through us is unconscious of itself. Hegel (1837/1987) claims

> World history begins its general aim—to realize the idea of spirit—only in an implicit form … namely, as nature—as an inmost, unconscious instinct. And the whole business of history … is to bring it into consciousness. (p. 30)

Meanwhile, spirit works itself out against itself. Hegel said "Spirit is at war with itself" (p. 69). Spirit is alienated from itself because the subjective side continually gets in the way of the objective side. Human beings, that is, continually get in the way of God's purposes. The objective side of spirit reflects God's will and is conscious of itself. Hegel said it is "the operation of coming to itself" (p. 23). And it comes to know itself through freedom. "World history is the process of the consciousness of freedom" (p. 24). However, as spirit progresses toward its self-consciousness it also necessarily becomes "connected with the degradation, destruction, annihilation of the preceding mode of actuality" (pp.

38–39). Thus, history is not happy but filled with conflict, struggle and pain. Hegel claims that "history is not the soil of happiness. The periods of happiness are blank pages in it" (p. 33). Hegel also refers to history as a "slaughter bench" (p. 27). For what purpose, Hegel asks, is this slaughter bench? For God's divine purpose. Did God, then, will the slaughter bench of the Holocaust? Wiesel (1982) wrote:

> I awoke on January 29th at dawn. In my fathers' place lay another invalid. They must have taken him away before dawn and carried him to the crematory. There were no prayers at his grave. No candles were lit to his memory. His last word was my name. A summons to which I did not respond. (p. 108)

Did Hegel's God will the slaughter bench of 6 million Jews? If so, Hegel's God is a scandal. This scandalous God is also a reasoning God for Hegel. Sometimes Hegel even talks as if reason is God. Reason, says Hegel, is "the law of the world and that, therefore, in world history, things have come about rationally" (p. 11). Like spirit, reason "determines itself in absolute freedom" (p. 15). Sometimes Hegel refers to reason as the *Idea*. The Idea, this transcendent something, is the prime mover of the world. The Idea, Hegel declares "remains in the background, untouched and uninjured" (p. 43) while the "particular exhausts itself in the struggle and part of which is destroyed" (p. 43). Human beings are destroyed, in other words, in the process of world history while the Idea remains safe and unharmed. Hegel calls this movement of the Idea in history the *cunning of reason* (pp. 43–44). Reason is cunning because it destroys whatever gets in its way while remaining free from injury.

Like spirit, the Idea divides in two parts: the absolute part and what Hegel calls *absolute free volition* (p. 32). The absolute Idea is God or the "substantial fullness of content" (p. 32). *Free volition* is the movement of the universe, the movement of people in the universe. However, "God and the universe have separated and set each other at opposites" (p. 32). The Idea "uses an external phenomena which in history present themselves directly before our eyes" (p. 26). History uses us as it pleases, we are but "hollow vessels" (Hillesum, 1986, pp. 28–29).

Some individuals throughout history, however, intuit God's purposes, according to Hegel (1837/1987). Here the subjective and objective sides of spirit coincide; here God's fullness of content and free volition coincide. "World historical individuals" (p. 39), or heroes, coincide with God's purposes. But I wonder what kind of heroes Hegel is talking about? World historical individuals, if they coincide with God's purposes, must also coincide with God's self-consciousness. Hegel's dream (or nightmare), then, is about consciousness. The goal of history is to get rid of what is unconscious. To me, Hegel squashes out the mystery of life because the unconscious is this mystery. Hegel's system smacks of what Freud (1909–1910) called the "arrogance of consciousness" (p. 39). Hegel believed that world history would fulfill its purposes by spirit's becoming ever more conscious of itself. But what exactly is this consciousness of which Hegel speaks? It is God, it is spirit, it is reason, it is little more than a mythical creature floating around, disembodied, pulling human beings into its web and closing off the future. Hegel's notion of consciousness is a ghost in the machine of history. The ghost of consciousness has prearranged the universe. The already made, the a priori principles to which world history is to unfold, weaves world history together without gaps, holes, or broken threads. Human beings need not worry, because God already has made up his mind, he has a plan. What God wants, God gets.

Of course, world history does not happen according to a plan. The coursings of history happen in chaotic, violent, and unpredictable ways. A Kleinian interpretation of Hegel might suggest that the Godhead, or the objective side of spirit, represents the good breast; the demonic, or the subjective side of spirit, represents the bad breast. The bad breast projects all of its hatred onto the world.

A Laplanchian reading of Hegel might suggest that the otherness within the self of God takes on demonic properties as it lashes out and destroys part of itself. The self of God, or the subjective side of spirit, cannot manage its own difference within, it cannot manage otherness. Thus, the repressed otherness projects its hatreds onto the world. The split-off self of the Godhead masters and controls world history. World history is controlled through violence. History is the unfolding of violence.

Hegel's system is sadistic. Spirit seems to take pleasure from the ruthlessness and cunning of reason. The polarization of good and evil, unconsciousness and consciousness, objective and subjective sides of the Godhead serve as defense mechanisms against complexities of God, world, self, and history. These kinds of dichotomies wipe out ambiguities and unresolvable paradoxes of lived experience. Hegel seemed afraid of uncertainty and the aporias of historical understanding. He seemed to have world history sewn up into a box. And out of this box comes Pandora's scandals.

The metanarratives of consciousness and reason have been deconstructed and questioned with the advent of post-structuralism and post-modernism. The notion of reason has been demonized, especially since the Holocaust. Some scholars even blame reason and progress and modernity for the rise of Hitler and the Nazis. Scholars tend to suggest that either fears of modernity, or conversely, the embracing of modernity played a role in the rise of the Third Reich. Reactionary modernism (Herf, 1984), anti-modernism (Young, 1997), the fear of technology and big business, these scholars argue, created the backdrop against which the Holocaust emerged. The wish for a more völkisch time when things were simple, rural, romantic, and back to nature seems to be a kind of thinking Nazis cultivated in the advent of modernity. Backward and romantic speculations about a time when life was rooted in 'blood and soil' are familiar words of both Hitler and Heidegger (Zimmerman, 1990). Völkisch thinking, which has had long history in German culture, is a symptom of reactionary sentiment. To conserve a nostalgic and idealized past is key. Tom Rockmore (1997) explains that,

> The Völkisch perspective, like romanticism with which it is allied, represents an approach to the problems of modern life which eschews rational solutions of any kind, including economic analysis, social reform ... in favor of an emphasis on human being in an often mystical sense. It differs from romanticism ... in the appeal to supraindividual, mystical forces and the stress on the people writ large. The importance of the individual is limited to the belonging to the group, typically the nation, the race, or both. Unlike romanticism, which is often apolitical, Völkisch thought is typically related to extreme forms of political conservatism and the most virulent types of nationalism. (pp. 36–37)

Modernity, progress, and reason are feared because each signals the turn away from the rustic, agrarian life. The urban, chaotic city life of big business threatens more simple ways of living. Völkisch thinking was not limited to country bumpkins, though. Many intellectuals, including Heidegger, embraced it.

Unlike trends associated with reactionary modernist sentiment, some scholars argue that those who embraced modernity, or who embraced the dreams of the Enlightenment set in gear the conditions that allowed the Holocaust to occur. Zygmunt Bauman (1995) believes that modernism, with its penchant for reason, perfection, progress, and optimism created the very conditions necessary for the Holocaust to occur. Bauman claims that Hitler was the "offspring of the modern spirit, of that urge to assist and speed up the progress of mankind toward perfection" (p. 199). The Holocaust was a "kingdom of reason, the ultimate exercise in human power over nature" (p. 198). Recall, Hegel's rational God willed a perfect kingdom as spirit comes to itself through the destruction of anything that gets in its way. Bauman suggests that our era is the "age of the camps" (p. 193). Bauman declares that the camps are places where difference is wiped out, where "efficient killing, scientifically designed and administered genocide" (p. 193) occur. Technology, a product of the modern spirit, created the conditions that set the stage for the horrors of efficient killing machines. Tom Rockmore (1997) suggests that according to Steven T. Katz, "many writers fail to give sufficient weight to the role of technology in Nazism since they overemphasize the reactionary, romantic aspects of National Socialism" (p. 355). There does seem to be a tension in the literature between those scholars who stress reactionary trends in Germany and those who stress the role of modernism and technology as potential backdrops to the Holocaust. Perhaps this polarization is too simplistic. Competing and contradictory sociocultural forces must be taken into account when interpreting the Holocaust.

Like Bauman, Tony Kushner (1994) calls for a critical look at modernity, suggesting that modernity and liberalism created the conditions for the Holocaust to occur. The lack of response on the part of Great Britain and the United States had much to do with the ways in which both of these countries embraced modernity and liberalism. Liberalism actually prevented the democracies from responding to the crisis until very late. The "liberal imagination" (p. 55), Kushner contends, worked against itself. That is, liberal ideas of tolerance, progress, optimism, and reason made it impossible for people to "think the unthinkable" (p. 74). Although Kushner points out that responses were not monolithic, generally speaking the United States and Britain did little to help the Jews. And this nonresponse was due in large part to liberalism and optimism. People in the West thought the crisis would just go away. Disturbed by the nonaction of the free world, Elie Wiesel (1995) writes

> The free world didn't care whether Jews lived or died, whether they were annihilated one day or the next. And so the sealed trains continued to shatter the silence of Europe's flowering landscapes.... I freeze every time I hear a train whistle. (p. 74)

Like Bauman and Kushner, Christopher Browning (1992) claims that Susanne Heim and Gutz Aly argue that reason and modernism set the stage for the Holocaust. Browning (1992) comments that for Heim and Aly, the Holocaust became possible primarily because of "the rational means employed by technocrats" (p. 60). Heim, and Aly suggest that the Final Solution was carefully and rationally planned out by an "intelligentsia [who] ... cooperated closely with one another in an interdisciplinary fashion" (cited in Browning, p. 60). These so-called *technocrats* embraced a "common vision and way of thinking—sober problem solving and rational" (p. 60). The specters of Hegel are echoed here.

Bauman, Kushner, Heim, and Aly all feel, in one way or another, that modernity itself, reason as the stepchild of modernity, created the very conditions that allowed the Holocaust to occur. But perhaps this kind of thinking is too simplistic, too reductionistic, too monocausal. How does one make the move from ideas about modernity to actions of mass murder? What happens between reason and killing? How does "the cunning of reason" (Hegel, 1837/1987, pp. 43–44) turn into the cunning of murder? I do not think it is enough to say that modernity and reason caused the Holocaust. As Saul Friedländer (1997) points out, the "major features of modernity itself ... do not alone constitute the necessary cluster of elements ... leading from persecution to extermination" (pp. 2–3). Jeffrey Herf (1997) drives this point home in his book:

> The message of the Nuremberg trials was that human beings and their political decisions had made Auschwitz possible—not being, fate, destiny, instrumental reason, the Enlightenment, modernity, or the West. (p. 208)

The tropes of the Enlightenment, instrumental reason, fate, and modernity, when used to explain or perhaps explain away the cause of the Holocaust, serve as defense mechanisms which cover over human complicity. The trope of modernity, when applied to the Holocaust, explains little about the makings of Auschwitz or the ways in which ordinary Germans perpetrated horrific crimes. Individuals made choices and these choices are what moved history along.

Unlike Hegel, Marx felt that individuals make history. Marx and Engels insist that "The first premise of all human history is, of course, the existence of living human individuals" (p. 147). Many times, Marx refers to man as the center of history. This emphasis on human agency runs counter to Hegel. Hegel's history is one that could press on without human beings. In fact, it is humankind that gets in the way of God's self-consciousness. Marx and Engels (1987) stress that human beings are central to history. "Its [history's] premises are men, not in any fantastic isolation or abstract definition, but in their actual, empirically perceptible process or development under definite conditions" (pp. 149–150). But the historical journey is not without difficulties. Our "alienation" and "self-estrangement" (p. 74) thwart the advance of history. Marx is not talking about alienated spirit after the fashion of Hegel, but rather he is talking about alienated self-actualization. The worker is alienated, both by the end product of labor and by the very activity of labor itself. Marx (1844/1987) claims that

> Whatever the product of labor is, he is not. Therefore the greater this product, the less he is himself. The alienation of the worker in his production means not only that his labor becomes an object, an external existence, but that it exists outside himself, independently, as something alien. (p. 72)

Labor, itself, alienates and it is the very activity of labor that causes "loss of ... self" (p. 74).

Bertrand Russell (1972) and Jean-Paul Sartre (1968) agree that, although Marx's philosophy of history is usually termed *dialectical mate-*

rialism (because Marx has said history makes us as we make it), still, human agency seems to weigh heavily over against the pressures of external circumstances. Whereas Sartre (1968) praises Marx's emphasis on human agency, Russell denounces it. Human beings are not the center of all things. Russell (1972) declares that

> Marx has many grave shortcomings. He is too practical, too much wrapped up in the problems of his time. His purview is confined to the planet, to Man. Since Copernicus, it has been evident that Man has not the cosmic importance which he formerly arrogated to himself. (p. 788)

Marx calls for a centering of the self in the scheme of things. Alienation of the self signals loss for Marx. But perhaps this understanding of the self is too simplistic. Unlike Marx's call toward centering the self, Laplanche (1999) suggests that what psychoanalysis teaches is just the opposite. In what he terms the *Unfinished Copernican Revolution* (p. 52), Laplanche calls for a "de-centering" of the self (p. 52). The self is "de-centered" by the "alien-ness" of the unconscious (p. 62). The unconscious "is precisely not our center, as it is an "ex-centric center" (p. 62). The "other thing" (p. 62) of the unconscious always makes us strangers to ourselves and to our own actions. We are both strangers in our being and in our doing. But this condition of strangeness does not prevent us from social engagement; it enhances it by keeping us open to the radical alterity of the other.

Thus, unlike Marx, Laplanche complexifies the notion of the self and turns the concept of alienation on its head. Alienation, or alien-ness, becomes an asset not an impediment. Despite the fact that I think Marx undertheorizes around notions of self and agency, I do think, however, that he is correct to say that human beings do indeed shape history and shape their lives. And like Jeffrey Herf (1997), I believe that when we examine the Holocaust, we must understand that the perpetrators made decisions to do what they did and they were not guided by anything other than their own conscience or lack of conscience. Still, human beings are not radically free, as Marx might suggest. Rather, freedom is always qualified and strained by institutionalized racism, sexism, homophoia, anti-Semitism and classism. But for Marx and Engels (1978), human beings can overcome circumstances even if they are "not free to choose their productive forces" (p. 137). Unlike Hegel, Marx and Engels suggest that history will be toppled not by criticism, not by

> resolutions into self-consciousness or transformations into "apparitions," "specters," "fancies," etc., but only by the practical overthrow ... revolution is the driving force of history. (pp. 156–157)

Conflicts will be brought on by class struggle and capitalism. Class struggles are caught up in the material forces of economic production. Terry Eagelton (1976) comments that for Marx "'forces' and relations of production forms ... the economic structure of society; or what is more commonly known by Marxism as the economic 'base' or 'infrastructure'" (p. 5). The superstructure, Eagelton points out, "produces laws and politics [and] a certain kind of state" (p. 5). For Marx, Eagelton contends, "certain ... forms of social consciousness" (p. 5) produce ideology that serve to "legitimate the power of the ruling class" (p. 5).

The forces of economic production and class struggles will be resolved with the development of the Communist state. Marx and Engels (1844/1987) suggest that Communism is the "specter ... haunting Europe" (p. 203). The bourgeoisie will eventually "disappear in the face of modern industry" (p. 219). Accordingly, the proletariat will emerge victoriously as a mature form of Communism births itself. Communism will move toward the future and will be a

> positive transcendence of private property ... the real appropriation of the human essence [Man's centering ego] by and for man; Communism therefore is the complete return of Man to himself. (pp. 102–103)

Clearly, Marx returns to a Ptolemaic universe where humankind re-centers itself in the world. Not only are human beings re-centered, but struggle will be overcome and the dialectic of history will resolve itself. Communism will win out and at last a happy ending to history will occur.

It is obvious that Communism has been a disaster. And it is also obvious that there is much more to history than class struggle. The narrowing of history, the reigning in of history, through the supposed adherence of real events to a priori principles suggests that Marx, not unlike Hegel, was uncomfortable with contingency, complexity and chaos. Again, I argue that preconceived systems like Hegel's and Marx's serve as defense mechanisms against the unknown, against the very instability and uncertainty that surround us, against our own strangeness and inner alterity, and against our position as strangers in the world. However, Marx's fundamental premise that human beings make history is an important one, but has been overshadowed by the specters of structuralism, especially within the discipline of Holocaust historiographies.

Since the 1980s overriding principles governing these debates have turned on arguments between intentionalists (Dawidowicz, 1975/1986; Goldhagen, 1997; Friedländer, 1997) and *structuralists* (Hilberg, 1961/1985; Mommsen, 1966; Browning, 1992/1998; Broszat, 1969/1981). I discuss these debates in subsequent chapters, but for now I suggest that the argument between intentionalism and structuralism turns on the question of whether subjects produce history, or whether history produces subjects. *Intentionalism*, much like Marxism, stresses that human agency and human choice make history, while *structuralists*, much like Hegel, stress the function of social structures, such as institutions, and the role these have in making history. It seems, for the structuralists, that human agency gets overshadowed by larger, socially constructed institutions. It is as if institutions and social apparatuses have a life of their own, a driving force of their own. Intentionalists tend to stress the orderliness and know-how of the Third Reich; structuralists tend to stress the chaos and happenstance of the Third Reich.

Lucy Dawidowicz (1975/1986) suggests that, ultimately, the problem with the structuralists' argument is that they have no way to determine blameworthiness. Dawidowicz (1975/1986) contends that structuralists cannot hold actors accountable.

> Structuralists regard political decisions as the by-product of the ... structures or functions, and not as an expression of the will or intention of the States' leaders. Accordingly, no human agent can then be held responsible for decisions or for their consequences. (p. xxvii)

As Charles Maier (1988) points out, Saul Friedländer criticizes structuralist approaches because they tend to obscure blame. Maier contends that "In Friedländer's view [structuralists] ... dissolve guilt for the horrors of Nazism. Responsibility for an unspeakable crime becomes diffuse and elusive" (p. 95). Maier (1988) claims that structuralists might counter these charges by arguing that responsibility for the crimes of Nazism shifts from a few leaders to the "whole Nazi apparatus" (p. 95). Thus, blame seems broadened.

I find that this debate over intentionalism and structuralism, although important, too narrow. It frames perspectives of Holocaust scholarship in a certain way that sanitizes history. This debate serves to obscure and shift attention away from the hideousness of the Holocaust. Intentionalism and structuralism are signifiers that operate to keep certain questions at bay and certain horrible thoughts abstracted and unreal. Windows into the world of Holocaust victims undo these abstractions. The window into the world of this horrific memory is beyond the thinkable. This haunting is beyond imagination. Passages from this past, passages of personal experience like the one below, sink into the unconscious in ways that abstractions do not.

> They started the motor and the two Gestapo men began to pour some liquid, like water, on the Jews. But I am not sure what while pumping, they were connecting the hoses to the other containers, one by one. Apparently, because of

> the slaking of the lime, people in the pit were boiling alive. The cries were so terrible that we who were sitting by the piles of clothes began to tear pieces of stuff to stop our ears. (Biskupi, cited in Langer, 1998, pp. 21–22)

Reading a passage like this one demands a certain psychological readiness on the part of readers. The intentionalist–structuralist debate serves as a defense mechanism against dealing with this kind of emotionally gritty material. Victims' and survivors' voices are hardly heard in historians' renderings—part of the reason might not just be epistemological, it may be psychological too. Many cannot stand reading these kinds of horrific narratives so they exclude and erase them.

THE VICISSITUDES OF HISTORIOGRAPHY

Alongside philosophy of history, the writings of historiography were often subsumed under the category of literature. But with the rise of scientism and positivism, history gradually became a discipline in and of itself. Eventually, history departed from both philosophy and literature. In contrast, during the 17th and early 18th centuries, history and literature were closely related, if not inseparable. Lionel Grossman (1990) explains that the "relation of history to literature was not notably problematic. History was a branch of literature" (p. 227). Crafting history was considered an art by many. The debates over history's artistic or scientific foundations continued long after the 17th and 18th centuries. Croce and Travelyan (cited in Stern 1973) argued that the craft of doing historiography was artistic. Dilthey (1907–1910/1962) suggested that historiography was a "hermeneutic art" (p. 139). Marc Bloch (1954) declared that "the very idea that the past as such can be the object of science is ridiculous" (p. 122). R. G. Collingwood (1922/1965) suggested that historiography embraced both art and science. Leopold von Ranke and J. B. Bury (cited in Stern, 1973), believed that historiography was a science. Some commentators suggest that questions around whether art and science serve as the foundations of historiography are misguided. Hans Kellner (1989) remarks that

> The problem is not whether history is best conceived of as art, a science, or both, or neither, but whether art or science or something else is the most adequate representational model for historical consciousness. (p. 34)

The connection between literature and history began to disintegrate, when literature, especially during the Romantic era (18th and 19th centuries), became elevated to the level of the "sacred" (Grossman, 1990, pp. 228–229). Conversely, with the rise of scientism, history writing modeled itself after the natural sciences, which sought to name universal laws governing human relations. Grossman (1990) comments that

> The separation of literature and historiography was institutionalized, by the breakup of what had once been the republic of letters—a society in which the historians, both of the Enlightenment and of the Early Romantic period ... had mingled freely with ... novelists, poets, philosophers. (p. 223)

The idea of interdisciplinarity, then, is nothing new. But with the age of specialization and separation of the disciplines, with the rise of scientism and positivism, interdisciplinarity fell out of fashion. What was in fashion during the late 17th century and early 18th century was history writing as "active reflection" and "judgment" (Kellner, 1989, p. 5). Yet, some thought that to judge historical actors anathema. Marc Bloch (1954) argues that historians should never judge their subjects. "Are we so sure of ourselves ... to divide the company of our forefathers into the just and the damed?" (p. 140). Similarly, Tony Kushner (1994) suggests that Holocaust historians should not condemn, but explain. But I think that historians can and do make judgments. Even if they think they are not judging, they are by the mere selection and omission of material. As R. G. Collingwood (1924–1925/1965) declares, "We are making a judgment" (p. 50) in what it is we wish to represent. Interpreting material in particular ways is already an act of judging.

It is interesting to note that many historians, John Weaver (in press) explains, do not consider historical scholarship legitimate before the arrival of Leopold von Ranke. Ranke, who lived from 1795 to 1856, marked a turning point in the discipline of history. Many consider him the father of modern history. Weaver remarks that

> The tradition of history writing is thought to have begun with Leopold von Ranke ... the tradition defines history as an almost strict recounting of the diplomatic and political events of the past. According to the principles of historicism, the historian was not to interpret any contemporary viewpoints or theories into the past because if done correctly, the spirit of the past era would come through the historian's recounting. Historicism will dominate as a way of writing history ... well into the 20th century. (in press)

Ranke believed that the historian could let the facts speak for themselves without any extraneous interpretation. The historian was to seem the invisible arbiter of facts. The historian's voice was to vanish amidst a mountain of evidence. But Carl Becker (1935) comments that "to suppose that the facts [could] speak for themselves is an illusion. It was perhaps the illusion of those historians of the last century who found some special magic in the word "scientific" (p. 249). And Marc

Bloch (1954) declares that to let facts speak for themselves "effaces" the historian (p. 138). Historians cannot efface themselves, though. The historian and her writings are one, no matter how much she tries to be dispassionate.

Ranke and Bury both engaged in doing what might be termed historical realism. They believed that words can mirror reality; facts can copy reality and capture the past. Fritz Stern (1973) remarks that "J. B. Bury's lectures of 1903 may be taken as the culmination of that earlier mood of certainty ... the historian's task was to reconstruct the past ... to establish cause and effect in history, just as the natural scientists did" (p. 20). But as I mentioned earlier, not all historians agreed with the so-called scientific nature of history; not all adhered to the naive belief that facts correspond to reality in an exact fashion. Grossman (1990) explains that Chladenius, Leibniz, and Bayle understood already in the 1700s that interpretation and "point of view" (p. 230) undermine correspondence theories when applied to historiography. If everyone is different, if everyone operates out of his or her own perceptions, how can facts correspond in any neat and tidy way to reality? Hayden White (1978) comments that

> four major theorists of historiography rejected the myth of objectivity prevailing among Ranke's followers. Hegel, Droysen, Nietzsche, and Croce all viewed interpretation as the very soul of historiography. (p. 52)

But Ranke and Bury won the day. Historical realism won out over against constructivism. John Weaver (in press) argues that the dominant mode of history writing still resembles Ranke's. Historians, though, are well aware that their interpretations shape their texts. But that historians of the Holocaust, for instance, do not overtly interpret their representations is commonplace. They might offer a few introductory remarks about their point of view, but they tend to shy away from being overly speculative, overly philosophical, or overly interpretive. This is problematic because the facts do not speak for themselves.

Weaver (in press) explains that history has been considered a social science since the 1960s. And still, most traditional accounts of history focus on political and diplomatic issues. These top-down approaches, as Tony Kushner (1994) calls them, ignore broader social categories. Recently, though, in Holocaust scholarship there is a movement toward doing what is called *Alltagsgeschichte,* or everyday history (Kushner, 1994; Browning, 1998; Kaplan, 1998). These bottom-up approaches examine the histories of labor movements, police battalions, women's struggles, and other facets of everyday life under the Nazis. However, *Alltagsgeschichte* has been criticized by some who feel that it might tend to avoid discussing the more important issues that concern high level officials who became ultimately responsible for setting policies during the rise of the Nazis (Friedländer, 1997). But Christopher Browning (1998) argues that *Alltagsgeschichte* "becomes an evasion, an attempt to "normalize" the Third Reich, only if it fails to confront the degree to which the criminal policies of the regime inescapably permeated existence under the Nazis" (p. xix). Still, the bulk of Holocaust historiography takes a top-down approach; most sources attempt to explain political or military struggles. It is interesting to note that the History channel on television follows this pattern as well. Many of the Holocaust documentaries presented on the History channel take top-down approaches. Cultural histories, or everyday histories, are absent.

THE VICISSITUDES OF HISTORICAL INTERPRETATION

Michel Foucault (1966/1994) comments that since the middle of the 17th century, during what he termed the *classical age*, textual interpretation, or exegesis, turned on the notion of "resemblance" (p. 17). The exegete's task was to reveal hidden meaning in the original text. Once this hidden meaning was revealed, the exegete's explanation was supposed to resemble the original text as closely as possible, thus the phrase 'a close reading.' "Search for meaning is [always about bringing] to light a resemblance" (p. 29). The exegete's goal was to produce true copies or at least "similitudes" (p. 30) of the original. Foucault notes that "commentary halts before the precipice of the original text, and assumes the impossible and endless task of repeating its own birth within itself" (p. 81). The purpose of writing commentaries or doing exegetical work was to mirror back the text, to try to get it right, to attempt to get a likeness, and to reveal the truth concealed and buried within the text.

Wilhelm Dilthey (1907–1910/1962) stressed these principles. He considered the work of the historian a "hermeneutic art" (p. 139). Although the historian "stands in the midst of the ruins" (p. 139) his goal is to get behind the text to get at the truth[s] of history. In order to tell the truth[s] of history, which "are universally valid" (p. 69) the historian must "determine the inner side" (p. 69) [of the mind of historical actors]. Dilthey argued that "Actions and their permanent outward results constantly help us to reconstruct the mental content from which they arose" (p. 76). Dilthey offered up a psychological hermeneutic. Some consider him to be the father of psychohistory. When we examine the bulk of the work that has been done in psychohistory, especially psychobiographies, the goal seems to be to get behind the mind of, say, Hitler (Rappaport, 1975; Binion, 1976; Waite, 1977; Langer, cited in Rappaport, 1975; Erikson, 1976; Bromberg, cited in Rappaport, 1975). But is it really possible to get inside the mind of anyone? Can we ever really know what motivates people? Can we ever determine what people's intentions are? Does diagnosing historical actors help? Even if the diagnosis of borderline personality disorder is correct when applied to Hitler and to Luther, what is it that we do not learn about these people?

Like Dilthey, R. G. Collingwood (1946) offers another kind of psychological hermeneutic when thinking about doing historiography. Like Dilthey, Collingwood suggests that the historian, if he is to get at the truth of history, must "think himself into ... the thought of its agent" (p. 213). The historian must attempt to delve into "the thought in the mind of the person by whose agency the event comes about" (pp. 214–215). Again, Collingwood assumes that we can actually get into the mind of historical actors.

When hermeneutics is used to reduce complex phenomena, to reveal a truth hidden behind a text, it becomes inadequate to its task. Hermeneutics should not be reductive, but productive and generative. To suggest that we can know what it was that made Hitler tick presupposes too much. Assuming that we can get behind texts to reveal truth suggests that truth stops somewhere, that truth must be absolute. Truth with a capital T is nowhere to be found. But the proliferation of interpretations around a single event suggests that many truths may emerge. But these truths do not lie behind the text. They emerge in the complex interaction of reader and text. Doing good interpretive work does not clarify truth, it complicates truthfulness.

Jean Laplanche (1999) calls for an "anti-hermeneutics" (p. 88). He worries that hermeneutics always works to squash mystery out of texts. "The notions of defense, conflict, compromise, condensation ... lose all their impact when psychoanalysis is reduced to a new version of hermeneutics" (p. 88). Even so, I think we can use hermeneutics to complicate rather than reduce, and therefore, I am not willing to renounce hermeneutics once and for all. If interpretations of texts, of history are done sensitively they will generate rather than reduce ideas. Interpretations are always tentative and partial. What it is that gets represented as Holocaust scholarship depends on the interpretation given by the historian. The shifting and changing trends in Holocaust historiography change the ways in which this event will be remembered by generations to come. New interpretations might not generate new material, but perhaps new interpretations will reflect the growing concerns of the next generation. With every new interpretation comes a new strangeness. As Dilthey (1907–1910) stresses, "Interpretations would be impossible if expressions of life were completely strange. It would be unnecessary if nothing strange were in them. It lives, therefore, between these two extremes" (p. 77).

The strangeness of interpreting historical texts lies not in our ability to get at the mind of the author, or even to get at the workings of our own mind, because much of our lives are covered over in unconscious traces. Rather, strangeness in interpreting historical texts comes out of sites of liminality, slips of the tongue, or what Freud would call *parapraxes*, proliferations of doubles, repetitions, ghosts, reversals, internal objects, or uncanny transferences. As Hans Kellner (1989) points out, "historical thought" becomes open through "the problem of disjunctiveness, interference, and destruction of information" (p. 34). The destruction of information has much to do with the ways in which historians repress difficult materials. As Hayden White (1978) comments, "there are always more facts in the record than the historian can possibly include in his narrative representation" (p. 51). It is what the historian chooses to throw away or exclude that might offer clues to her own psychological resistances to the material. "By filling in the gaps," White contends, the historian interprets (p. 51). But what is it about these gaps and lapses and absences that become troubling? It is in the not-said that we should turn our attention.

It becomes clear in Holocaust scholarship that gaps in historical representation emerge around victims, women, gays, and lesbians. These representations in Holocaust studies have been, for the most part, considered "unfitting subjects" (Talburt, 1999, p. 59). We must disturb the memory text of history and examine these unfitting subjects, as Susan Talburt might call them. These historical subjects are considered "unfitting" by many traditional historians because matters of gender and sexuality are taboo and not considered appropriate to discussions around the Holocaust. But there is a movement, albeit a small one, mostly by feminists and queer theorists, to move these so-called unfitting subjects into the discussion. Historical writing shapes memory by erasing subjects.

FIVE

Memory Text of Holocaust Histories

Häftling: I had learnt that I am *Häftling*. My number is 174517; we have been baptized, we will carry the tatoo on our left arm until we die. (Levi, 1996, p. 27)

The definition of *Häftling* is prisoner. But the word prisoner does not, and cannot, capture what it must have been like to have lived through Auschwitz. Primo Levi survived Auschwitz, but forever remained a prisoner to its memory. The memory of Auschwitz, though, eventually overpowered and killed him. Primo Levi committed suicide like many other Jews returning to life after Auschwitz.

Through the prisms of memory, the term *Holocaust* arrived on the scene in the 1960s, but not without debate. This is a contested term, a contested site of representation which serves "to separate this particular massacre from other historical instances of genocide" (Marrus, 1987, p. 3). But some Jews are offended by the term Holocaust. Berel Lang (1990) explains that the word *Holokautima,* which is found in the septuagint, is a "Greek translation of the Hebrew *Olah*, which designates the type of ritual sacrifice that was to be completely burned" (p. xxi). But the Holocaust had nothing whatsoever to do with ritual sacrifice, with the divine. There was nothing sacred about it. Lang (1990) points out that many Jews prefer the term "shoah" which means "wasteland" or "destruction" (p. xxi). The term *shoah* is taken from the books of Isaiah and Proverbs. Whether one embraces the term Holocaust or shoah, the crucial and significant point here is to respond to the event in an intellectually and emotionally sensitive way. With "non-postponable urgency" Emmanuel Levinas (1969) remarks, the other "face" of the other, demands a response (p. 212). The others of this wrenching history demand a response; the face of 6 million dead others demands attention. And so respond we must. Levinas (1995), a Holocaust survivor, declares that we must respond to the call before it is too late:

> With the indulgent attitude toward mortality which we call the historical conscience, each of us has to wait for the occasion and recognize the call addressed to us. To respond to the call of the perishable instant! It must not come too late. (p. 184)

An historical consciousness and conscience should be an ethical one. Doing work on the Holocaust is an ethical task, and I feel that I have been called to address this difficult memory; I have been called out of my own unconscious, called out of a place that has no name. As a third generation American Jew, a third generation Jew after Auschwitz, I feel that it is my responsibility to grapple with this event. As Geoffrey Hartman (1996) claims, "the enormity of the event … blocks thought and leads to a black hole that swallows the haunted interpreter" (p. 1). Indeed, I am haunted by the memory of Auschwitz. But, despite being haunted by this horrific past, I am bound by a "promise of truthfulness" (Wyschogrod, 1998, p. 10) to remember the Holocaust, to remember both the living and the dead, to remember my Jewish ancestors.

The memory of the Holocaust is unique, a particular Jewish tragedy. One of the important points about the term *Holocaust* is that it designates the uniqueness of this tragedy. Michael Marrus (1987) stresses that "Holocaust specialists have presented a strong case for the "centrality" of anti-Semitism in Nazi ideology, or the "uniqueness" of the Holocaust, even by the grim standards of 20th century massacres" (p. 8). As David Weinberg (1996) points out, it was the trial of Adolph Eichmann that drove this point home. "Of particular significance was the emphasis that the Israeli prosecutors placed on the specificity of the Jewish tragedy" (p. 22). The Holocaust was not merely a humanitarian tragedy, it was rather a specifically Jewish one. It was not a tragedy like other tragedies. Charles Maier (1988) claims that "suggesting the comparability of the Final Solution to other genocides opens the way to apologetics. It facilitates a literature of evasion" (p. 1). The Holocaust signifies a radical alterity that must not be subsumed under the notion of the same. The attempt to subsume the Holocaust under the notion of the same, to suggest, in other words, its likeness or resemblance to another tragedy smacks of "normalization" (Maier, 1988, p. 70). To think that the Holocaust is like something else is to trivialize it.

The position which allows for comparability is one that is embraced by neo-conservative historians in Germany. Neo-conservatives often compare the Holocaust to Stalinist crimes. Charles Maier (1988) explains that

> The central issue has been whether the Nazi crimes were unique, a legacy of evil in a class by themselves, irreparably burdening any concept of German nationhood, or whether they are comparable to other national atrocities, especially Stalinist terror. (p. 1)

The debate around the issue of comparability surfaced during what is termed the *Historikerstreit* in Germany in the 1980s. Fiercely opposed to comparability, Jürgen Habermas charged neo-conservative historians like Andreas Hillgruber, Ernst Nolte, and Joachaim Fest with "relativizing" the Holocaust (cited in Maier, 1988, pp. 1–2). Ernst Nolte, in a move of projection, shifts blame from the Nazis to the Bolsheviks as the "original perpetrators of global annihilations" (cited in Friedländer, 1993, p. 34). Saul Friedländer explains that, according to Nolte, the Nazis acted out of desperation and "copied the Bolsheviks" (p. 34) because they feared that if they did not kill Jews in camps, the Bolsheviks would kill the Germans. The *Historikerstreit* entertained debates like these. The key issue here turns on national identity. The question becomes, how could historians frame history in Germany to bolster national identity and national pride? If they shifted blame to other perpetrators, or if they leveled the Holocaust and suggested that it was similar to other tragedies, the hope was that Germans would not feel so bad about having been complicit during the rise of the Third Reich. Jürgen Habermas suggests that the *Historikerstreit* signaled a "new nationalism" (cited in Maier, 1988, pp. 1–2). This new nationalism served to erase the past, or at least rewrite it, so as to become less awful.

Comparisons between victims and victimizers also works to unwrite history. The so-called *Bitburg* Affair demonstrates this morally repugnant stance. The year was 1985, the 40th anniversary of the end of the Holocaust. When President Reagan visited the *Bitburg* cemetery in Germany, where both the *Wehrmacht* (German army) and Nazi SS are buried, Jews protested. The protest concerned these issues. Initially President Reagan did not wish to visit a concentration camp. As historian Raul Hilberg points out, Reagan declared that he did not want to go to a concentration camp because he did not wish to "reawaken the memories and so forth, and the passions of time" (cited in Hilberg, 1986, p. 19). After pressure, however, and as an aside, Reagan did visit Bergen-Belson. But to make matters worse, Reagan then compared Jewish victims with Nazi SS, who he also considered "victims" of history. ""Reagan: F in history," a French newspaper headline declared" (Hartman, 1986, p. 11). It is repugnant and offensive, especially for Jews, to level victims and victimizers.

Many Jews were offended at Reagan's visit for another reason: Nazi SS were buried at *Bitburg*. Why honor perpetrators of horrible crimes? Would Reagan's visit have created such controversy if SS had not been buried there? If he would have only commemorated the *Wehrmacht* would it have made any difference? This depends on what it is people think about the German army and their role in the Holocaust. José Brunner (1997) points out that neo-conservative historian Andreas Hillgruber has argued that the *Wehrmacht*

> fought in the name of their nation and protected their families and women from death ... rather than aiding and abetting genocide—their deeds were not only innocent but heroic. (p. 269)

But evidence to the contrary abounds. It has long been known by historians that not only were the *Wehrmacht* soldiers not innocent but rather they were directly complicit in "aiding and abetting genocide." Omer Bartov (1997) explains that the *Wehrmacht* was deeply involved not "only in killing pows and partisans ... but also, in a direct and massive manner, in the implementation of the Final Solution" (p. 172). Thus, it does not make sense to draw a clear distinction between Nazi SS and the *Wehrmacht*, for they were both guilty of war crimes. Hence, Reagan's visit to *Bitburg* probably still would have created controversy even if Nazi SS were not buried there; although his *Bitburg* visit was aimed at reconciliation with Germans, it turned out to be an utter disaster, and if anything, it further alienated Jews.

> I saw people being sent to the gas chamber. I lived a block opposite the gas chamber and could see from my window people going into the building. There was a tall chimney and I could see flames coming from inside the building and never saw these people come out. (Szafran, cited in Zeiger, 1960, p. 188)

Dora Szarfran's deposition, taken at the Eichmann trial, is a reminder that these mass murders were carried out by human beings, who were doctors, teachers, soldiers "ordinary Germans" (Browning, 1998; Goldhagen, 1997; Friedländer, 1997). The smoke from the crematoriums is said to have been so thick that it produced a black cloud which hung densely overhead. The smoke could be seen for miles. The smoke was so thick that it made the sun turn black, hence the metaphor the black sun of Auschwitz. The smoke covered the walls of the train station at Auschwitz. People said they could smell burning flesh for miles away. How could they do it? I ask this question every day. How could they do this? When I attend synagogue and look around at all these Jewish people, at all these Jewish *children*, the question rings in my ears, How could they do it? I am aghast.

A crisis of representation and erasure of memory is happening now around the Holocaust. The so-called revisionist historians are, as Pierre Vidal-Naquet (1992) suggests in the title of his work on Holocaust denial, *Assasins of Memory*. Revisionists claim that (a) the Holocaust is a hoax, (b) that the numbers of deaths reported are exaggerations, (c) that the gas chambers did not exist, and (d) that the Holocaust was actually a Jewish plot to acquire the state of Israel. Deborah Lipstadt (1993) comments that the United States Holocaust Memorial Council receives many complaints from high school teachers that their students believe these fallacious claims. Lipstadt (1993) explains that

> High school teachers have complained that when they teach the Holocaust in their classes, they increasingly find students who have heard about Holocaust denial and assume it must have legitimacy. (pp. 3–4)

This is troubling especially since the last generation of Holocaust survivors are dying off, and within one generation they will not be able to testify to the horrors through which they lived. The burden of memory is on us.

That the Holocaust happened, that 6 million Jews were massacred is historical reality. As Georg Iggers (1997) explains, "historical accounts refer to a historical reality, no matter how complex and indirect the process is by which the historian approximates reality" (p. 147). A historical reconstruction attempts to get at the truthfulness of the event. A construction, a narrative, may shift our viewpoints around the event, but still it leaves the truthfulness of the event intact. Louis Mink (1987) remarks that "of course our interpretations and state of knowledge may change, but either Caesar visited Britain or he didn't" (p. 93). But doing interpretive work around the Holocaust is not just about changing states of knowledge. It is also about changing states of the psyche. Repression and its unconscious formations alter our viewpoints around historical events. Repressed memory might determine beforehand what it is an historian excludes in her interpretation. Interpretation of historical reality does not mean anything goes; it does not mean that radical relativism will do. Some interpretations are better than others; some interpretations are completely inadequate, some are outright lies.

Scholarship around the Holocaust is generally divided into three areas: *perpetrator*, *victim*, and *bystander* histories. Historians tend to specialize in one domain or another, rarely crossing boundaries. Saul Friedländer worries that Holocaust historiography has become too specialized and fragmented so as to obfuscate. Friedländer (1993) remarks:

> the image of the Nazi era presented by German and foreign historians, in becoming so diversified and complex, is perhaps blurred: the sheer multitude of specialized studies on the minutest aspects of this epoch tends to erase the sharp outlines of certain central issues, be they conceptual or ethical. (pp. 5–6)

The balkanization of Holocaust scholarship can produce, for the researcher, an overwhelming array of material which may become difficult, if not impossible, to sift through. What I would like to do here is draw out some of the broader questions that are raised when looking at the three broad areas of Holocaust scholarship (perpetrator, victim and bystander historiographies) and touch on key issues that Friedländer worries are being obscured. I argue that psychological mechanisms such as transference, repression, denial, projection, reversal and introjection may shape and determine what gets represented as Holocaust historiography in the first place.

PERPETRATOR HISTORIES

> The first time I came face to face with a German soldier was in 1940, when I was ten and a half.... The Germans wore goggles, black leather jackets, shiny high boots. In their powerful mechanized equipment they looked like giants from outerspace. At that moment I felt we had lost the war. (Jeruchim, cited in Rosenberg, 1994, p. 139)

German soldiers seemed like giants from outerspace, says Holocaust survivor Simon Jeruchim. It is this seemingly alien nature, this bizarre portrait of Germans, that echoes in many early Holocaust histories. Social psychohistorians (Reich 1933/1945; Adorno, 1950; Horkheimer, 1940; Fromm 1941/1969) and psychobiographers (Binion, 1976; Rappaport, 1975; Waite, 1977; Erikson, 1976) tended to emphasize the pathological, and hence, alien nature of German society. According to Peter Marthesheimer, the Germans' willingness to follow Hitler, "led to the psychopathology of a whole nation" (cited in Markovits & Noveck, 1996, p. 406). Wilhelm Reich (1933/1945) argued that Germans, under the sway of Hitler and his Nazi henchmen, got themselves embroiled in "a psychotic situation" (p. 29). Martin Broszat (1969/1981) suggested that the rise of Nazism was, in part, due to "the general pathology of German nationalism" (p. 29).

According to Wilhelm Reich, German pathology was caused by "sexual regression" (1933/1945, p. 26). Reich argued that German men became willing to "submit" (p. 25) to "authoritarian order" (p. 25) because they were "masochistic" (p. xi). Boys suffered at the hands of authoritarian fathers and consequently felt that they needed to identify with someone, namely Hitler, who could satisfy their masochistic needs. Hitler, the sadist, then filled the gap psychologically, especially for German men. Reich (1933/1945) comments that

> Sexual regression aids political reaction not only through this process which makes the mass individual passive and unpolitical but also by creating an interest in actively supporting the authoritarian order. (p. 26)

The so-called "mass individual" or collective German culture, had a basic flaw, an "irrational structure" (p. xvi) that allowed for the very condition of "fascism" (p. xvi) to arrive on the scene. Reich remarks that "fascism is not the deed of a Hitler or Mussolini, but the expression of the mass individual" (p. xvi).

Like Reich, Adorno (1950) suggested that German collective psychopathology was due to what he termed the "Authoritarian syndrome" (p. 759). This syndrome was caused by a tendency toward a "sadomasochistic resolution of the Oedipus complex" (p. 259). Similarly, Erich Fromm (1941/1969) declared that German society had a "symbiotic relationship" (p. 246) with Hitler, as he was the sadist and Germans masochists. The "authoritarian character" of German society allowed for the

> simultaneous presence of sadistic and masochistic drives. Sadism was understood as aiming at unrestricted power over another person more or less mixed with destructiveness; masochism as aiming at dissolving oneself in an overwhelmingly strong power and participating in its strengths and glory. (p. 246)

Unlike Fromm, Reich (1933/1945), and Adorno (1950), Ackerman and Jahoda (1950) claim that Germans, because they had authoritarian parents, were afraid to show weakness, and consequently became sadistic. As Robert J. Lifton (1986) stresses, many "early descriptions of Auschwitz and other death camps focused on the sadistic and viciousness of Nazi guards, officers and physicians" (pp. 14–15).

All of this pathologizing of German society is, however, problematic. To suggest that all Germans behaved in sadomasochistic ways is simplistic. Of course, there are many accounts of sadistic camp guards and passive German citizenry. But as Marion Kaplan (1998) points out, many Germans exhibited neither sadistic nor masochistic behavior. Lifton (1986) explains that, "sadism and violence alone would not account for the killing of millions" (pp. 14–15). One of the most serious problems of these early studies turns on blameworthiness and responsibility. If German society is pathologized, if Germans have collectively gone mad and are considered alien and abnormal, they can be exonerated from perpetrating crimes, for who would try the insane? "To dismiss Hitler or Himmler (or collective German society) as madmen or fiends, incomprehensible to "normal" people, is to say that critical judgment of them is not possible" (Waite, 1977, p. xvii). Germans are not demons. Germans are not aliens from outerspace. Germans are people. Since at least the 1980s, scholars have stressed that German crimes were committed by ordinary people. Lifton (1986) comments that what troubled him while doing research on the Nazi doctors was

> the ordinariness of most Nazi doctors.... [who were] neither brilliant nor stupid, neither inherently evil nor particularly ethically sensitive, they were by no means demonic figures—sadistic, fanatic, lusting to kill. (pp. 4–5)

Langer (1998), Kelman (1976), and Browning (1998) agree with Lifton that Germans, by and large, were neither sadistic or psychopathic. Like the label "psychopaths," the label "authoritarianism" conceals more than it reveals. It keeps us from thinking about the complexities of the responses and actions of perpetrators. To say that all Germans have authoritarian characters is to essentialize and simplify.

Like the label *authoritarian*, the term *Fascist* also becomes problematic because it too conceals more than it reveals. Wilhelm Reich (1933/1945) claimed that Fascism was the "basic emotional attitude of man in an authoritarian society" (p. ix). Reich contended that Fascism was a "mixture of rebellious emotions and reactionary social ideas" (p. x). But the term Fascism explains little. Saul Friedländer (1993) argues that

> "Fascism" as an overall tag ... shielded many of them [Germans] from the specificity of the Nazi past, and such ideological generalizations became deeply embedded in subsequent historical discourse. (p. 125)

Recall, East German historiography became saturated with rhetoric of anti-Fascism. Communists blamed former West Germans for the Holocaust. West Germans were referred to as Fascists. But this anti-Fascist rhetoric is problematic because not only does it obscure, it shifts the onus of blame on West Germany. Jeffrey Herf (1997) explains that

> The dominant German Communist anti-Fascist discourse suggested that its exponents were "anti-Fascists" who were only incidentally German and thus only incidentally bound up with the burden of German history. (p. 56)

The East German government has traditionally only honored Communist resisters of Fascism. Communists in the former East Germany just three years after the war "abolished the Jewish anti-Fascist Committee and arrested its leaders" (Herf, 1997, p. 119). Herf remarks that with the recent opening of the Stasi Archives in Berlin, historians have learned that Communists who helped Jews found themselves in trouble with the police. And many Jewish Communists, along with their non-Jewish compatriots landed in jail. Herf (1997) relates that

> those who returned from Mexico ... those Communists such as [Paul] Merker, [Leo] Zukerman, and others who in the spirit of Communism wartime anti-Fascism, had emphasized Jewish issues ... now fell under a cloud of espionage accusations. (p. 64).

Anti-Fascism also meant "government initiated anti-Semitism" (p. 117). Jeffrey Peck (1996) is not confident that the former East German mentality has changed much with reunification.

Early Holocaust scholarship also embraced what is termed the *Sonderweg* thesis. Before 1933, *Sonderweg*, which means special path, suggested that Germany was superior to other nations. After all, Germany produced Beethoven and Bach. Many major German historians, John Weaver (in press) claims, appropriated this position of superiority before 1933. Weaver explains that after 1933, Hans Ulrich Wehler argued that Germans had taken the wrong path. Now, *Sonderweg* designated deviance. German historians felt that "somewhere Germany had gone wrong" (Maier, 1988, p. 103). Martin Broszat (1969/1981) claims that whereas Germany may have progressed economically, she lagged behind socially and politically. Like Broszat, Thorstein Veblen (cited in Maier, 1988) argued that

> Germany had borrowed Britain's advanced technological achievements without having had time to internalize the values of workmanship and democracy ... The concept of a lag between economic and political modernization continued to mark influential historical interpretations. (p. 104)

However, the *Sonderweg* thesis has come under attack. Charles Maier (1988) stresses that Germany "was hardly a feudal society" (p. 108). Maier asks what it is German historians mean when they suggest that Germany diverted from the West? What "West" are they talking about? Exactly what were Germans diverting from? Maier argues that the *Sonderweg* thesis is nothing more than "a complacent or apologetic notion that Germany had been seized by demonized forces" (1988, p. 106). After 1945, then, the implication is that Germany was no longer off track, but squarely on track once again. The *Sonderweg* thesis implies that after 1945 everything was fine again in Germany. Germans, after the war, for the most part, were not held responsible for their crimes, so that in fact, many were put back into positions of power. Former Nazis became judges, teachers, and attorneys. Scholars stress that there was an uncanny continuity between pre-1945 and post-1945 German society. Thus, the *Sonderweg* thesis has been dismissed by many historians primarily because it served as an apologetic.

More recently, Holocaust scholarship has been guided by the intentionalist–structuralist debate. Christopher Browning (1992) comments that the intentionalists "explain history through the ideas and decisions of individuals [and these historians emphasize] the "continuity" of Hitler's goals and "the central role of Hitler" (p. 3). Conversely, structuralists stress "improvisation and cumulative radicalization produced by [the] contradictory nature [of] ... chaotic decision[s]" (p. 3).

Intentionalists generally argue that Hitler had a "blueprint" (Goldhagen, 1997; Dawidowicz, 1975/1986) or plan to murder the Jews all along. Dawidowicz looks to *Mein Kampf* for evidence of Hitler's plan. Other historians, Browning (1992) explains, look to Hitler's 1939 *Reichstag* speech. It is here that Hitler talks of a bloody solution to Germany's problems. Browning (1992) comments that

> The programmatic view is based primarily upon the statements made by Hitler, such as those in the late 1920s threatening a "bloody" solution through the sword or his famous 1939 *Reichstag* prophecy that the outbreak of war would mean the destruction of the Jewish race. (p. 26)

Some caution that despite these early pronouncements of murder, despite Hitler's ravings in *Mein Kampf*, it becomes difficult to prove whether he actually intended all along to kill millions of people. Saul Friedländer (1997) remarks that the Holocaust was not a "predetermined enactment of a demonic script ... [nor was it] haphazard, involuntary, imperceptible and chaotic" (p. 5). Lucy Dawidowicz (1975/1986) claims that structuralists offer up an apologetic because they obscure blame. "By removing the moral aspect of decision making in the Hitler era, the structuralists initiated a new cycle of apologetics" (p. xxvii).

The intentionalist–structuralist debate echoes ideas found in Hegel and Marx. Recall, Hegel's work suggests that history produces subjects. Subjects have little agency, as spirit moves through the world. Of course, structuralists are not mystical like Hegel, and they certainly do not argue that history is akin to some spiritual entity moving like a phantom through the world. However, structuralists do argue that Nazi apparatuses functioned in ways to move history. This kind of explanation leaves little room for human agency. The notion of an apparatus seems obscure. What is an apparatus? How can we assign blame to an apparatus? The rhetoric of apparatuses (Hilberg, 1961/1985) obfuscates and may serve to depersonalize and sanitize what it was that individual perpetrators did. Apparatuses do not kill, people do. People bleed, people die. Perpetrators have names and faces. On reading depositions taken at the Eichmann trial, it becomes very clear that the rhetoric of apparatuses conceals the human complicity, the humanness of crimes perpetrated.

> I identify Number 21 on photograph Z/4/7 as an SS kitchen chief of number 1 kitchen at Belsen. I have been told that his name is Erich Basch.... I was standing near the door to the kitchen. There was a girl prisoner ... Basch ... when

> he was about 3 meters from her he fired 2 or 3 shots ... at this girl. I saw the girl fall to the ground and blood coming from her head. (Silberberg, cited in Zeiger, 1960, p. 172)

The above particular perpetrator was named Erich Basch. Basch was not an apparatus, he was a human being who shot and killed a girl at point blank range. Daniel Goldhagen (1997) stresses that historians should attach faces and names to perpetrators. He wants to "restore them to their identities" (p. 6). Goldhagen declares that he wants to let the reader see that these were people who killed, and these people are garbed in what Goldhagen considers to be "obfuscating labels, like "Nazis" and "SS men"" (p. 6). He stresses that we should call "them what they were, Germans" (p. 6).

Intentionalists, like Goldhagen, argue that subjects produce history and are responsible for their actions. This position echoes that of Marx's. Here, intentionalists stress that we can examine what individuals did and make judgments about their actions and hold them responsible for crimes. This is the power of the intentionalist argument. Clearly Eichmann was an individual, not an apparatus, and he had to be held responsible for what he did.

Raul Hilberg's (1961/1985) early work anticipated structuralist accounts of perpetrators. Michael Marrus (1987) comments that Hilberg's work "offers a magisterial synthesis on a scale that no one has matched before or since ... [Hilberg's] remains the most important book that has been written on the subject" (p. 48). Although Marrus praises Hilberg, others criticize him and consider him a scandal. Hilberg writes in his memoirs that for 30 years he has "almost been buried under an avalanche of condemnations" (p. 137). Hilberg (1961/1985) argues, generally, that Jews were passive and did not resist the Nazis, and in fact, "hasten[ed] their [own] destruction" (p. 28). Hilberg contends that "In many cases they failed to escape while there was still time and more often, still, they failed to step out of the way when the killers were already upon them" (p. 26). Hilberg contends that "Jewish institutions [were] ... an extension of the German bureaucratic machine" (1996, p. 127). Jews were led like sheep to slaughter. It is this image which has gotten Hilberg in so much trouble. Oscar Handlin, Arno Lustiger (cited in Hilberg, 1996), and a host of other Jewish historians since Hilberg have tried to overturn this image. As Tony Kushner (1994) explains, responses of Jews were complex, and it is this complexity that Hilberg did not take into account.

Contrary to what Hilberg maintains, Yehuda Bauer (1989) suggests that Jews did resist. Bauer explains that

> In the *Generalgouvernment* there were three armed rebellions ... four attempted rebellions at Kielce, Opatów, Pilica, and Tomaszów Lubelski ...

> [there were] rebellions in six concentration and death camps Kruszyna, Krychów, Minsk Mazowiecki, Kopernik, Sobibor, and Treblinka. (p. 143)

Still, Bauer points out that Jews could not always resist because they had little access to guns. Without guns, resistance was impossible. Jews fought back with what they had and did what they could do but the Nazis were just too strong. In the camps, according to Hermann Langbein (1996), there was organized resistance. This, Langbien writes, is a fact that tends to get overlooked or obscured.

> It is little known that there was resistance in the camps—in defiance of an inconceivably brutal and totally effective system of terror—resistance to the killing of human beings ... not just individual resistance, but organized resistance. (p. 2)

So the debate about resistance rages. The image of Jews, passively marching like sheep to slaughter has been the impetus for these counter arguments. And it was Hilberg who initiated the debate. I do think he undertheorized around the complexities of Jewish responses. It seems that scholars can come to little agreement on how much or how little Jews actually resisted.

I consider Hilberg to be a structuralist, not in the same way as Broszat (1969/1981) or Mommsen (1966), because unlike them, he argues that Hitler was responsible, and unlike them, he argues that the actions of the Nazis were carefully thought through. Hilberg (1961/1985) remarks that the Nazis knew just what they were doing. But Hilberg's discourse is similar to structuralist discourse. He argues that the Nazi "apparatus" (p. 55) churned like an "engine of destruction" (p. 55), like a "sprawling" and "far-flung bureaucratic machine" (p. 53). It was the "sheer mechanism of destruction" (p. xi) that concerned Hilberg. Robert J. Lifton (1986), like Hilberg, remarks that it was the "bureaucracy of killing: the faceless, detached bureaucratic function" (p. 15) of murder that allowed perpetrators to carry out such hideous acts. The bureaucratic nature of mass murder allowed for a "routinization" (p. 15) of killing to numb the perpetrators enough so that they could detach themselves from what they were doing.

What exactly is an engine of destruction? Why all this mechanistic language? Lawrence Langer (1998) writes that "the very image of machinery ... tends to obscure individual offenders and obscure the identity and the catalyst of the very culprits who initiated and carried out the crime" (p. xii). It is this mechanistic language that becomes troubling for me. Although I understand that Hilberg suggests that the Holocaust was a complex web of complicity, I believe that this web is made up of people, and it is to these individuals we should turn. Structuralists' accounts of the Holocaust, like this one, suggest that people do not produce history, but rather, historical structures (mechanisms, networks of power, engines of destruction, and so forth) sweep people into the web of history, into events.

Although Hilberg's work is problematic, I want to suggest that Hilberg is an important historian. He does stress, albeit problematically, the complex web of complicity of perpetrators. That is, Hilberg attempts to locate perpetrators in a broader network of power structures; he attempts to show how intertwining systems of bureaucracy aided the process of carrying out mass murder. But most of all, Hilberg becomes important because he is one of the earliest Holocaust scholars to suggest that Nazi SS were not the only group of people who became complicit. Hilberg (1992) stresses that "All components of German organized life were drawn [in]" (p. 20). If this is the case, then ordinary Germans became just as blameworthy as Nazi SS.

Martin Broszat (1969/1981), structuralist par excellance, argues that the Nazis operated as "a growing system of rival power groups" (p. xi) who "improvised" (p. xi) in the form of a "polyocrac[ies]" (p. xi) which competed for power with Hitler. These so-called polyocracies engaged in a "wild proliferation of National Socialist power" (p. 139). Broszat's portrayal of the Nazi era is one of utter and complete chaos. The Nazis lacked any "direct and systematic leadership" (p. xi). Thus, Broszat is led to the conclusion that "below Hitler there was no overall political responsibility" (p. xi). But how could Broszat maintain such a claim? In one sentence he exonerates all Germans complicit in Holocaust crimes. Lucy Dawidowicz (1975/1986) calls Broszat's interpretation "bizarre" (p. xxvi). She criticizes him for offering up a "science-fiction-fantasy of government by automation, robotistically driven by an internal law of motion" (p. xxvi). Not only does Broszat rule out political responsibility of middle- and lower-echelon leaders, according to Dawidowicz he also suggests that Hitler's place in all of this was secondary. Broszat "downgraded Hitler's role" (p. xxvi). The implication here is that the rise of the Nazi era was so chaotic and so haphazard that it becomes hard to pinpoint the real culprits. But is this just an apologetic? Broszat claims that Germany suffered from a "collective neuroses," a society out of control, a society gone mad. A society gone mad cannot be held responsible for its actions. Something is out of joint here. Broszat's work signals, to me, repression.

Repressed memory shapes historians' work. One can get a better understanding of perhaps why Broszat (1969/1981) writes about the Holocaust the way he does when one examines his so-called "plea for historicization." Broszat, in a well known debate with Saul Friedländer (1997), argues that German historians must become more objective by separating their own personal memory of the Holocaust from their rendering of the Holocaust in historical accounts. Broszat declares that he does not want to distance himself from the event; he wants to lessen "the moral loading" (Rüsen, 1997, p. 123) of writing about the event. But still, it seems to me, that despite his claim, he does distance himself from the past. He wants German historians to become more objective so that they can do their work without emotional upheaval. It seems that Broszat wishes to repress the memory of the Holocaust by suggesting that it is necessary for historians to separate their memories of the event from the work that they do around the event. How is this possible? When the memory gets repressed, the historiographies produced end up being, as Dawidowicz put it, bizarre. Jörn Rüsen (1997) comments that,

> by historicizing National Socialism, Broszat wishes to overcome the historical estrangement of Germans and their identity in relation to that era. Friedländer interrogates this project, wondering whether a normalization in the historical patterns of German identity can be achieved at the cost of neglecting the special quality of National Socialism in historical perspective. (p. 119)

Here again, for so many German historians the question turns on national identity and national pride. If historians are old enough to remember the Holocaust, how can they write history pretending that remembering the event is irrelevant? Here we see the implications of drawing sharp distinctions between history and memory. Friedländer has often argued that these sharp distinctions cannot be drawn, that the relation between history and memory is fuzzy, especially if the historian works on recent history. Personal memories of Auschwitz and of the Nazi era have got to affect the writings of German historians. It seems to me that Broszat's plea to separate memory, and his refusal to admit that this memory affects historians, sounds the Freudian theme of negation. But for Freud (1925/1989), a negation signals an affirmation of some sort. For a very strong 'no' a very strong 'yes' lurks in the unconscious. Broszat doth protest too much. I wonder what it is that he does remember and why this memory bothers him so much to call out for forgetfulness. Broszat's plea serves as a defense mechanism against his own memories.

Christopher Browning (1992), unlike Martin Broszat, calls himself a moderate structuralist. He takes a "middle position" (p. 5) between intentionalism and structuralism. Browning argues that the Nazi regime was divided by "factionalism and infighting" (p. 76). Planning "emanated from the center with receptivity and accommodation in the periphery" (p. 76). Taking up the "evolutionary position," Browning still contends that Hitler was ultimately responsible. Like other structuralists, Browning suggests that the Nazis, because they embraced a sort of evolutionary scheme, improvised as they went along.

The important move that Browning has made, I believe, is toward doing what is termed *Alltagsgechichte.* Unlike most perpetrator histories since Hilberg, Browning (1996) does not focus on "middle-echelon perpetrators," but rather, he focuses on the "little men" (p. 27).

Browning's work attempts to humanize and not demonize the killers. Because he suggests that it is human beings who kill, because he suggests that it is the human conscience that makes decisions and shapes history, I would consider him closer to the intentionalists than the structuralists.

Christopher Browning's (1998) work, *Ordinary Men: Reserve Police Battalion 101 and the Final Solution in Poland,* has been overshadowed by Daniel Goldhagen's (1997) *Hitler's Willing Executioner's: Ordinary Germans and the Holocaust.* The Goldhagen controversy, which I discuss later, caught the eye of the popular press and consequently, led to submerging Browning's book in the background. What is interesting is that both books deal with a similar topic: ordinary German complicity during the Holocaust. Ordinary men, who were not Nazis, but who were reserve police, willingly engaged in brutality, murdering innocent people. Ordinary men willingly murdered Jews. Yahuda Bauer (1997) attributes Goldhagen's popularity, at least with lay readers, to his simplistic argument:

> I believe that the real reason [Goldhagen is so popular] is the very simplicity of the argument, its manichaen (black and white) character. A complicated phenomenon is seemingly explained in the most simple fashion: the Germans killed the Jews because they wanted to; they wanted to since the mid-nineteenth century, and maybe before that too. And that's all there is to it. (p. 71)

Unlike Goldhagen's simple explanation, Browning (1998) offers up what he calls a "multilayered approach" (p. 215). His treatment of police reserve battalion 101 is complex. He does not demonize, yet he does not exonerate either. Browning's is a more sympathetic approach than Goldhagen's. Goldhagen tends to demonize Germans.

Browning (1998) bases his book on "judicial interrogations" (p. xviii) of 125 men who served in reserve police battalion 101. These interrogations were conducted in the 1960s. Browning's research led him to believe that not only did some of these men repress their memories of what they did to Jews, but some lied outright. What is disturbing is the way in which many of them, according to Browning, utilized projection, to cover over their hatred for Jews. Browning (1998) describes this projection as it had implications for Germans' relationships with Poles. He comments that

> While the policemen's testimonies offer scant information concerning German attitudes toward Poles and Jews, they contain very frequent and quite damning comments on Polish attitudes toward Jews. (p. 155)

Germans often considered Poles second-class citizens; in fact, many Germans hated Poles and many Poles were anti-Semites. But the very "omission" (Browning, 1998, p. 73) of policemen's own Jewish prejudices during these interrogations reveals something about their attitudes toward Jews. It is in the not said that we begin to understand something lurking in repression. Browning (1998) contends that the men of reserve police battalion 101 were given the choice of not participating in shooting Jews, of "stepping out" (p. 71). Only 12 out of 500 men took up the offer of Major Trapp (who was affectionately called Pappa Trapp). Why did only 12 men step out? Browning suggests that most of the policemen felt the "pressure" to conform (p. 71) and had "a lack of time for reflection" (p. 71). Goldhagen (1997) refutes these claims. He suggests that Browning is merely excusing here and that Germans murdered because they wanted to. Conformity and lack of reflection had nothing to do with it.

Browning (1998) asks, "How did a battalion of middle-aged reserve policemen find themselves facing the task of shooting some 1,500 Jews in the Polish village of Józefów, in the summer of 1942?" (p. 3) They faced the task initially with difficulty. Some of the men displayed "sheer physical revulsion" (p. 74), some expressed "resentment" and "bitterness" (p. 76). The Józefów Massacre was carried out essentially by what Americans would consider the equivalent of a national guard unit made up of weekend warriors, not professional soldiers. These were not professional soldiers; they were everyday men, middle-aged men, far beyond the age for military service. Nonetheless, these ordinary men killed Jews by the scores. Some were killed in a face-off. Some were killed at point blank range. Browning (1998) explains that

> When the first truckload of 35 to 40 Jews arrived, an equal number of policemen came forward and, face to face, were paired off with their victims.... Kammer then ordered the Jews to lie down in a row. The policemen stepped up behind them ... and on Kammer's orders fired in unison. (p. 61)

But the policemen did not always aim well. Skulls were blown off, blood splattered everywhere. Some of the policemen intentionally missed. If they did not aim right they had to shoot several times. The account that Browning (1998) portrays is completely disgusting and gruesome. Some perpetrators became sick and threw up; some ran into the woods in hysterics. "When the men arrived at the barracks in Biłgoraj, they were depressed, angered, embittered, and shaken" (p. 69). However,

Browning (1998) stresses that after a while, the policemen became numb to what they were doing. After killing 10 or 20 Jews or more "they became increasingly efficient calloused executioners" (p. 77).

It is interesting to note that in Goldhagen's account of police reserve battalion 309, it seems that the men had little difficulty in killing. Goldhagen's (1997) portrait of ordinary Germans is quite different. He gives the impression that the Germans were natural born killers who suffered little from pulling the trigger. Browning, on the other hand, tries to paint a more complex picture. But he does not exonerate or apologize for the men of reserve unit 101. He simply paints a picture that is probably more truthful than Goldhagen's.

Browning relates that not only were reserve policemen involved in killing villagers, they were also directly involved in the Final Solution. Reserve police were involved in the *Einsatzgruppen* in 1941 in Russia and mowed down scores of Jews with machine guns. It was after this event that the Germans decided to use gas instead of guns, because gas was more efficient and caused Germans fewer psychological problems than shooting their victims face to face. It is interesting to note that in post-war trials, the leader of the reserve police, Kurt Daluege, denied that these men had anything to do with direct executions. It was this kind of myth that protected ordinary Germans from feeling, in any way, responsible. Often, one hears the protest that Germans were simply following orders, or that the reserve police and regular army were not complicit; they were only doing their duty. But stepping out of the line of duty was not a punishable offense. These Germans had choices.

Browning (1998) points out, unlike Goldhagen, that "ordinary Germans" were "not of one mind" (p. 216). The irony about reserve police battalion 101 is that most of the men were from Hamburg, which according to Browning, was one of the "least Nazified" (p. 48) cities in Germany. These men were not really interested in politics. Some of them, Browning suggests, were not anti-Semites at all. These ordinary men were not raving, murderous lunatics who thought only about killing Jews. Rather, these men incrementally became killers; their transition from ordinary men to mass murderers was not without difficulty.

Unlike Browning's sympathetic, complex portrayal of the role ordinary Germans played in the Holocaust, Daniel Goldhagen's (1997) portrayal of ordinary Germans is unrelenting, unsympathetic, and outright demonizing. Goldhagen is an intentionalist, although he would probably refuse the label because he argues that the intentionalist–structuralist debate a "misnomer" (p. 10). Goldhagen, however, argues in typical intentionalist style. Hitler, he contends, had a "blueprint" (p. 86) for the Holocaust. This blueprint could be traced back to *Mein Kampf*. Hitler intended all along, says Goldhagen, to murder the Jews. Not only that, but the "Nazis were remarkably consistent" (p. 132) and "Hitler never waivered" (p. 134) from his plan. Recall, Browning (1992) contends that intentionalists usually argue for "continuity" (p. 3) of Hitler's goals and this is just what Goldhagen suggests. For Goldhagen, unlike Broszat, the Nazi era was not one of chaos and disorganization; Hitler and his henchmen knew just what they were doing. Goldhagen (1997) argues that Germans killed Jews because they wanted to, and because Germans embraced what he terms *eliminationist anti-Semitism* (p. 132). This so-called eliminationist anti-Semitism was "shared" (p. 132) among all Germans. Clearly, anti-Semitism is more complex than this, and I find it hard to believe that an entire nation shared one brand of anti-Semitism. It is also unlikely that all Germans wanted to kill Jews. Perhaps many Germans wished that Jews would emigrate, but I cannot believe that all Germans wished for the mass annihilation of Jews.

Unlike Browning, Goldhagen (1997) contends that ordinary Germans "would easily become genocidal executioners" (p. 185). This claim is in stark contrast to Browning's. Recall, Browning went to great lengths to demonstrate the difficulties many Germans initially had when they began killing Jews. Goldhagen refutes this claim and says killing was easy for Germans; they were natural born killers. Why did they do it? Because they wanted to. Goldhagen declares that "it is cognition and values, and only cognition and values, that in the last instant moves someone willfully to pick up his hand and strike another" (p. 21). Goldhagen argues that the men of reserve police battalion 309 "became instantaneous *Weltanschauungskriegen,* or ideological warriors" (p. 190).

Goldhagen has been taken to task by other historians for several reasons: First, his explanation is monocausal and simplistic. There were many causes for the Holocaust and although anti-Semitism was an important factor it was not the only factor. Further, Goldhagen has oversimplified the term as well. There are many brands of anti-Semitism but not all kinds lead to murder. It is ironic that Goldhagen stresses that "studies of the Holocaust have been marred by a poor understanding and or under-theorizing of anti-Semitism" (p. 7). But I think he has a poor understanding of the complexities of anti-Semitism. Not all Germans embraced an "eliminationist" model of anti-Semitism. Historically, there have been many varieties of anti-Semitism, as shown previously. Hans Mommsen (1997) argues that Goldhagen oversimplifies his entire approach to the Holocaust, he reduces the complex to the simple. He

> is driven by the determination to deny every mixture of ideological fanaticism, of psychopathological aberration, of moral indifference and bureaucratic perfectionism, even of "the banality of evil." (p. 36)

Although I do not agree with Mommsen's explanation here, the point is that Goldhagen narrows his explanation so much as to make it sound as if his is the absolute and authoritative understanding of the Holocaust, which is the fact that all Germans wanted to kill Jews because they all embraced a deadly variety of anti-Semitism. Mommsen (1997) points out that Goldhagen's argument implies that the collective German spirit embraced an "innate" (p. 36) kind of anti-Semitism, although Goldhagen denies this charge. But one gets the impression that Goldhagen suggests the collective guilt of Germans, as this anti-Semitism must have been innate. Goldhagen also denies this, but all the same, this is the impression one gets from reading his work. Among historians, the notion of collective guilt is no longer a tenable one. Since at least the Eichmann trial, most historians would suggest that what is at stake is individual guilt and individual responsibility. Further, the notion that Germans had some innate thing that caused them to kill is also untenable. There is no essential Germanness. All Germans are different.

Goldhagen has also been taken to task for making errors. He suggests that, for instance, he is the first historian to discuss the role of ordinary Germans in Holocaust historiography. Pollefeyt and Colijn (1997) remark that Von der Dunk criticizes Goldhagen's "distorted depiction of Holocaust literature to underlie his own originality and he finds especially steep Goldhagen's contention that he is in fact the first one to focus on ordinary executioners" (p. 5). Other scholars are upset at Goldhagen's arrogance. Yehuda Bauer (1997) comments that his "overbearing attitude" and his refusal to "take into account" (p. 62) the works of other historians simply will not do. In Goldhagen's notes in his book, he takes to task every major Holocaust historian and argues that their ideas are completely misguided. He says that ordinary Germans did not kill because they were coerced, which is what Sarah Gordon argues (p. 490); they did not kill because they were "blind followers of order" (p. 490) which is what Friedländer, G. P. Gooch, Stanley Milgram, and Hannah Arendt argue; they did not murder because of "social psychological pressure" (p. 490) which Goldhagen suggests is Browning's contention; they did not kill because they were "petty bureaucrats" (p. 490) which is Heim and Aly's and Mommsen's position. No. According to Goldhagen, Germans killed because they wanted to. Each of these other historians has something to offer but it seems that Goldhagen dismisses all of the them.

I attended a Goldhagen lecture in New Orleans. When people asked him questions he was arrogant and dismissed nearly every questioner. I thought him a very defensive young scholar. And this becomes evident in his work. Pollefeyt and Colijn (1997) remark that Goldhagen's "book is of no value to historians. There are no new, previously unknown facts" (p.

5). Well, I would not go this far. I do think that what Goldhagen has done is to cause a terrific uproar in the historical community, and to the general reading public he has become a sort of cultural hero. His book is widely read by lay persons and has been translated into many languages. He is known worldwide. His book is one of the few in recent years to capture so much public attention. I think that lay readers like his book because it is a very emotional one. His anger comes out on nearly every page. I must say that on my first reading I was swept up in his book as well. Yet, despite all of the criticisms, I think that Yehuda Bauer (1997) is right to point out that Goldhagen has brought the problem of anti-Semitism out into the open once again. This is a problem that gets buried, I think, in all the minutiae of Holocaust scholarship. Goldhagen has raised popular consciousness in such a way that most historians have not. Most everyday people never read history. They are confronted with the past, and with the Holocaust through popular culture, primarily through film. It is amazing that Goldhagen's work has captured the attention that it has. But still this does not make his book a good one either. The Holocaust memory will not die. These controversies, these contested sites of representation attest to this. Sometimes this struggle is fraught. The burden of memory proves heavy.

> May 1944: a transport arrives at Auschwitz-Birkenau ... Elie Wiesel, age fifteen, his father, mother, and little sister, Tzipora, are among them. Separated by the SS, the boy loses sight of his mother and sister, not fully aware that the parting is forever. (Berenbaum & Roth, 1989, p. 371)

We must not lose sight of the fact that debates and controversies around what it is scholars do when they talk about the Holocaust may serve to repress, distort, distance, rigidify, and alter memory of this horrific event. We must never forget that ultimately we are talking about the murder of 6 million Jews. We must never forget that history is about people. Getting lost in scholarly debates might serve to prevent the researcher from really thinking about these horrors. Intellectualization serves as a defense mechanism to keep emotion at bay. Researchers must try to avoid the trap of intellectualization.

The literature on perpetrators is immense and continues to proliferate. Nothing has been written about so much and we still know so little. I have painted a very broad picture of some of the debates in Holocaust historiography around perpetrators. I tried to highlight what I thought some of the major issues have been. My picture is partial and incomplete. Earlier, I suggested that historians are subject to the workings of their own psychological repressions. Although we can never get into the mind of an historian to find out why it is that he or she represented the Holocaust in a particular way, we can assume that emotional responses and transferential relations with subject matter matters. These responses shape what it is historians write about and exclude. I am convinced that unconscious traces are deposited in these texts, and it is these strangenesses that defy translation. There is always a remainder, a something left over, an ineffable residue lurking in these texts. Historians cannot even begin to capture the hideousness of Auschwitz; Auschwitz leaves us with traces, screen memories, and disgust. There is always something left over, something beyond representation, phantoms lurking between the sites of historiography and the actual past. Memory of this event haunts. Like Friedländer (1997), I believe that historians who can remember the event cannot separate that memory from their work. If they attempt to repress the memory, their representation of the event tends to reflect this repression in some way. The memory of the event and its subsequent historiography are interconnected.

VICTIM HISTORIES

In most Holocaust historiography, victims' voices do not appear much. Tony Kushner (1994) explains that

> The first major historians of the Holocaust, Leon Poliakov in France and Gerhard Reitlinger in England [notably two non-Germans] were in close agreement that the voice of Jews themselves would be used sparingly in their narratives.... 'Authenticity' was thus required and it was assumed that evidence from the victim was somehow less ... objective. (p. 3)

It seems a symptom of repression on the part of historians that victims are not included in the traditional accounts of the Holocaust. Part of the problem is the distinction historians make between history and memory. When these two categories are dialectally opposed, memory is seen as something beside the point, unreliable, and soft. Is it that historians have a difficult time dealing with the emotional horrors that victims report? Is it easier, psychologically, for historians to examine train schedules, rather than look at painful accounts of unthinkable suffering? Many historians claim that it is more important to do histories of perpetrators than of victims because if we are to understand why or how the Holocaust happened, we must first examine the perpetrators. Of course this is true. Still, I find it curious that victims' voices are absent from most perpetrator historiography.

Although perpetrator accounts of the Holocaust have managed to exclude victims' voices, one can turn to other kinds of writings to hear what they have to say. The repressed has returned, in fact, in a great proliferation of memory. Victims' voices are scattered in diaries: The Diary of Anne Frank (1989); The Diary of Eva Heyman (1981); Child of the Holocaust (1988); The Diary of Etty Hillesum (1983); in memoirs: Delbo

(1990); Levi (1990); Bettelheim (1971); Wiesel (1995); Anger (1981); Friedländer (1979); Geve (1987); Nir (1989); in studies about children: Lukas (1994); Rosenberg (1994); Klarsfeld (1996); Kamenetsky (1984); Stein (1994); Wardi (1996); Boguslawska (1975); Dwork (1991); Eisen (1988); Holliday (1991); Lifton (1988); in studies on ghettos: Ringelblum (1974); Cholowski (1980); Gutman (1984); Heydrecker (1990); Katz (1970); Marks (1975); and in studies on camps: Donat (1979); Kogan (1975); Dobroszycki (1984); LeChene (1971); Smith (1995); and Langbein (1996). Victims' voices are scattered throughout these and many more writings.

As a curriculum theorist, it is my responsibility to uncover historical memory that has been the most repressed and the most marginalized. The two most marginalized memories of the Holocaust are those of women, and of gays and lesbians. Generally speaking, issues around gender and sexuality are still considered taboo subjects for many who do work on the Holocaust. Thus the literature around these two subjects is limited in comparison with the enormous amount of literature on perpetrators. I next tease out some of the debates on gender and sexuality, and then move to a discussion around repressed memory and what it is that psychoanalysts and psychotherapists have discovered by working with Holocaust survivors and their children.

As I mentioned earlier, one of the unfortunate consequences of driving a wedge between memory and history is the validation of history and the denigration of memory. Memories of victims have traditionally gotten squashed out of Holocaust narratives. When memories of victims do appear, they are distorted primarily because victims and survivors have been portrayed as an "amorphous mass" (Hilberg, 1992, p. x). This facelessness of victims is partly a result of the way in which historians have couched their debates. Abstractions tend to wipe out humanness. Isaiah Trunk (1979) explains that

> One of the results of this one-sided concern with the Nazi aspect of the war and the Holocaust is the mistaken notion that, within the immense bureaucracy and technology of genocide, the Jewish victims were passive objects of the "process." (p. ix)

The rhetoric of apparatuses, technocrats, machines, and networks of power shape not only the way we understand perpetrators, but also shapes the way we might think about victims. The absence of victims in these accounts gives the impression they were not even part of their history, that they were led like sheep to slaughter. Saul Friedländer (1997) remarks that this assumption needs to be interrogated. The responses of victims is far more complex than one might think. Friedländer comments that

> In many works the implicit assumption regarding the victims' generalized hopelessness and passivity, or their inability to change the course of events ... have turned them into a static and abstract element of the historical background. (p. 2)

Jewish responses to the rise of Nazism differed, of course. Some fled, some hid, some believed they could live with Hitler and just ignore him. But as Yehuda Bauer (1989) points out, many more Jews fled than is commonly remembered. Bauer comments that "Contrary to conventional wisdom, most German and Austrian Jews, some 410,000 out of 700,000, did manage to leave the Third Reich" (p. 146). However, many of the Jews fled to countries that were not friendly to Jews. In fact, many were rounded up by collaborators and sent back to Germany.

Gender made a difference here too. Women were more eager, by and large, to leave Germany than were men. Marion Kaplan (1998) declares that "As emigration became more and more crucial, women usually saw the danger signals first and urged their husbands to flee Germany" (p. 63). Men were more reluctant to leave because they were tied to their businesses. But in the early years, if men decided to leave, some left without their wives because they thought only men would be endangered. In fact, women were in greater danger than men. Joan Ringelheim (1993) suggests that more women than men were deported from the Lodz ghetto to Chelmno death camp. More women than men were deported from Theresienstadt to Auschwitz. More men arrived than women in the displaced persons (DP) camps in 1945 because more women had been killed. Ringelheim argues that men were put in camps that "offered some possibility for survival" (p. 399). Schindler's List included only 200 women, while 1,000 men were asked by Schindler to work for him. Some Jews who were lucky enough to appear on Schindler's list survived the Holocaust. But Ringelheim (1993) stresses that

> The numbers begin to show a stark and disturbing reality. It can no longer be doubted that being male or female mattered.... Sexism attended anti-Semitism ... as it attends all forms of racism ... Anti-Semitism, racism and sexism were not separated in the theory of the Nazis. (p. 400)

Women were also targeted if they had children or were pregnant. These women were killed immediately on arrival in the concentration camps. Gisella Perl, a Jewish doctor who was deported to Auschwitz, performed as many abortions as she could to save women from being sent to death. Perl (1993) remarks that she did not believe what it was the Nazis were doing to pregnant women until she witnessed their executions with her own eyes.

> A few days after the arrival of a new transport, one of the SS chiefs would address the women, encouraging the pregnant ones to step forward because they would be taken to another camp where living conditions were better.... Group after group of pregnant women left Camp L. Even I was naive enough ... to believe the Germans, until one day. (p. 113).

Perl comments that one day she saw these women being executed with her own eyes. This sight must have been unthinkable. How could they do it? If women got past "selection," Sybil Milton (1993) contends, they faired better than men. Milton claims that "women appear to have been more resilient than men, both physically and psychologically to malnutrition and starvation" (p. 227). Still, more women than men died during the Holocaust. Women were subject to medical "experiments," as were gay men, and this was also a factor in higher mortality rates. Rittner and Roth (1993) explain that so-called Ravensbrück "rabbits," as the Nazis called them, or women at Ravensbrück, were subjected to "tortuous medical "experiments" [which] wasted women ... infections were induced, limbs amputated, and wartime wounds replicated" (p. 9). Gay men also suffered due to these so-called experiments. Klaus Müller (1980) reports that "At Buchenwald ... an SS doctor performed operations ... the insertion of a capsule which released testosterone; some of the men died during the operation" (p. 12). These so-called medical experiments are beyond comprehension. One of the most difficult books for me to read, emotionally, was Robert J. Lifton's (1986) work on Nazi doctors. There is something particularly insidious about the part doctors played in the Holocaust. Doctors' roles in the Holocaust are often overlooked, Lifton tells us. The doctors decided, willy-nilly, who would live and who would die. They were waiting at the off-ramps when Jews stepped outside of the trains. They decided—left or right—one side meant death, the other life. They were there, at the killing sites, at the crematoriums. The Nazi doctors orchestrated the Holocaust more than some would like to believe. Women and gay men made up the largest percentage of victims, in part, because the Nazi doctors decided that they might benefit from experimenting on them.

Some scholars argue that the emphasis on gender and sexuality distorts the memory of the Holocaust because it turns it into a debate over sexism or homophobia (Fagin, Ozick, cited in Rittner & Roth, 1993). These scholars argue that if the Holocaust is made into an example of sexism, for instance, the larger picture is lost. However, it makes little sense to separate out racism, sexism, homophobia, and anti-Semitism. I think we get a fuller picture of the Holocaust when a multilayered approach is taken.

Not all women were led like sheep to slaughter. Some women were engaged in underground movements, and in revolts. Sybil Milton

(1993) declares "There were open revolts in which women participated at Sobibor, Treblinka, Auschwitz, and possibly Bergen-Belson" (p. 231). Isaiah Trunk (1979) suggests that lower- and working-class Jews adjusted better than middle- and upper-class Jews. By implication, lower- and working-class women were probably more likely to be involved in active resistance, such as the camp revolts, whereas middle- and upper-class women resisted in other ways. Of course, middle- and upper-class women had a better chance to escape Germany simply because they had the money to get out.

Similarly, eastern and western European Jewish women responded differently. The more assimilated Jewish women were with their Christian neighbors the better chance they had of surviving. Because, for example, Jewish women in western Europe were not assimilated, as were their husbands due to business exchanges with Christians; they had "no extended Christian family to protect them" (Ofer & Weitzman, 1998, p. 14). Middle-class Jewish women were not forced to work and their isolation from Christian neighbors hurt them. But in Poland, Ofer, and Weitzman suggest, the situation for women was very different. Because women were mostly working class, they were forced to assimilate with Christians and Poles. Thus, their ability to speak Polish helped them "pass" (p. 4) and hence some would escape.

Sara Horowitz (1998) points out that women have traditionally been represented by men in Holocaust historiography. These representations have been distorted. "In many narratives by men, women are portrayed as peripheral, helpless, and fragile, as morally deficient; or as erotic in their victimization" (p. 367). But Rittner and Roth (1993) paint a different picture. These scholars explain that many women were resistance fighters. But Ruth Linden (1993) cautions that not all Jewish women were resistance fighters and to give this impression is false. Linden (1993) comments that "Scholars now recognize that there was indeed, significant Jewish resistance.... Yet an oversimplified, idealized view of Jews as "victims" ... or self-conscious resistance fighters has obscured our understanding" (pp. 84–85). The point here is that women's experiences during the Holocaust differed from one another. Class status, the ability to fight back, assimilation, age, and geography all affected the ways in which women responded. Just as women experienced the Holocaust differently from men, so too were experiences for heterosexuals and homosexuals different. Gender and sexuality mattered.

Currently, there is little documentation on lesbian experiences during the Holocaust. There seems to be more literature on gay men, but not very much literature on this group either. Vera Laska (1993) explains that "while homosexuals were treated in a manner that even within the concentration camp framework was ghastly ... the lesbians, were seldom hunted down for special treatment" (p. 263). As Klaus Müller (1980) suggests, "only gay men were made criminals under Paragraph 175. We know much less about the persecution of lesbians" (p. 11). Richard Plant (1986) comments that "Most lesbians managed to survive unscathed. Fortunately, they fell outside the universe of Himmler's sexual obsessions" (p. 116). If lesbians did survive the camps, the memories are yet to be written. Sybil Milton (1993) suggests that lesbian life stories during the Holocaust are virtually non-existent primarily because of the "inhibitions of survivors and historians" (p. 231). Perhaps it is the historians' homophobia that keeps these memories hidden. Historians, the keepers of memory, have painted a picture of the Holocaust that makes lesbian experience invisible.

1934 marks a turning point in the history of gay life in Germany. Richard Plant (1986) explains that when Hitler demolished the SA, and ruthlessly had its homosexual chief, Ernst Röehm, murdered, the pace of arresting gay men increased. "During a 15 week period in 1934, the Berlin Police and the SS arrested more homosexuals than the Weimar Police did in 15 years" (p. 90). Heinrich Himmler was one of the chief architects behind the murder of Röehm. Plant (1986) states that for Himmler, homosexuality

> was to be diagnosed as a contagious disease. The plague was highly dangerous because it affected the young.... Himmler was repeatedly to urge chiefs of the Hitler Youth to purge former leaders of the old Rover youth movement, which ... he judged to be strongly homoerotic. (p. 102)

It was paragraph 175 that, in 1935, made it illegal to even look as if you were gay, and if anyone suspected gay activities, the suspicion alone could get you arrested. When gay men were put in camps they were subjected to brutal treatment. Pierre Seel (1997) recalls a scene in which a gay man is literally torn apart and killed by a German Sheperd:

> The loudspeakers broadcast some noisy classical music while the SS stripped him naked and shoved a tin pail over his head. Next they sicced their ferocious German Sheperds on him: the guard dogs first bit into his groin and thigh, and then devoured him. (p. 43)

Not only were gay men subject to brutalities such as these, they were also "treated with contempt by their fellow prisoners" (Müller, 1980, p. 13). Unlike their fellow prisoners who were liberated after the war, gay men never felt liberated. Seel (1997) remarks that "liberation was for others" (p. 88). Gay men were treated as criminals not only in Germany but also in France. In fact, in Germany, Paragraph 175 was not repealed until 1969 (see Plant, 1986), and in France, homosexuality became legal only in 1982. Because gay Holocaust survivors were considered criminals, they did not receive restitution from West Germany after the war.

Heinz Heger (1980), whose memoirs inspired the 1979 play *Bent* by Martin Sherman, recalls some of the meaningless tasks Nazis forced gay men to perform. These tasks were meant to humiliate, and humiliate they did:

> Our work, then, was as follows: In the morning we had to cart the snow outside our block from the left side of the road to the right side. In the afternoon we had to cart the same snow back from the right side to the left. (p. 35)

Bent was eventually made into a film and it is here that we see the scene Heger describes above. In a Beckettian landscape, two men carry snow with their bare hands back and forth all day. Hermann Langbein (1996) comments that this kind of meaningless "work" occurred in many camps. Langbein (1996) contends that

> Since work was intended as punishment, many performed meaningless tasks, the kind that really wears a person down. Only members of units that were charged with maintaining the operation of the camp and its workshops escaped such demoralizing activities as swiftly carrying rocks to a certain place and then carrying them back the same way. (p. 15)

The humiliation of these tasks, according to Heger (1980), resulted in many suicides, as men would run into electrified fences or throw themselves in front of carts filled with rocks and clay and "human bodies would fly through the air, and limbs would be crushed to pulp" (p. 35). Of course, there are many accounts of sexual torture carried out by SS guards. Seel (1997) comments that after liberation, he "returned as a ghost" (p. 91). Müller (1980) remarks "ours is an empty memory" (p. 13). During the course of my research I was disturbed to discover that literature concerning gender and sexuality was limited. This signals a denial of memory. Jews are not just Jews. We are engendered, we are heterosexual, homosexual, queer.

The repression of memory is evident in the lives of many Holocaust survivors. It is to these various repressions I want to turn. More specifically, I want to examine what it is that psychoanalysts and psychotherapists have discovered in their work with Holocaust survivors. It is important to keep in mind, though, that no matter what psychoanalysis teaches about the human psyche and its vicissitudes, it cannot define what it means to suffer, nor can it name the pain of Holocaust survivors. To think that psychoanalysts have the answer is simply naive. However, psychoanalytic theory may help us to keep Auschwitz strange. The otherness of this event must be kept intact, otherwise it risks domestication.

Bergman and Jucovy (1990) suggest that psychoanalysts felt ill-equipped to treat Holocaust survivors, especially during the early years after liberation. "The theoretical position of psychoanalysts, many of whom were classically Freudian ... did not appear sufficient to conceptualize and explain the bewildering array of symptoms" (p. 8). The bewildering testimonies of Holocaust survivors demand a different kind of listening. *Listening with the Third Ear*, Theodor Reik's (1948/1998) work on psychoanalysis, might help us hear these voices in a way that lends an otherness to Holocaust survivors' experiences. As Brent Davis (1996) remarks

> Listening, rather, is more toward an imaginative and conscientious participation in the unfolding of the world. Immediate, intimate, implicating, and interactive. (p. xxvi)

A conscientious participating when listening to Holocaust survivors' memories means that readers/listeners must have a certain psychological readiness to allow survivors to speak without censorship, and without censoring the unconscious of the other or the other of memory. The immediacy of experiencing Holocaust survivors' memories requires a certain kind of distancing. To keep intact what I term the *not-me* of the event is crucial, especially for the reader/listener who did not actually live through the black sun of Auschwitz. Still, psychological distance does not guarantee that readers and listeners will not experience some kind of traumatic effect through the listening. Sheldon Roth (1995b) states that there are three kinds of trauma: one is external, another is developmental, and the third is intrapsychic. Roth claims that "those of us not directly involved can be traumatized by the third, intrapsychic conflict" (p. 88). Thus, listening with the third ear might open one up to this kind of conflict. It is nearly impossible to avoid psychic upheavals while working with the texts of the Holocaust. Reading survivors' testimonies and Holocaust texts generally impacts not only the ways in which we approach "difficult knowledges" (Britzman, 1998, p. 119), but it also affects the ways in which we approach the other. Transferential relations with these texts mark the reader in uncanny ways and leave her changed. The "ruins of memory" (Langer, 1995, pp. 195–196) leave their traces in our skin.

1938, the year which marks *Kristallnacht*, was a decisive moment in the history of Jewish and German life. As I stated earlier, it was not until *Kristallnacht* that Jews began to fear that their lives could be in danger. Marion Kaplan (1998) explains: "Psychologists who studied refugee memoirs determined that almost 40% of memoir writers did not give up psychologically until 1938 or 1939" (p. 129). It became enormously difficult to understand what was happening and part of the problem,

Kaplan (1998) suggests, is that "normalcy" of "German daily life" (p. 9) prevented Jews from grasping the severity of their situation. Ambivalent messages from German friends and signs of "loyalty" (pp. 43–44) made it even more difficult to believe that Nazis would kill Jews, that most of German society would become complicit in one way or another. So many underestimated Hitler's power. As I mentioned earlier, even Sigmund Freud had a difficult time leaving Austria. Peter Gay (1989) traces Freud's reluctance to leave.

> 1938 ... Freud refuses to believe it, in any event, he says he is too old to leave the country.... 1938 ... Nazis march into Austria, greeted by cheering throngs.... March 15 ... Ernst Jones reaches Vienna persuading a most reluctant Freud that it is time for him and his family to leave.... March 22 ... Anna Freud [is] summoned to [the] Gestapo ... the trauma persuades Freud to make every effort now. (pp. x/vi–x/vii)

If Freud had difficulty leaving, difficulty believing what was happening, imagine what it must have been like for the everyday person, for the non-introspective person, for working class nonpolitical people or for middle-class Jews who were apolitical. Not only did Freud underestimate the power of Hitler and the complicity of German society, he also underestimated the callousness with which many of the perpetrators would eventually carry out their crimes. Dan Bar-On (1993) explains that in 1930, Freud said that horrific atrocities could not be perpetrated without psychic splitting. Freud believed that perpetrators of hideous crimes "could not remain psychologically intact for long. Guilt feelings of great intensity might drive them crazy or kill them" (Bar-On, 1993, p. 195). But Bar-On points out that Germans, by and large, did not go crazy and hardly any committed suicide after Auschwitz. The converse, however, was true for Jews. Many suicides had been reported after *Kristallnacht* in the ghettos, in camps, upon liberation and afterwards. The burden of memory killed German Jews (and Jews from other countries outside of Germany), not German non-Jews. However, there is evidence that subsequent generations of Germans have suffered psychological damage from the effects of denial and repression.

Like her father, Anna Freud underestimated the psychic effects of trauma in children who survived the Holocaust. Kestenberg (1990) explains that Anna Freud thought that young children who had survived the horrors of the camps would heal relatively easily after the war. But Kestenberg claims that she was wrong on this. Young children did not heal easily; in fact, they suffered deeply.

> This early impression [of Freud's] was not born out by the facts.... Shalom Robinson (1979) in an Israeli mental hospital revealed that the psychic dam-

> age to children traumatized during the Holocaust was most severe in those who were persecuted before the age of three. (p. 85)

This psychological damage suffered by survivors cannot be defined, named, or "cured." To label this suffering is to trivialize it. Post-traumatic stress syndrome, survivor syndrome, depressive reactive disorder, and reactive aggressive disorder are labels that trivialize and reduce suffering to neat and tidy categories. Jack Terry (1984) remarks that

> The survivor has been avoided, blamed, "syndromized;" exploited and rarely understood.... I suggest that the unconscious contempt for the survivor plays a role in generalizations and clarifications such as "survivor syndrome." (p. 139)

Pathologizing survivors is troublesome and highly problematic. It is difficult, however, to avoid doing this because classical psychoanalytic theory is pathologizing. But again, a Laplanchian or post-Freudian reading of psychoanalytic theory may help us not to pathologize, but rather, to translate these so-called symptoms as a form of radical otherness and strangeness.

> We turned toward the grave and then he turned around and asked, 'Whom shall I shoot first?' ... I did not answer. I felt him take the child from my arms. The child cried out and was shot immediately. And then he aimed at me. (Yosselesvka, cited in Gilbert, 1985, p. 421)

Mass graves, shootings, torture, burnings, beatings, gassings, medical "experiments," and starvation are simply unimaginable, unthinkable, and in a certain sense, beyond representation. Most academics know nothing of this kind of torture. Yet, academics writing about the Holocaust must remember this fact: It is arrogant to assume that we can understand fully what these experiences were like. Holocaust memory burns a hole in one's psyche. There is always a lack, a void, and an otherness that marks these memory texts.

Martin Gilbert (1985) reminds us that in 1941 the death camp at Chelmno was up and running. "The first 700 Jews were being transported to the death camps at Chelmno ... Roosevelt's day that would 'live in infamy' was also the first day of the Final Solution" (p. 240). But Roosevelt, as we will discover later, did not give a whit about the fate of the Jews. The trains kept rolling into Auschwitz and America and Britain did little to rescue the Jews.

When Jews were first deported to the camps, psychologically, they had to turn to stone or they would not be able to survive. Defense mechanisms such as dissociation actually helped some Jews survive. Martin Wangh (1984) explains that,

> Profound psychic shock enveloped those who newly arrived at the death camps.... Shock was followed by apathy. Recovery from these states would occur only by means of psychic splitting ... denial ... numbing, derealization. (p. 197)

Jews who could not allow defense mechanisms to operate lessened their chance of survival. Yet, even if defense mechanisms were intact, it did not necessarily make a difference, because Germans murdered indiscriminately. Still, defense mechanisms saved some, at least for a while. Kaplan (1998) reports that "a recurrent theme in Victor Kelemperer's diary was his and other's attempts to deaden their feelings" (p. 53). Camp life did not offer chances to grieve.

Delayed grief haunted many Holocaust survivors long after liberation. In fact, Yael Daneli (1989) stresses that expressing grief while in the camps probably would have threatened survival. "During the war, mourning endangered victim's lives. As with any prisoner's behavior which might have slightly deviated from that of the totally obedient automaton the Nazis expected, grieving had to be suppressed" (p. 428). Delayed grief returns in all kinds of somatizations. Repressed grief comes back. There seems no end to it. As Dori Laub (1992) points out, "The trauma is thus an event that has no beginning, no ending, no before, no during and no after. The absence of categories that defines it lends a quality of otherness" (p. 69). Despair, which is marked by a "lapse of duration" (Laplanche, 1999, p. 242), tells much about the workings of the unconscious. As Freud suggested, the unconscious is timeless, it knows no division between past and present. Holocaust survivors' nightmares attest to this. An event that happened years ago gets replayed over and over again as if the events which transpired happened yesterday. Repressed memories find a way of returning through unconscious traces, splitting the ego and continuing to push against consciousness. As Dina Wardi (1996) explains in her work with Holocaust survivors that,

> We thus witness an excessive use of the mechanisms of defense, denial, and compartmentalization, which became vital for the preservation of some basic integrity of the ego. But the excessive use of these mechanisms necessarily lead to structural changes in the ego itself. Emotional experiences that flood and terrify the ego eventually bring about internal splits and rifts. (p. 13)

Structural changes in the ego are marked by continual utilization of defense mechanisms when they are no longer needed. Depersonalization, numbing, and depression set in and become sedimented over time. Memories haunt.

> The old, the sick and the babies ... were placed on stretchers and taken to the edge of the huge mass graves. There, the SS man Irrman shot them and pushed them into the graves with his rifle. (1985, Reder, as cited in Gilbert, p. 414)

It is simply impossible to integrate these kinds of memories into the psyche. The notion of working through the past is probably naive. There is no working through the Holocaust. Perhaps there is only a coping with.

According to Rashkin (1992), Holocaust survivors and psychoanalysts Nicolas Abraham and Maria Torok (1992) suggest that traumatic memories get "lodged" like "phantoms" (p. 27) in the psyche. These memories are not wholly repressed but they hover in a place that is located between remembering and forgetting, between the unconscious and the conscious. These phantoms, then, get introjected or "implanted" (Laplanche, 1999, p. 258) in another and this is what Torok (1992) calls "transgenerational haunting" (cited in Rashkin, p. 27). Sometimes transgenerational hauntings are triggered by secrets. What is muffled reappears in ghostly forms. Many Holocaust survivors, especially immediately after liberation, entered into a pact of silence about what it was that they experienced. But these secrets and these silences mark subsequent generations in different ways. Rashkin (1992) explains that Abraham and Torok believe that

> The unspeakable secret suspended with the adult is transmitted silently to children in "undigestable form and lodges within his or her mental topography as an unmarked tomb of inaccessible knowledge." (pp. 127–128)

These entombed memories leave "cryptic traces of an unspeakable drama" (p. 157) in another, infinitely regressive infinitely "repressive family history" (p. 157). Like Abraham and Torok, Shaton and Rosenfeld (cited in Kestenberg, 1989) feel that memory gets "encapsulated" or "intrapsychically jailed" (p. 386) neither exactly repressed or denied, but marking a site between repression and denial, between forgetting and remembering. Memory haunts and hovers like a ghost. Distance in time from these memories does not bring psychological relief for many. In fact, the reverse may be true. Aaron Hass (1996) points out that "As most [survivors] enter old age, a phase characterized by reintegration, reinterpretation, and reminiscence, trauma that had been successfully buried may come to life" (p. 23). This Freud would call *failed repression*. Repression has failed because memories which have been buried now push through to consciousness. But the memories that surface do not mirror the original memories; they take on their own shapings and coursings.

Precisely how generations pass along repressed memory is not clearly understood. These are "enigmatic messages" (Laplanche, 1999,

p. 80) that get transferred from one generation to the next. Whether survivors tell their stories to their children or not, intergenerational trauma is likely, if not unavoidable. If survivors keep secrets, these secrets somehow get "implanted" (p. 259) in their children's psyches. Children will phantasize about their parents' experiences during the Holocaust whether or not it is spoken about. Dori Laub and Nanette Auerhahn (1984) suggest that it does not matter whether the child actually witnessed his or her parents' persecution. "Children imagine trauma or, rather, experience it through identification" (p. 153).

A symbiotic relation usually develops between parents and children if they are Holocaust survivors, analysts reveal. It is this symbiosis that causes children of Holocaust survivors to suffer later on in life. Holocaust survivor parents become psychologically enmeshed with their children through the telling or not-telling of the past. Many times the children, for the parents, symbolize "all the relatives who perished" (Wardi, 1996, p. 6). Thus, the children have, it seems, a double identity. Dina Wardi (1996) explains,

> Many survivors preserve the memory of family members in their children and name them after dead relatives.... This is not a mere identification with those who perished, but a more complex mechanism—A transportation of the world of the past; during the course of which a divided ego is created in which two or more identities exist simultaneously. (pp. 94–95)

Usually girls, who are referred to as "memorial candles" (p. 31), carry the burden of memory. When survivor's children reach the age of 30 or so they sometimes seek therapy. One of the reasons they seek therapy, according to Wardi, is that they have difficulties individuating themselves from their parents. Maud Mannoni (1999) explains that another reason children seek therapy is guilt. Child survivors, even second generation children who were born after Auschwitz, may suffer from a terrible sense of guilt, especially when the "survivor [or children who were born after Auschwitz] reaches the age when his own parents were deported" (p. 39). These guilt feelings may result in what Mannoni considers "serious somatizations ... depression, fractures, angina" (p. 39).

Intergenerational trauma, even into the third generation, is real and refuses to just go away. Of course, the ways in which these memories affect second and third generation Jews vary widely. As Dominick LaCapra (1994) suggests, "especially in cases of severe trauma, one may never fully transcend the past and that one should be ... respectfully attentive to the voices of victims" (p. 3). Being respectfully attentive requires that we listen "with the third ear" (Reik, 1948/1998). Listen to Emmanuel Ringelblum's (1958) report about Auschwitz:

> A great many dispatches are arriving from Oswiecim [Auschwitz] with news of the death of inmates. People are forced to exercise under showers for three hours there; this produces inflammation of the lung[s] and death. (p. 38).

Ringelblum's reports from Auschwitz refuse assimilation into consciousness. A third generation Jew like myself, without actually having experienced the Holocaust, cannot imagine what this must have been like. I do believe that difficult memories like this one mark the unconscious in ways that cannot be named. Freud (1915) commented that "the unconscious of one human being can react upon that of another without passing through the conscious" (p. 194). Because Holocaust memory texts are so emotionally difficult to deal with, I think that the reception or introjection of these texts bypasses consciousness, depositing residues into the unconscious. What happens once deposited there is a mystery. Sometimes these images will re-appear in strange forms in nightmares. Sometimes the reader of these texts changes in uncanny ways. Lifton (1986) explains that after he finished his research on Nazi doctors he was no longer the same.

> As I reached the end of this work, many people asked me what it had done to me. My answer has usually been, "A great deal," followed by a change of subject. The truth is that it is still a little too early to tell. One cannot expect to emerge from a study of this kind spiritually unscathed. (p. xiii)

I would add to Lifton's comments that one cannot expect to emerge from this work psychologically unscathed either. The unconscious messages transferred from text to reader and the reader's transferential relations with these texts, shape and reshape the reader's unconscious in uncanny ways.

BYSTANDER HISTORIES

Holocaust scholarship has moved in its own uncanny ways since the 1960s. It has moved from what Tony Kushner (1994) calls "Hitlercentric" perspectives to "one incorporating the role of 'ordinary people' in its execution, the involvement of non-Germans in the occupied or Nazi influenced countries, the impact on Jews themselves and the presence of bystanders" (p. 11). Thus, at this juncture I turn first to two collaborating countries, France and Italy, and then examine two bystander countries, Britain and the United States. Here I am interested in looking at the complexities of response to the Holocaust and the ways in which repressed memory and psychological denial play a role in shaping the memories of the Holocaust in these various countries.

One of the disturbing facts about collaborators is that there were so many willing non-Germans who were not only complicit but directly involved in carrying out brutalities against Jews. Latvians, Lithuanians and Ukranians actually volunteered their services to aid the Germans during the actions of the *Einsatzgruppen* in Russia in 1941. Here scores of Jews were mowed down with machine guns. Paul Webster (1991) remarks that in France, under the leadership of René Bousquet, "There was no lack of French police ready to work directly for the Gestapo. By the end of the war, it was estimated that about 30,000 French were working with the Nazis" (p. 108). Many Italians were willing partners in crime too. Despite the fact that 85% of Italian Jews had survived the Holocaust, according to Susan Zucotti (1996), 6,800 were deported and murdered. When Germany occupied Italy in 1943, Eichmann sent to Italy "Jew hunters" and "thousands of Italian Fascists ... were eager to help" (p. xxvi).

What becomes difficult for me not to repress is the fact that so many European countries collaborated with the Nazis. Raul Hilberg (1992) reminds us that collaborating countries included Italy, Bulgaria, Rumania, Hungary, Slovokia, Croatia, Norway, France, and The Netherlands. We can also add to this list Switzerland. Tom Bower (1998) comments that in November of 1940,

> two hundred of Switzerland's financial and political leaders—the pillars of that nation—petitioned their government to show greater sympathy toward the Nazis.... While Europe shuddered before the apocalypse, Switzerland was aligning itself with evil.... The hopes of many refugees ended in Switzerland and they were murdered soon afterwards. But their money remained secure, too secure, in Switzerland's banks.... A country whose citizens ... boasted to their neighbors about their enviable wealth, was quite knowingly profiting from blood money. (pp. xiii–xiv)

It is difficult as a Jew to take in, psychologically, the fact that we have been so despised as a people historically. Do these hatreds ever die? While in Rome this summer, I saw spray painted on a wall near the Colosseum, "The Holocaust was a hoax." I know that anti- Semitism is alive and well but I have difficulty believing that Holocaust deniers and Jew haters are everywhere, even in Rome. This constant reminder that Jews are still despised unsettles me continuously. According to Albert Memmi (1966) Jews live in a "pathogenic condition" (p. 268). Lawrence Kritzman (1995) comments that for Memmi "Jewishness can never be anything beyond the mere reification of torment, the reflection of a problem that the Jewish subject internalizes" (p. 105). The question is how not to internalize hatred. But this presents difficulties, especially when much of Europe and America has had a history of anti-Semitism.

One of the few countries that has not had a history of anti-Semitism is Italy. This was one of the reasons I wanted to travel through Italy recently. I was shocked to see anti-Semitic graffiti in Rome. But then again, Italy did collaborate with the Nazis, although their collaboration was not total and did not come close to the viciousness of Vichy. The history of Italy usually brings to mind Fascism and Mussolini. Of course, there is more to Italy's history than this yet these are the lasting impressions that many Americans share about Italy. Many Italian intellectuals, Furio Columbo (1996) suggests, have traditionally only remembered the past in this way too. Italian intellectuals "felt purified by the great wave of the anti-Fascist crusade, by participation in the Resistance ... Fascism had not only been defeated by the Allied troops. It had been beaten by partisans.... But in that manner an entire past was erased and the Holocaust was forgotten" (p. xi). The internal resistance against Fascism covered over and repressed the memory of Italy's collaboration with the Nazis, although by and large, most Italians were not involved and not complicit.

The question that Suan Zuccotti (1996) raises around Italian collaboration is important. She asks why Italians became complicit in the first place as anti-Semitism never really took hold in Italy. Daniel Carpi (1994) explains that "There is widespread agreement among scholars ... that Italy was a country, (or even the only country) where anti-Semitism did not strike roots" (p. 241). Nevertheless, racial laws, roundups, and deportations were carried out in Italy. Approximately 6,800 Jews were deported and murdered. In light of the fact that Italy never had a history of anti-Semitism, Italy's complicity becomes puzzling. It is crucial to understand that in France, it is estimated that 76,000 Jews were deported to concentration camps, and Marrus and Paxton (1981/1995) contend that only 3% of those deported survived. In Italy, 6,800 Jews were deported. These numbers tell two different stories.

Zuccotti (1996) believes that so many Jews survived in Italy because unlike France, Poland, Belguim and The Netherlands, which were occupied by the Nazis for five years, "the Holocaust began late in Italy [and] ... by September 1943 most Italians had heard about the deportation of Jews" (pp. 272–273). Moreover, most Italians wanted nothing to do with deporting Jews.

Scholars agree that Italians did everything they could to save Jews in the occupied territories of Greece, Southern France, and Tunisia. Zuccotti (1996) explains that Italians "resorted to every imaginable scheme and subterfuge to resist repeated German demands for the deportation of Jews. They ignored Mussolini's directives" (p. 75). Not only did the Italians ignore Mussolini, they ignored the Nazis and the Vichy police.

The irony, though, is that Jews living on Italian soil were not protected from arrest and deportation. Jews were arrested and deported and betrayed by Fascists and non-Fascists alike. Unlike Jews in other countries, Italian Jews who were summoned to the police often did not show up. Zuccotti (1996) remarks that "Italian Jews seemed to have shared with their Catholic compatriots an amiable inclination to ignore the law" (p. 275).

Like Italy, France has traditionally suffered from repressed memory about its collaboration with Germany during the Holocaust. Until the 1970s, the French generally erased Vichy's complicity. David Weinberg (1996) declares that "for more than three decades after liberation, French society denied its painful wartime past and ignored the fate of its Jewish inhabitants under Vichy" (p. 31). Stanley Hoffman (1981) reports that the first book written on Vichy, by Robert Paxton, was greeted with hostility by the French reading public. It was not until the mid-1980s that the Ministry of Education in France agreed "to include discussions of French complicity in the deportation process in classroom textbooks" (Weinberg, 1996, p. 36). Elizabeth Bellamy (1997) argues that France has taken longer to come to terms with repressed memory of the Holocaust than has Germany. Bellamy suggests that

> The psychic phenomena of memory, forgetting, melancholia, and repression all converge on vichy as the locus of France's characteristic ... "inability to mourn" and they serve as a vivid demonstration that Frances' *Aufarbeitung* has been delayed much longer than Germany's. (p. 13)

Wyman (1984/1998) and Bellamy (1997) agree that France, before the 1970s, engaged in a myth of resistance, what Bellamy calls "France's customary narratives of resistance heroism" (p. 14). But even in the resistance movement anti-Semitic attitudes were prevalent. Traces of repression, in the form of denial and reversal, are evident in the ways in which French officials, immediately after the war, rationalized Vichy's complicity.

These rationalizations and denials manifested themselves around many different issues. In post- war trials, one of the most blatant examples of repressed memory is that many argued that France became complicit with Germany because of coercion. Robert Paxton (1975) explains that,

> Marcel Peyrouton traced the anti-Jewish legislation of 1940 to German pressures and said that the Germans threatened 10,000 hostages in 1942 if the French did not tighten those laws even further. (p. 142).

But scholars generally agree that Vichy's anti-Semitic policies were homegrown. The Germans did not care what the French did. They never threatened the French and they did not demand any kind of anti-Semitic policies be set in place. The French, it seems, wanted to demonstrate to the Germans that they could be even more anti-Semitic than the Germans to win German approval. But as Paxton (1975) contends, "Neither diplomats nor soldiers at Berlin cared a fig for Vichy's internal acts" (p. 142). Vichy authorities wanted to out do the Nazis. And on one occasion they did. Here I am thinking of the deportation of children from Vichy to Auschwitz. It is estimated that about 6,000 children in 1942 alone were deported without the approval of the Germans. Even the Germans shuddered at Vichy. Marrus and Paxton (1981/1995) report that what transpired at Vichy shocked the world.

> During 1942, according to Serge Klarsfeld's estimate, 1,032 children under the age of 6 years old were sent to Auschwitz from France, along with 2,557 between 6 and 12, and 2,464 between 13 and 17. (p. 263)

This would be the greatest shame of Vichy. It is unthinkable that children under the age of 6 would be put on cattle cars and shipped off to Auschwitz. Children! I am aghast. Klarsfeld (1996) has maintained that after this horrific event occurred, the Catholic Church stepped in to intervene and help prevent more incidents like this one. But Paul Webster (1991) writes that Klarsfeld is mistaken about this. Webster claims:

> There are other French historians, even inside the Catholic Church who ... point out that both Cardinal Gerlier and Cardinal Suhard went to see the head of State on 29 October 1942 to pledge their loyalty at a time when deportation trains were still leaving. (p. 132)

It becomes very difficult to believe that the Church would actually pledge loyalty to Vichy. But, of course, we now know that the Church was compliant all along (Cornwell, 1999). The Church has recently justified their silence during the Nazi era, claiming that they remained silent to save Jews. Clearly this is a move of denial.

Xavier Vallet's postwar trial defense offers up a similar kind of reversal. Vallet was responsible for setting anti-Semitic policy. Vallet argued that because the French mainly hunted foreign-born Jews and that anti-Semitic policies were directed toward them, that Vichy actually engaged in a policy in which "Jews had been saved. Vichy, the argument went, had served as a shield" (Marrus & Paxton, 1981/1995, p. 344). But in point of fact, 76,000 Jews were deported from Vichy. How could anyone rationalize that?

Like Vallet, police chief René Bousquet, in a move of reversal, suggested during the postwar trials that he was, in fact, "defiant" (Webster, 1991) against the demands of the Nazis. But this clearly was not the case.

> Recent research has destroyed the image of a defiant Bousquet, which he projected during his trial. He often lied over his responsibility in planning the round-ups, even covering up a crucial meeting with SS chiefs. (p. 107)

Like Bousquet, Pierre Laval, who conducted the deportation of children from Vichy to Auschwitz, pretended that he was a "lone wolf" (Paxton, 1975, p. 67) who got in over his head and kept his "colleagues in ignorance" (p. 67). But according to German archives, this lone wolf image is untrue. Paxton reports that we learn from these archives that Vichy's complicity was "much more broadly shared" (p. 67). And, like Bousquet and Laval, Marshal Pétain was portrayed in postwar trials as a "manipulated old man" (Webster, 1991, p. 7). Yet this portrayal is not accurate either. Marrus and Paxton claim that it was not a coincidence that anti-Semitic laws came into existence just 12 days after Pétain's arrival in office. Marrus and Paxton (1981/1995) explain some of the implications of setting in place anti-Semitic laws:

> The law of 22 July 1940—rushed into effect only twelve days after Marshal Pétain's role as head of state.... Eventually over fifteen thousand lost French citizenship ... including about six thousand Jews.... The law of 4 October 1940 ... authorized prefects ... to intern foreign Jews in "special camps" (p. 4).

Clearly, this is not the work of a manipulated old man. This is the work of a man with a mission. Twelve days after taking office, Pétain began to ruin the lives of Jews with the stroke of a pen; Pétain knew just what he was doing.

Denial and reversal take time to get worked through. It has taken French society many years to begin to come to terms with their collaborationist past. Bellamy (1997) and Hoffman (1981) agree that, at least since the 1970s, France has begun to "lift the veil of repression" (Bellamy, p. 14) and to remember its complicity.

Although Italy, France, Britain, and the United States played radically different roles during the Holocaust, there does seem to be a consensus among scholars about a fundamental attitude that ran through all four countries: indifference. Even after the war, the French continued their attitude of indifference. Hoffman (1981) remarks that, "Simone Weil, who survived deportation, told of the indifference with which Jewish survivors were met when they returned to France" (p. x). Like the French, many Italians, at least those Italians who were not living in occupied territories during the war, remained indifferent. Furio Columbo (1996) explains that although "many Italians never became enemies of the Jews or informers for the Germans ... [they did not oppose] ... the racial laws [but] simply pretended to avoid seeing the implications" (p. xiii). To pretend that the racial laws did not exist or to rationalize them was to remain, in essence, indifferent to the Jews. But in occupied territories, Italians were anything but indifferent.

Similar to Italy and France, Britain remained, for the most part, indifferent. Wasserstein (1988) reports that although Churchill was sympathetic to the Jewish tragedy, he was blocked by "his subordinates [who got submerged in] an ocean of bureaucratic indifference and lack of concern" (p. 395). Feingold (1995) suggests that the U.S. State Department was being bogged down with "indifferent ... decision makers" (p. 175). David Wyman (1984/1998) declares that neither British nor American government officials gave one whit about the Jews. In fact, "the American State Department had no intention of rescuing large numbers of European Jews" (p. xii). Roosevelt demonstrated, "indifference to so momentous an historical event as the systematic annihilation of European Jewry [which] ... emerges as the worst failure of his presidency" (Wyman, p. xv).

Against these scholars, Tony Kusher (1994) suggests that the term "indifference" is not helpful. Kusher claims that *indifference* is too simplistic a term to explain the complexities of response to the Holocaust. By and large, Britain, especially on examination of labor movement responses, was not indifferent, but rather "essentially ambivalent" (p. 46). Kushner attempts to suggest that responses to the Jewish tragedy were not monolithic. Indifference seems to suggest a monolithic response.

I think Kushner is right to point out that there were a variety of responses to the Jewish catastrophe. At the end of the day, it is really quite impossible to tell what it was people felt, if they felt anything at all. However, the actions of the allied countries leads me to believe that government officials, for the most part, in both Britain and the United States did not care enough or do enough to save European Jews.

In both Britain and the United States, top government officials blocked opportunities for refugees to escape Europe at every turn. This seems to suggest more than an attitude of indifference; it seems to reveal contempt. And it is this contempt for Jews that disturbs me. Perhaps seemingly sympathetic responses served as gloss for a deeper hatred for Jews. If British officials were truly sympathetic, they would have acted differently. But the White Paper policy remained intact through the duration of the war. The White Paper policy limited the number of immigrants allowed to go to Palestine to 75,000. But as Wasserstein (1988) points out, "barely half ... had been admitted" (p. 52). Part of the rationalization for not allowing many refugees into Palestine sprang from paranoia that German spies would be among the refugees and threaten "the international security of Palestine" (p. 49).

A similar kind of paranoia filtered into the U.S. State Department. Feingold (1995) refers to this paranoia around Jewish refugees as a "security psychosis" (p. 172). By 1940, immigration to the United States was impossible. Breckenridge Long, who was Head of the State Department, argued that "Germany had infiltrated the refugee stream with agents" (Feingold, p. 172). But spies were never discovered.

David Wyman (1984/1998) remarks that the U.S. State Department amassed what he called Paper Walls, which made it nearly impossible for refugees to land on U.S. soil. These Paper Walls were made up of "four feet long" visa applications. Refugees found themselves in an Orwellian nightmare because they had difficulty reaching American Consuls in Axis territories, and those who escaped from Axis territory were not thought to be in danger, so State Department officials decided there was no need for them to come to the United States. Wyman (1984/1998) explains that "where Jews were in acute danger, in Axis-held territories, there were no American Consuls to issue visas. But those who escaped to countries where consuls continued to operate were not [considered to be] in acute danger" (p. 127). The U.S. State Department, in short, made certain that European Jews would not be able to reach American soil. The chief architect of these Paper Walls was Breckenridge Long. Long was, clearly, a Jew hater. Wyman (1984/1998) declares that

> Long, an early admirer of Hitler and Mussolini came to head the Special Problems Division of the State Department almost by accident.... It was the caprice of this single individual that could make the difference between life and death. (p. 86)

It is hard to imagine that the head of the U.S. State Department was an admirer of Hitler and Mussolini.

Information about the Holocaust was known. Ever since *Kristallnacht* in 1938 German policy toward Jews was no secret. However, both Britain and the United States censored news and even cut it off. Walter Laquer (1981) explains that in 1942 the Jewish Telegraphic Agency received word from a certain Reigner from Europe that approximately 4 million Jews had been exterminated. But Long cut off such reports after yet another telegram was sent. In Britain, Reigner's telegraphs were completely dismissed. Officials dismissed the reports as "Jewish Agency 'sob stuff' calculated to engender greater sympathy for Zionist efforts to get more refugee immigrants into Palestine" (Cesarani, 1996, p. 607). It was not as if the British did not know what was happening. Cesarani (1996) reports that as Jews were being deported to Auschwitz from Hungary these "deportations were known in Britain virtually as they took place" (p. 609). But the British government did little to help the Jews.

What is perhaps the most scandalous of all is that the Allies, when they had the chance, did not bomb the rail lines to Auschwitz, which could have potentially saved many Jews. Wyman (1984/1998) contends that Roosevelt was urged by The Jewish Committee to consider bombing the rail lines but he never did. It was not that the rail lines were located in some remote region; it was not that bombing the rail lines would have thwarted the war effort either. In fact, Wyman declares that "a total of 2,700 bombers traveled along or within easy reach of both rail lines on the way to targets in the Blechhammer—Auschwitz region" (p. 311). But because "rescue was not part of its mission" (p. 307) the military bypassed Auschwitz as the sealed trains continued to their destination.

William Rubenstein (1997), an ultra-conservative historian, argues that bombing the rail lines at Auschwitz would have done little to save Jews. Rubenstein's position reflects that of the Franklin Roosevelt Institute, which seems to suffer from denial. In Rubenstein's (1997) work he argues, against the grain of Holocaust scholarship, that the United States actually had a "liberal" immigration policy toward Jews and that Roosevelt did everything he could to help the Jews. How could Rubenstein make the claim that the U.S. had a liberal immigration policy? This is clearly not the case. The thrust of Rubenstein's argument is that no matter what Roosevelt would have done he could not have saved Jews anyway. But clearly, many scholars argue that Roosevelt could have made a difference but saving Jews simply did not interest him.

It is difficult to understand why the allied countries abandoned the Jews, as the title of Wyman's book suggests. And it is even more difficult to squarely face the fact that our own President Roosevelt turned his back on Jews at a time when we needed him most. Feingold (1995) remarks,

> The president, so beloved by American Jewry, did not have the spiritual depth to fathom the crucible being experienced by European Jewry, the historical insight and intelligence to understand the meaning of Auschwitz for his time in history. (pp. 176–177)

I remember how much my own grandparents loved Roosevelt, like so many of their generation. How shattered they would be if they only knew the truth.

SIX

Memory Text of Holocaust Novels

Holocaust scholarship is generally separated into two broad realms. On the one side, Holocaust historiography abounds; on the other side we find the work of Holocaust fiction and the work of literary criticism. I think that educators should have some grasp of both of these worlds. Historiography is crucial for understanding this event while fiction evokes emotional and intellectual registers that historiography does not. My aim in this chapter, then, is to examine Holocaust fiction. In this chapter, I look at Jewish novels and German (non-Jewish) novels, side by side. My treatment of Holocaust literature is unlike the work done by literary critics. Literary critics, who do work on Holocaust novels, tend to be divided into those who examine exclusively German (non-Jewish) texts, or those who examine exclusively Jewish texts. Literary critics who study either German (non Jewish) or Jewish texts tend not to cross over and look at the other side. This not-crossing-over is myopic. An either/or framework limits the horizon of understanding. A both/and approach is better. Here my framework is broadened. I suggest, therefore, that educators need to read both German and Jewish texts alongside one another. I am not arguing, however, that one can get the whole picture by reading these texts side by side. Understanding is always partial. But I am suggesting that a broader encounter with this material is necessary if we are to call ourselves educated people.

Historical novels are an expression of memory. Like the craft of doing history, novel writing is a kind of systematization of memory. Writers organize, select and narrate. Novel writing, however, is not reducible to memory, because writers, even if drawing on their own memories, are constrained by the narrative form. Memory seems not to be constrained in the same way, although we remember via "quasi narration" (Casey, 1987, p. 44). Edward Casey (1987) argues that what is lacking in memory is a narrator who tells a story. Memory is more like a "pastiche" (p. 72). Even novels that are written in the form of a pastiche seem more tightly woven than a memory. Personal memories function out of sites of repression, denial, and projection and may therefore determine, to a certain extent, the ways in which novelists select, imagine, and construct the past.

The writings of historians share certain features with the writings of novelists. But I suggest that, at bottom, historical writing is not reducible to the writing of historical novels. History shares with literature its narrative and imaginative form. History is both a construction and reconstruction of the past. I maintain that history constructs the past by drawing on memory, perception, and imagination. Historians select and omit events and express their thoughts by narration. Further, historians attempt to reconstruct the past by drawing on archives, artifacts, testimonies, and other kinds of documents. Although historians rely on imagination to systematize and interpret, they are ultimately constrained by the methodology of the discipline in order to ensure that they get at an approximation of the truth about the events of the past.

Novels that are historical rely on narrative to express the imagination of the writer. These novels, like historical texts, are constructions that draw on memory, perception, and imagination. Novelists, too, select and omit what they deem relevant to their stories. Historical novelists may also draw on artifacts, archives, testimonies and other kinds of documents, but they do not have to use evidence to support their claims in the same way that historians do.

Psychologically, fiction may evoke different kinds of transferential relations in the reader than historical accounts of the Holocaust. Reading Holocaust novels may trigger more intense emotional engagement than reading historical texts. And the emotional response of the reader is complexified by her relation not only to the text but to the otherness that the text evokes in her unconscious. Peter Brooks (1987) comments that

> The advantage of such a transferential model, it seems to me, is that it illuminates the difficulties and productive encounter of the speaker and listener, the text and the reader, and how their exchange takes place. (pp. 12–13)

This exchange takes place, as one unconscious (the text) interferes with another (the reader). Andre Green (1986) remarks that the text will inevitably "leave behind ... scattered traces of the primary process on which it is constructed" (p. 338). Because these scattered traces of unconscious processes get introjected into the reader's psyche, it becomes important to become aware of the ways in which different kinds of Holocaust novels affect the reader.

Realism, metaphor, and irony deposit different kinds of traces in the reader's psyche. Novels written by Jews and novels written by Germans who are not Jewish impact readers differently, depending on their ethnicity and gender. Therefore, I suggest that researchers, if they are to grapple with what I call the *memory text of Holocaust novels*, need to read broadly. Different genres written by both Jews and Germans help readers experience different kinds of transferential relations with the memory of this event as it gets handed down to us in fiction. Writing Holocaust fiction is not wholly acceptable, especially in Jewish circles. In fact, for some Jews writing fiction around the Holocaust is considered anathema. Alvin Rosenfeld (1980) reminds us that it was Adorno who claimed early on that turning the Holocaust into art is "not only impossible but perhaps even immoral" (p. 13). Lawrence Langer (1975) remarks that "there is something disagreeable, almost dishonorable, in the conversion of suffering of the victims into works of art" (p. 1). Some, like George Steiner, call for silence. Steiner argues that art trivializes (cited in Langer, 1975). Like Steiner, Reinhard Baumgart and Michael Wyshogrod feel that the Holocaust should not be turned into art (cited in Rosenfeld, 1980). Following Adorno, Baumgart declares that Holocaust literature does a terrific injustice to victims because it domesticates and exploits. Sara Horowitz (1992) claims that "in the ongoing initial discourse about the Holocaust and its representation, the status of imaginative literature as a serious venue for reflection about historical events comes repeatedly under question" (p. 1). Literature that glorifies suffering, that exploits victims, that offers redemptive messages, that turns suffering into "an affirmatively posited transcendence" (Adorno, 1966/1995, p. 361) does indeed run counter to an ethical sensibility and does not do justice to the memory of the Holocaust. These scholars are right to point out the pitfalls of writing fiction around the Holocaust. But I argue that there are other ways of writing fiction about the Holocaust which avoid these problems. The alternative to artistic expressions of silence is not a good one. Silence represses memories; silence shuts off and shuts out literary representations leaving a void in the heart of memory. Silence cannot be maintained because the repressed returns. The repressed returns in ways that haunt, in ways that will do tremendous damage to Jewish and German psyches. Dori Laub

(1992) comments that "silenced memory ... finds its way ... through an uncanny repetition of events that duplicate ... the traumatic past" (p. 65). For survivors, memories, if not written about, talked about, or thought about get repressed and surface later in nightmares, somatizations, depersonalizations, and depressions. However, writing about the past in an imaginative way does not always undo repression either. Sometimes writing fiction retraumatizes. It is no coincidence that so many Jewish Holocaust fiction writers have committed suicide. There is nothing liberating about writing Holocaust novels. Writing is a way of coping.

One of the most obvious worries, especially for Jews, is simply that fiction lies, it fabricates and falsifies. Holocaust fiction, for some, seems to "add nothing substantial to our understanding of those events but instead gives fodder to the historical revisionists" (Horowitz, 1992, p. 20). Many people believe that (legitimate) historical accounts are more appropriate than literary ones. However, historians are not the only keepers of memory, and certainly, their interpretations are not the most authoritative. Novelists have something to say about this past, and imaginative constructions evoke emotional responses in ways that historical accounts do not. Both historical and literary representations of the Holocaust, if they do justice to the memory of the victims and survivors, have something to offer. Neither form of representation should be placed over against the other. Both are equally important in shaping our understanding of this event. Literary and historical representations help us keep the memory of the Holocaust alive. Yehuda Bauer (1988) remarks that reading historical accounts actually enrich our readings of fiction.

> Without a return to the arduous task of actually knowing something about the Holocaust, the symbolic descriptions that occupy, quite legitimately, the center of the literary stage in Holocaust literature, become just another escape route for the superficial. (p. 7)

I do not believe that literature is "escapist." Maxine Greene (1995) and Mary Aswell Doll (2000) argue that literature grounds us in lived experience. Doll suggests that fiction is not "mere;" rather, it can serve to "disturb the status quo. Feelings thought to be central get routed. Peripheral imaginings begin to take root" (p. xii). Fiction is not fluff. As Doll suggests, fiction is about living and dying and there is nothing superficial about that. Reading historical accounts alongside literary ones helps us to encounter different perspectives and thus broaden our experience as readers. James Young (1988) argues that "literary and historical truths may not be entirely separable" (p. 1). Because they are not entirely separable it makes sense to read them both.

Many argue that literary representations of the Holocaust are indeed appropriate expressions of memory. Yet, there is much disagreement about appropriate genres. More conservative scholars contend that the realistic novel best represents the Holocaust (Rosenfeld, 1980; Lang, 1990; Bosmajian, cited in Ryan, 1983; Trommler, cited in Ryan, 1983). Realist novels James Young (1988) terms "docu-novels" (p. 51) because they are written in a documentary style. These scholars feel that literary representations of the Holocaust should attempt to get at the truth of this event. It seems that the assumption here is that truth is unmediated. Accordingly, the documentary style is the closest thing to the real because words can represent things. Sara Horowitz (1992) claims that Berel Lang, for instance, calls for the "bare chronicle" (p. 20). Hamida Bosmajian (1983) argues against using metaphor and irony because they merely serve as a "psychological defense against memories that threaten to become overwhelming" (cited in Ryan, p. 19). Rosenfeld (1980) declares that "there are no metaphors for Auschwitz" (p. 27). Frank Trommler claims that metaphor "obscures the reconstruction of the German past" (cited in Ryan, 1983, p. 19).

It seems to me that what undergirds the argument for what Young (1988) calls "docu-novels" (p. 51) is the belief that texts can correspond to reality, unproblematically. This assumption is what I have called the classical position around representation. But texts do not correspond to reality in neat and tidy ways because they are mediated by language, perception, memory, repression, projection and all kinds of complex psychological mechanisms. Texts are translations of events and these translations are slippery and necessarily perspectival. But perhaps the real issue underneath these debates around genre has little to do with the genre itself. The real issue, Sarah Horowitz (1992) says, turns on truth.

> At issue is not simply the stylistic competence of a particular writer but also the truth, authenticity, and morality of the writing, its connection with the philosophical, political, metaphysical implications of the Nazi genocide. (p. 25)

Truth is not absolute. Nowhere do absolute truths exist. Scholars, therefore, who argue for the legitimacy of documentary style fiction are, I think, naive. I think they suffer from literalism.

Mary Aswell Doll (2000) makes a strong case against literalisms. She argues that "the problem is not illiteracy but rather literalisms.... Texts are everywhere being literalized: copied" (p. xiii). The idea that fiction must literally represent truth or literally represent the events of the Holocaust lacks depth and is built on what I consider to be a misguided presupposition. No matter how literal one tries to be, no matter how much one attempts to match up words with memories of past events, slippage is everywhere. Memories have memories of their own. And words cannot capture the past in a neat and tidy way. Imagination, belief, and repression always interfere with representations. However, it is understandable why Holocaust survivors felt the necessity to tell the truth, to tell their story in a documentary way. Aharon Appelfeld (1994) explains:

> The first writing about the Holocaust was in the documentary style.... To write about oneself, about one's personal feelings, seemed selfish and vulgar.... The interior was locked away. (p. x)

Appelfeld continues by saying that for many survivors "deviation from memory was sinful" (p. xii). But Appelfeld remarks that he could not get a likeness to his past and his memory was too slippery and changeable. The harder he tried to write in a documentary style, the more stifled his writing became. Ernst Van Alphen (1997) points out that for many, "literary representations of the Holocaust are especially valued if they make people think of literature as little as possible" (p. 18). Appelfeld (1994) argues that testimonies, memoirs, and documentary novels serve actually as repressive mechanisms because they bury emotions. Documentary novels serve to block deeper emotions, according to Appelfeld (1994):

> If you read the many collections of testimony written about the Holocaust, you will immediately see that they are actually repressions, meant to put events in proper chronological order. They are neither introspective, nor anything resembling introspection, but rather the careful weaving together of many external facts in order to veil the inner truth. (p. 14).

As against Appelfeld, I argue that testimony and memoirs are important genres when examining the Holocaust. The question is, What do people use testimony for? Is it used to block thinking and feeling? If so, Appelfeld's contention is right. Testimony, if used to just report facts, is a way of not thinking and not feeling and may serve as a repression. However, if testimony is used to unblock thinking and feeling, if testimony is used to communicate with others or to communicate with the self, then it does not serve repressive ends. If writing or testimony or memoir aims at capturing the literal truth, whatever that is, it lacks depth, in part, because I believe that it censors primary process thinking. Docu-realism is the kind of writing that is guided by secondary process thinking, writing that gets hedged in by categories, dates, times, places, names, and so forth. But because writing is always already a translation, an embellishment, it still leaves traces of primary process thought in the text. If the writer censors deeper emotions, these traces get blocked and repressed. When writing moves against the unconscious and censors, it reads without depth and texts tend to get flattened out. The novel, then, becomes explanation. Surely a novel could be more than this. James Macdonald (1995) teaches that if understanding is merely rational (as it is in docu-realism), it serves to cut off emotion. A text that gets flattened out because it squashes feeling dulls. James Macdonald (1995) teaches that thinking needs to embrace feeling or it

> leaves out the thinker, his or her own horizon or place in the universe, with its associated urges feelings and impulses. The main purpose of rational thought is to explain things, so that we may predict and control things. Explain means to "flatten out." (p. 173)

If the writer were more open to primary process thought, free association and dreams, the text might open out toward unconscious traces. Here, a deeper text surfaces. It is here, in the mode of primary process thinking, that metaphor finds a home. Metaphoric texts do seem richer and deeper than texts that attempt to get a likeness; metaphor opens the doors of perception and leaves the otherness of the text open rather than closing it off.

James Young (1988) comments that "part of the impulse [against metaphor] may stem from a traditionally positivistic attitude toward metaphor as a frivolous and merely decorative and trivializing influence" (p. 19). This attitude may also be a move against unconscious processes that open texts out onto many layers and levels. Texts are like dreams in that the latent and manifest content compete for attention. Freud (1900a/1900b) suggests that it is not so much the manifest content that is crucial; it is the latent content of a dream that is important. It is here that the trajectories of associations and jagged wanderings open out onto the otherness of lived experience. Metaphors evoke these kinds of openings.

The use of metaphor in Holocaust novels does not mean that the text does not point toward the horizon of truth(s). Metaphorical writing, at least for me, seems to deposit more disturbing traces in my psyche. I respond to metaphor in more emotionally intense ways than I do to documentary texts. Documentary texts serve their purpose, of course, but I simply prefer Holocaust novels that are metaphorical because they seem to move me more intensely. Thus, metaphorical writings are not forms of defense mechanisms, as Bosmajian (cited in Ryan, 1983) claims; on the contrary, I feel that literalisms and documentary realism can serve as defense mechanisms. I argue that an openness to the otherness of the unconscious keeps us from turning Holocaust literature into a glorification of suffering. Lawrence Langer (1975) remarks that

> The will of the reader is drawn into an autonomous milieu of the work of art and is subtly transformed—disfigured ... to see imaginatively both the rela-

> tionship between empirical reality of the Holocaust and its artistic representation in the work of literature, and the fundamental distinction between both of these worlds.... The reader is temporarily an insider and permanently an outsider, and the very tension resulting from this paradox precludes the possibility of "pleasure" Adorno mentions. (p. 3)

That readers are permanently outsiders to the event, if indeed they have not actually experienced the black sun of Auschwitz, is what openness to the otherness of the text ensures. This is why we cannot say after reading Holocaust fiction that we understand the event in any absolute way, because we never will. But these texts do provide "a framework for responding" (Langer, 1975, p. 2). And respond we must. Holocaust fiction writers, I believe, have an ethical responsibility to approximate the truthfulness of this event, whether they tell their tales in an ironic, metaphoric, or realistic mode. But truthfulness does not mean literal truth. Fictional accounts must do justice, in some way, to Holocaust memory.

Holocaust novels written by Jews and German non-Jews are important for us to read. However, some argue that German writers, who do not represent Jews in their novels, should not be considered part of the Holocaust canon. Alvin Rosenfeld (1980) argues that Günter Grass should not be included in the Holocaust canon because Jews are rarely represented in his texts. Dismissing German writers, as if they have nothing to say erases memory and further represses the German past. Rosenfeld misses a crucial point about the invisibility of Jews in German texts. This invisibility tells much about the ways in which German writers have not come to terms with the past. The absence of Jews in Holocaust texts signals what Dan Diner calls a "negative symbiosis" (cited in Gilman, 1995, p. 43) between Germans and Jews. The glaring absence of Jews in these texts may signal the presence of negativity Germans feel toward Jews and or the presence of negativity in Germans themselves around this event. The cloud of memory haunts Germans. But the memory Germans bury is inextricably tied to Jews.

A German psychotherapist, in an interview with novelist Ursula Hegi (1997), contends that her "Germanness plays an important role with Jews [she] ... works with ... it has to be acknowledged. We have to understand that we understand each other through that. Over and around and through that" (Katherina, cited in Hegi, p. 273). Whatever "Germanness" means, it always already means a symbiotic relation with Jews; Germans carve out their identities in the ways in which they absent Jews from their psyches or their worlds. What happened in Germany between 1933 and 1945 cannot be erased; Jews will always leave traces in the psyches of Germans. Freud (1925/1989) might suggest that it is to these negations that we must turn because underneath the no is a yes. No, Jews do not appear in German novels. Yes, Jews haunt Germans. Jews are present in their absence. Germans and Jews will always be in complex interrelations with each other. Difficult memory haunts and entangles whether we like it or not. And so it is to this difficulty we must turn.

The ethical responsibility of Holocaust fiction writers, according to Aharon Appelfeld (1994), is to counter facelessness, the facelessness Germans imposed on Jews during the Holocaust. Jews were reduced to numbers, to subhuman creatures, to massless ash. "In their explicit wickedness, the murderers reduced Jews to anonymity, a number, a creature with no face. And in fact, years of suffering slowly erased the image of humanity from within the Jews" (p. 22). It is to the face of the other we must turn. But the face of the other is not abstract; it is the face "of the individual, the individual whose father and mother gave him a name, taught him their language, gave him their love, and endowed him with their faith" (pp. 21–22). The continued facelessness of the Jew in German fiction attests, perhaps, to a failure to see Jews as Jews, to see Jews as human beings. This failure to see the other as other is due to all kinds of psychological resistencies to the memory of the Holocaust. It is up to second, third, and fourth generation Germans to put the face of humanity back on Jews, to see Jews as Jews and to put them back in their writings, back in their expressions of memory.

JEWISH NOVELS

At this juncture, I next turn to Holocaust fiction written by Jewish writers. Cynthia Ozick's (1989a) *Rosa* and *The Shawl* (1989b) are companion pieces about a Holocaust survivor named Rosa. Rosa's daughter Magda was murdered in a concentration camp by a Nazi guard. Magda was thrown against an electrical fence and died instantly. The memory of this haunts Rosa, ruins her life, and drives her beyond the bounds of sanity. Rosa clings to the shawl in which she tried to hide Magda before the Nazi flung her daughter against the fence, before Magda was electrocuted. Magda haunts Rosa.

Rosa is a detached shadow of herself. "Someone who is already a floating angel, alert and seeing everything, but in the air, out there not touching the road" (Ozick, 1989, p. 13). She is a "madwoman" (p. 13) who is but a mere "shell" (p. 16) of a human being. Those who escaped from the horrors of the camps, Rosa suggests, are now "burned out" (p. 16) and resemble "scarecrows" (p. 23). The narrator of this novel describes Rosa as being "skinny" (p. 23) like a "ragged old bird with worn feathers" (p. 23).

Rosa calls herself a "shell" (p. 16) of a human being. Sander Gilman (1995) contends that the issue of invisibility is pervasive among German

Jews. "There are dangers in being too visible a Jew in Germany today" (p. 34). Gilman suggests that many German Jewish writers, especially women, attempt to negotiate a space between their feelings of invisibility and their need to become visible through their writing. But because they are afraid to come out with their Jewishness, it makes the writing task all the more difficult.

Ozick's character Rosa emphasizes how the very discourse about "survivors" makes her feel worse, more invisible. "Consider also the special word they used: Survivor. Something new. As long as they didn't have to say human being. It used to be refugee.... A name like a number.... Blue digits on the arm.... They didn't call you a woman anyhow" (pp. 36–37).

Rosa points out that the term *survivor* is obfuscating. It serves to take away the face of the individual and the individuality of suffering; it is a term that conceals and covers over. The word survivor also erases the engendered nature of suffering. Rosa declares, "They didn't call you a woman" (pp. 36–37). As Marion Kaplan (1998) stresses, "There is a relation between gender and memory" (p. 8). There is a relation between gender and suffering. Women suffered differently from men while in the concentration camps, as discussed earlier. In Ozick's novel, Rosa's face is given back to her to drive home the point that Holocaust survivors are not numbers and are not without gender. Aaron Hass (1996) remarks that frequently "Jewish survivors are often seen as a unitary phenomenon" (p. 7). But Rosa's deconstruction of the term survivor interrupts preconceptions that level survivors into one massless, faceless thing. Lawrence Langer (1998) comments that Ozick "refuses to tell a story of the triumph of spirit, the vindication of suffering through transcendence ... closure is impossible" (p. 123). Rosa is a madwoman who talks to her shawl and pretends that her daughter is alive. She never assimilates into her new life after Auschwitz, she is always clinging to memory, clinging to her dead daughter.

Like Ozick's Rosa, Greta Weil's (1984) unnamed narrator in *My Sister, My Antigone* is also a Holocaust survivor who feels detached from herself psychologically, haunted by facelessness. "A strangeness that eludes clear definition but seems to be growing steadily. A sense of distance between myself and other, myself and objects" (p. 11). The narrator declares that she is "being hollowed out" (p. 76) by life after Auschwitz. Recall, Rosa in Ozick's novel referred to herself as a mere "shell" (p. 16). Both of these characters, then, experience feelings of detachment, derealization, depersonalization and invisibility. Dina Wardi (1996) teaches that Holocaust survivors who seek psychological treatment suffer from "an excessive use of the mechanisms of defense, denial and compartmentalization" (p. 13). Defense mechanisms such as detachment and depersonalization helped Jews to survive while in the camps, but their continued use led to "internal rifts and splits [in the ego]" (Wardi, 1996, p. 13). In Rosa's case, the rifts and splits became manifest by psychotic episodes. Unlike Rosa, the unnamed narrator in Weil's novel flirts with insanity but never actually crosses the border. "I am distraught almost to the point of madness. I brush along the walls, getting gray paint on my clothes, cob webs in my hair, yet I lack the strength to run through the wall, to go really mad" (p. 77).

Weil's narrator is unnamed perhaps because she feels she has no identity, no face. The Germans have succeeded in making her faceless. She has introjected their poison. This unnamed narrator asks whether identity loss is such a bad thing after all. "Is loss of identity really such a mistake? Would I have been better to remain a German Jew in Munich all my life?" (p. 148). Remaining in Germany probably would not have been a good move for her. Sander Gilman (1995) suggests that Jews who remained after the war are, in the last analysis, "masochists" (p. 42). However, being a masochist has its advantage, Gilman contends. He says that German Jewish writers, who are masochists for living in Germany, are able to gain a certain amount of "control" (p. 47) over their sadistic counterparts, non-Jewish Germans. The Jewish writer is able to create "worlds of words, they can function in a position of dependence while claiming their own control over the world" (pp. 43–44). A "negative symbiosis" (Diner, cited in Gilman, 1995, p. 43) signals this sadomasochistic relationship between Jews and Germans. Some suggest that dialogue between Germans and Jews is impossible. Jack Zipes (1991) contends that Jew are seen by some Germans as "potential Nazis" (p. 9) primarily because of the tensions in the Middle East. Zipes explains as follows:

> What matters is that there is a great tendency among Germans to operate on Jews as stereotypes, and this tendency has been exploited by anti-Semites to transform Jews into Nazis. This operation is typical of the new German–Jewish symbiosis put forth by Henyrk Brodker, one of the most outspoken critics of German anti-Semitism ... it is the German who will never forgive the Jews for Auschwitz. (p. 23)

In a move of reversal, some Germans see themselves as victims of history, while Jews have become the perpetrators. Some of Ursula Hegi's (1997) interviews with Germans reflect this position. An interviewee, Joachim, says to Hegi, "And yet this[is] constantly thrown in their faces: Look at what your grandparents did. No race wants to be responsible for what its ancestors did. It's exactly the way Jews were being discriminated against" (p. 168). Hans-Peter, another interviewee, says to Hegi, "I feel a connection to blacks because I too have been prejudiced [sic] against" (p. 141). The perpetrator's grandchildren see themselves as the victims of history. They often comment that they are sick of hearing about the Holocaust. These remarks signal a refusal to take responsibility for at least discussing the ways in which second and third generation Germans might intelligently criticize their parents and grandparents. A critical memory would not lapse into victimization, which, for Germans, is completely inappropriate. Non-Jewish Germans are not victims of history, Jews are. Attitudes like these among Germans signal repressed memory and denial, and they foster a lack of social and moral responsibility. Part of the problem is that most Germans never make contact with Jews, at least in Germany. This absence creates the space for bizarre phantasies to emerge about Jews. Katharina Ocshe (1994) points out that in Germany "the probability that a non-Jew would ever meet a Jew is very small" (p. 113). Thus, hostility cannot be worked out if German Jews and German non-Jews do not talk face to face.

This negative symbiosis between Germans and Jews is evident in the language used to talk about these two groups of people. Ocshe (1994) reveals that currently in Germany there is much debate over how Jews are to be named. If non-Jewish Germans address Jews as a separate group by saying, for instance, Germans and Jews live in Germany, a problem arises. This division between Germans and Jews "robs the Jews of their citizenship, as if they were also not Germans" (p. 114). Furthermore, Ocshe comments that "those who prefer the expression "Jews in Germany" or "German Jews" reject the label "Jewish German" as inappropriate. For the "Jewish German" the expression "Jews in Germany" is an exclusionary term" (p. 114). Difficulties around the discourse of Jews and Germans is a symptom of the difficulty Jews have living in Germany, and signals the difficulty non-Jewish Germans have managing difference. Throughout this text, I struggle with these terms. I have sometimes experienced confusion when thinking that Germans may also be Jews, because so often in the past (before doing my research) I thought of these categories as being separate. My own confusion signals to me some kind of repression in my psyche. This is why it is helpful to read writings by German Jewish writers. Peter Gay's (1998) *My German Question: Growing up in Nazi Germany* has helped me understand the ambivalence around the German Jewish identity. As an American, I think I have particular difficulties understanding this ambivalence primarily because I have not personally experienced it the way a German Jew would. Being a third generation American Jew presents its own particular difficulties, but these difficulties are not as fraught. Jews might raise questions around assimilation into American culture and certainly issues of assimilation are troubling. Yet, I do not struggle over what to call myself. Calling myself a Jewish American or an American Jew makes little difference. These words do not carry the same weight, if you will, as German Jew or Jewish German. Throughout this entire text I feel uneasy around the question of naming.

The real uneasiness, though, concerns the ways in which Jews negotiated a space with non-Jewish Germans, especially right after the war. So to answer Weil's (1984) narrator's question, then, about remaining in Germany, one would have to say that it would not have been the best place for her. Having to deal with the complexities of negative symbiotic relationships with Germans would create a tremendous strain for a Jew. It is probably not impossible for Jews to live in Germany, some Jews probably live a good life there now.

Weil's narrator expresses a terrible sense of guilt for surviving the Holocaust. In fact, guilt consumes her. It is for this reason that she psychologically aligns herself with Antigone, for Antigone is her opposite and her heroine. Antigone "sneaks out under the cover of darkness to where Polyneices lies unburied.... Protest! Protest!... She pulls up clods of earth with her bare hands, throws dirt on the bloody flesh" (p. 15). Antigone did what she could never do, bury the dead. Unburied Holocaust victims haunt her. For not being able to even throw dirt over the dead, to grant the dead the dignity of a proper burial, she punishes herself by being buried in guilt.

Psychoanalysts are generally in agreement that many survivors suffer from guilt. Analysts term this *survivor guilt*. To incorporate the dead into living memory, the survivor becomes attached to guilt and to mourning. Yael Daneli (1989) comments that,

> Survivors fear that successful mourning may lead to letting go thereby forgetting the dead, and committing them to oblivion.... Many children of survivors also share this sentiment and, like their parents, hold onto the anhedonia, guilt, shame and pain. (p. 440)

I doubt that Holocaust survivors can ever experience so-called "successful" mourning whereby they let go and go on, but the investment in grief and the investment to the dead keeps them trapped in what Abraham and Torok call a "crypt" (cited in Rashkin, 1992, p. 157). Encrypted memory perpetually haunts because it hovers between memory and forgetting.

Like Ozick and Weil, Ida Fink's (1997) collection of short stories, *Traces*, is also about women survivors of the Holocaust. Only here, the reader sees traces of these characters, as if traces are the only thing left. We only get a brief glimpse into the lives of various characters. Eugenia, Sabina, and Julia are underweight to the point of being nearly invisible, faceless. Eugenia is "petite and fragile" (p. 72) with "thin legs" (p. 97); Sabina is "tall, and thin" (p. 97) and her hair is "thin, lanky and limp" (p. 97). These women are wasting away; survival after Auschwitz does not mean liberation. Eugenia "proclaimed that she wished to die in an automobile accident" (p. 71); Sabina has a "startled expression, as if she knew in advance that the world and its inhabitants had nothing good in store for her" (p. 97); Julia "floated away ... and soon all one could see was the black cloud rising above her" (p. 184). The Holocaust has left its indelible stain on these women. They remain faceless, invisible, and haunted. These characters had introjected and incorporated into their bodies the bad object of Nazi dehumanization. They have become perpetually depersonalized. These women could never again regain a sense of self, forever they would remain fragmented and detached. There can be no liberation from the Holocaust. "Memory is not only a spring flowing from the well of the past, but also a tomb, whose contents cling like withered ivy to the mind" (Langer, 1991, pp. 195–196). Memory is not only a "monument to ruin" (Langer, pp. 195–196) for Holocaust survivors, it is also a monument to ruin for children and grandchildren of survivors, for second and third generation Jews after Auschwitz.

In Cheryl Pearl Sucher's (1997) novel entitled *The Rescue of Memory*, readers are introduced to a Jewish character named Rachel who is the daughter of a Holocaust survivor. She is not, however, "rescued" by memory; rather, she wishes she could be rescued away from it. Rachel is torn between remembering and forgetting as her father continuously tells her his nightmarish stories. At one point Rachel says, "The truth was, I wanted to forget" (p. 95). But she cannot forget and insists that her purpose in life is "collecting remnants of memory" (p. 96). She suffers nightmares of her dead mother and scores of other family members killed during the Holocaust. Although the war is long since over, Rachel confesses, "Emily and I often stayed awake at night waiting for disaster to come" (p. 100). Aaron Hass (1996) states that "many children of survivors await a repetition of the persecution their parents experienced. Their homes [are] ... shaded by ominous clouds and peopled with ghosts and demons" (p. 7). Rachel is a "memorial candle" (Wardi, 1996, p. 31). She is chosen by her father as the bearer of memory. Wardi (1996) says:

> According to Heller (1988), the survivors tended to choose girls more than boys for the role of 'memorial candles,' perhaps because the Halacha prescribes that it is the mother's religion rather than the father's that determines the religion of the child. (pp. 31–32)

Wardi suggests that being the burden of a 'memorial candle' is sometimes too great. It creates a double identity, an enmeshed identity not only with the parents but with all the dead relatives who perished during the Holocaust. Rachel, in Sucher's (1997) novel remarks that

> Each year on the Day of Atonement, I attend my father's synagogue to say a prayer in honor of the souls whose name I have been given. Inscribed on the raised copper plates and illuminated by lemonflame bulbs, the names read Ruchel Wallfisch and Channah Sureh Greenblatt. Bathed in the pale golden light, I wonder what else of theirs is mine. (p. 30)

Rachel also wonders about difficulties she has individuating herself from her father. She sees his face whenever she looks in the mirror. Symbiosis with surviving parents and with the dead is what brings children of Holocaust survivors to therapy. (Wardi, 1996). These children have difficulty carving out their own identities. They also suffer from guilt. These complexities for children of Holocaust survivors transcend any neat and tidy diagnosis. Kestenberg (1990) reports that there has been considerable debate over whether or not to label symptoms "under the heading of 'survivor's child syndrome'" (p. 83). Kestenberg suggests that this label is simply not accurate because symptoms, if any emerge, are too various to be reduced to this label. It is hard to avoid "transgenerational haunting" (Rashkin, 1992, p. 22). Transgenerational haunting is real. It can ruin lives. And it seems that psychoanalysts are baffled by these uncanny ghosts. Sammy Speier comments that even the language analysts use to describe these hauntings is problematic. These hauntings appropriate a language and a coursing of their own. Speier, (1993) said that

> The implications of the experience of concentration camp survivors for the psychic illness of their children are much debated today; even the term "psychic illness" shows that the traditional diagnostic vocabulary of psychic illness is insufficient. (p. 63)

Speier suggests that there are no sufficient diagnoses for people who have "grown up with the fear of extermination" (p. 63). I argue against pathologizing Holocaust survivors and their children. Pathologizing and diagnosing covers over the horrors of suffering. Diagnosing keeps us from thinking about the complexities and the individuality of suffering (Salvio, 1999). Diagnosing is a form of naming that serves to box in something that is simply beyond name, beyond form, and beyond representation. There are no words to describe the depths of suffering, the depths of the empty holes left by absences and deaths.

At this juncture I contrast these novels, written by Jewish women, with novels written by Jewish men. I argue that gender matters in matters of novel-writing and in matters of memory. Memory is engendered. Texts written from a "male frame" differ from those written by women.

Bruno Schulz's (1934/1977) novel *The Street of Crocodiles* is a surrealistic tale. Schulz's narrator anticipates the danger to come, as the Nazi's, or crocodiles, begin crawling the streets. The narrator of this novel tells readers about his mad father. "He remained for long periods without moving, except to flap his arms like wings" (p. 43). Engaging in "childlike self-absorbed twittering," (p. 49) he thinks that he is at once a bird and a cockroach. Kafka's (1916/1992) novel *The Metamorphosis*, like Schulz's novel, allows readers to witness the transformation of Gregor Samsa, who turns into a roach. Like Kafka's Samsa, Schulz's narrator explains that his father

> lay on the floor naked, stained with black totem spots, the lines of his ribs heavily outlined.... He moved with many-limbed, complicated movement of a strange ritual. (p. 115)

Soon, however, this hallucination fades, and the narrator reports that after his brother came home with news of the end of the world (I believe he is referring to the Nazi accession to power), his father "put his head in the chimney shaft of the stove" (p. 157) and when he opens the flue, his father sees through "its dark abyss, where a smiling homunculus slept forever in luminous sleep, enclosed in a glass capsule, bathed in flourescent light, already adjudged, erased, filed away" (p. 160). The Jews of Europe had already been adjudged, erased, and filed away as Hitler arrived on the scene in 1933.

One interpretation of this story could suggest that the narrator's father is a raving lunatic. But at a certain level, the father understands what is happening and he anticipates what is to come, albeit in a psychotic state. The streets are filling up with crocodiles. These crocodiles, these ugly, horrible Nazis, are taking over and will soon come for their prey. They are coming.

Instead of becoming emaciated, as many of the characters did in novels written by women, Schulz's character becomes larger than life to the point of becoming surreal. This complete and utter alienation from others drives him to transform his being into other beings. He changes his face into that of another. He removes his face and becomes transformed into a creature, a non-human creature. Jews were hunted down like subhuman creatures; Eichmann called his men Jew Hunters, and he sent them everywhere to capture their prey. The feeling of being hunted down like a subhuman creature is unthinkable. Yet, it was this feeling of being hunted that drove many Jews to despair and suicide. Those who intuited that they could not escape often took their own lives. Like many others, Schulz did not have the chance to escape. But he did not take his own life, it was taken from him. Schulz was murdered in 1942. Ficowski (1977) explains:

> On November 9, 1942, on the streets of Drogobych ... there commenced a so-called action carried out by the local sections of the SS and the Gestapo against the Jewish population. "Black Thursday," brought death to some 150 passerby. Among the murdered ... was Bruno Schulz, a former teacher of drawing at the local high school. (p. 13)

There was nowhere to run by 1942, for the crocodiles were everywhere. Hardly anyone was willing to help Jews. The free world would "cast a cold eye" (Yeats, 1938–1939/1989, p. 325).

Schulz's (1934/1977) text is written like a dream or a nightmare. It is couched in metaphor and surrealistic imagery. It forever slips through interpretations and leaves marks of unconscious traces on the site of interpretation.

Analyst Andre Green (1994) talks about the difficulties of doing interpretive work around texts. He suggests that we treat a text as if it were the unconscious of another person. Green remarks:

> When the analyst ventures outside the analytic situation, in which he is in direct contact with the unconscious, as it were, he must proceed with caution. The work of art is handed over to the analyst; it can say nothing more than is incorporated in it and cannot, like the analysand, offer an insight into the work of the unconscious. (p. 47)

Whether we are analysts or not, Green's comments become important because he suggests we move with caution when doing interpretive work. The text is not an analysand, but it is the text of an other. Someone writes a text and leaves her traces in that text. But the writer has vanished; she is no longer present. Her absence, though, is marked by traces deposited in the site of the text. One moves cautiously and offers tentative interpretations, never approaching arrogance by claiming to have the authoritative interpretation.

Interpretations around metaphorical images become slippery because metaphor resonates with primary process thinking. Time is slippery, place is slippery, things converge in unusual ways. This is a world that is, as Martin Stanton (1997) would say, out of order. A smiling homunculus, birdman, and roachman all exist simultaneously. Schulz's text evokes strange transferential relations, feelings that cannot be named, thoughts that refuse categorization, ideas that refuse clear understanding, always slipping, slipping into unnamable horrors. Immersed in the vortex of being, immersed in the coming to power of Hitler, one could not possibly know the implications of what was to come. Schulz captures the confusion and sinisterness of Germany during the early 1930s. Something out of joint signaled doom.

Unlike the surreal landscape of Schulz's novel, Simon Wiesenthal (1976) writes a realistic novel entitled *The Sunflower* which tells the tale of a Jew who grapples with the problem of forgiveness on encountering a dying SS solider. This is the story of Simon, a Jew who survives the Holocaust. This is also the story of Karl, a Nazi who dies in a hospital during the Holocaust. Simon tells about his first encounter with Karl. "Although the place was in semi-darkness I would now see a figure wrapped in white, motionless on the bed. I tried to trace the outlines of the body" (p. 34). Karl needs to "confess" (p. 35) his crimes to a Jew, to Simon, so that he can feel absolved of his sins before death. Simon comments, "I began to ask myself why a Jew must listen to the confession of a dying Nazi soldier" (p. 39). Karl tells the awful tale of setting a house ablaze with Jews inside and finishing them off with the toss of a hand grenade. Wiesenthal's story is based on real events that not only happened to him during the Holocaust but happened to millions. In fact, Martin Gilbert (1985) reports an event that occurred in Bialystok, Russia in 1941. Szymon Datner recalls that

> From everywhere, the unfortunate people were driven in the direction of the great synagogue, which was burning with a great fire, and from which horrible cries came out. (cited in Gilbert, 1985, pp. 160–161)

According to Martin Gilbert, 800 Jews died in this fire.

Karl, the SS man in Wiesenthal's novel, is one of the many Germans who burned Jews alive during the Holocaust. Karl begged forgiveness from Simon the Jew. It is not insignificant that Karl is wrapped from head to toe in gauze and is blinded by his gauze. Karl is blinded by his act, he is blinded by his guilt and blinded by his request for absolution. Simon, however, sees that forgiveness is impossible. In fact, during Karl's testimony, Simon remains silent. Karl's punishment is silence. Simon declares, "I stood up and looked in his direction, at his folded hands. Between them there seemed to rest a sunflower … without a word I left the room" (p. 55). The sunflower might be a metaphor for dying with dignity, a death visited by flowers on the grave and by "butterflies" (p. 20).

The Bitburg cemetery might be such a place, a place where Nazis and the *Wehrmacht* soldiers are buried in Germany. But for Jews there were no graves, and there was no such thing as death with dignity. Simon, in Wiesenthal's (1976) novel, remarks "for me there would be no sunflower. I would be buried in a mass-grave, where corpses would be piled on top of me" (p. 20).

The Judeo-Christian tradition teaches that we must always forgive, no matter what. The virtue of absolute forgiveness seems inscribed in our skins. This teaching falls short in the face of Auschwitz. I argue that the virtue of absolute forgiveness be unlearned. Sometimes it is better not to forgive. Rabbi Barri Dov Schwartz reminds us that Wiesenthal once said that the Church "will fail us through its forgiveness" (cited in Wiesenthal, 1976, p. 5). Herbert Marcuse suggests that "the easy forgiving of such crime perpetuates the very evil it wants to eradicate" (cited in Wiesenthal, p. 169). Martin E. Marty comments that "non-Jews and perhaps especially Christians should not give advice about Holocaust experiences to its heirs" (cited in Wiesenthal, p. 172). Marty remarks that forgiveness around this issue may be little more than "cheap grace" (p. 177). Cheap grace slides down the slippery slope to forgetting. Marty says, "will we not soon forget to tell these stories?" (p. 174).

My experience reading these texts has been what I term a *continual not-me*. As a Jew, I identify with Jewish people who have suffered and died during the Holocaust. But this identification is partial because I did not experience these things directly. On another level, I disidentify with these texts because I will never wholly understand these kinds of experiences. A potential danger when reading fiction is psychological merging with the characters. Many students wish to identify with characters in fiction; they wish to find a kinship with the characters. Many long for a mirror. But as Jacques Derrida (1991) warns, "the misfortune would be the mirror itself" (p. 200). I argue that a jagged edge between my eye/"I" and the text must always remain or I shall become symbiotic with the text. Holocaust texts are other and must remain so. The alterity and strangeness must remain. If I merge psychologically with the text, I may think that it is possible to understand what it was like to live through or after Auschwitz. This is impossible and it is arrogant.

Ultimately, I must separate myself from the text. Suzanne de Castell (1996) teaches that we must engage in readings ""against the grain," readings which are not only against the grain of the text, but against the grain of the world" (p. 31). Reading against the grain is a way to open spaces between my "I" and the eye of the text, or the unconscious site of the text. De Castell argues that we must "refuse the literal" (p. 31). The literal is the mirror itself, the that's-me of reading, the identification and consequent submerging of the reader into the text. The unconscious site of the text, the unconscious traces deposited by the author, shatter this identification. Rather, a dialectical movement between reader and text is necessary, an identification-dis-identification, which keeps the otherness of the reading process intact. The effects of literary representation of the Holocaust on the site of the reader must remain mysterious. Perhaps it takes years to tell what it is these readings and interpretations do to the reader.

For a Jew, the experience of reading Holocaust texts might be very different from that of a Christian. For a German non-Jew, the experience is still different. One's situatedness makes a difference in the ways reading is experienced. I also believe that it makes a difference if the author of the novel writes from a Jewish , or a German non-Jewish, perspective. And it makes a difference if the author is male or female. My reading of Holocaust novels written by Germans produces a different experience than when I read those written by Jews. But at the end of the day, whether novels are written by Jews or Germans, I agree with Lawrence Langer (1991) that "all Holocaust art, whether memoir, biography, or fiction, is built on a mountain of corpses, so it can never be an account of celebration, a triumph of form over the chaos of experience" (p. 127).

GERMAN (NON-JEWISH) NOVELS

Here I turn to Holocaust novels written by non-Jewish Germans. James Young (1993) remarks that "in every nations' memorials and museums [and I would add works of fiction] a different Holocaust is remembered, often to conflicting political and religious ends" (p. ix). Certainly, a different Holocaust is remembered by Germans than by Jews and we see this as the Holocaust is represented in myriad forms in German literature. German novelist Günter Grass (1985) stresses the importance of responsibility to confront the past.

> The Germans ... cannot evade their responsibility. The more inoffensive they try to seem, the greater the dread they inspire in their neighbors.... No amount of talk about the innocence of the Germans who had not yet been born or about the crimes of other people can relieve them of their guilt. (p. 76)

A member of Hitler Youth, a high school drop-out, winner of the 1958 *Gruppe* 47 Prize, and recent winner of the Nobel Prize for Literature, Günter Grass, consumed by his own sense of guilt, is driven by an ethical responsibility to tell the story of the Holocaust over and over again in his novels. Grass is unusual. He began writing Holocaust novels shortly after the war as he wrestled with what had gone wrong. But for many Germans, this wrestling was belated. Margaret Mitscherlich-Nielson (1989) writes,

> After the defeat [of Germany] there was first an abrupt derealization; the past simply faded away like a dream.... The manic effect to undo, the enormous collective effort to rebuild, a kind of national therapy, made permanent denial and repression possible for the majority of Germans. (p. 406)

Martin Heidegger, for example, never apologized, never recanted his position, and said little about the Holocaust during his entire life. Heidegger was a member of the Nazi party and, according to Karl Löwith (1992), one of Heidegger's students, Heidegger even wore a swastika.

Heidegger was responsible (as Rector of the University of Freiburg 1933–1934) for the firings of many Jewish professors. Michael Zimmerman (1990) tells us that "far from dissociating himself from the party in 1934, Heidegger continued being a dues-paying member of the Nazi party (card number 312589, Gau Baden) until 1945" (p. 40). Like Hitler, Heidegger wanted the university to be 'Jew free.' Like Hitler, Heidegger called himself the "Führer." Heidegger prevented many Jewish doctoral candidates from finishing their degrees. He clearly aligned himself with National Socialism and with Hitler (Rockmore, 1997; Zimmerman, 1990). We learn in "Only a God can Save Us: The Spiegel's Interview with Martin Heidegger" (1966/1981), published posthumously at Heidegger's request, that Heidegger turned his back on his teacher, Edmund Husserl, who was Jewish, and even took Husserl's name out of the acknowledgments of the fifth edition of *Being and Time*. Heidegger did not attend Husserl's funeral. Heidegger and Karl Jaspers had a falling out because Jaspers' wife was Jewish. Tom Rockmore (1997) says, "We have learned more disquieting details about Heidegger's treatment of Hannah Arendt" (p. xiv). Michael Zimmerman (1990) comments that one of the few times Heidegger talked about the Holocaust, he did so in a most disturbing way. Zimmerman remarks that

> In the late 1940s, in an extremely rare reference to the Holocaust, he said: "Agriculture is now a motorized food industry, essentially the same thing as the fabrication of cadavers in the gas chambers of the extermination camps, the same thing as the blockades and the reduction of countries to famine, the same thing as the fabrication of hydrogen bombs." In this astonishing statement, Heidegger glided over the fact that the Holocaust was a *German* phenomenon involving the slaughter of millions of *Jews*. Instead, he chose to view the Holocaust as a *typical* episode in the technological era afflicting the entire West. (p. 43)

Zimmerman is correct to point out that the Holocaust was a unique event and should not be leveled as a "typical episode" of the West. Heidegger's odd comparisons (e.g., motorized agriculture to cadavers in gas chambers) make little sense. However, Heidegger's logic of comparability echoes that of neo-conservative, revisionist historians who argue that the Holocaust was like any other massacre in the 20th century. Leveling massacres makes it easier for Germans to sleep at night. One slaughterhouse is just like another. This kind of thinking makes the Holocaust seem less reprehensible. As I mentioned earlier, it was Jürgen Habermas who raised clear objections to issues of comparability around the Holocaust. Clearly, this kind of thinking suffers from denial and repression, let alone insensitivity.

Heidegger remained virtually silent on the Holocaust all his life. It is this silence that commentators worry about. What was Heidegger concealing? There is still much we do not know about Heidegger because the Heidegger archives in Marbach are under lock and key to this day. Apparently, Hermann Heidegger, son of the great thinker, has a watchful eye on his father's personal correspondences which are not open to public examination (Rockmore, 1997).

Some scholars, devoted to Heidegger's philosophy, attempt to excuse him by suggesting that Heidegger the man was different from Heidegger the philosopher. Some think that Heidegger's Nazism really doesn't matter after all because he was a great thinker. But there are many Heideggerians who now question these assumptions. Tom Rockmore (1997) comments that "Attention focused on Heidegger's Nazi inclinations by Farías, Ott, and others (e.g., Pöggeler, Marten, Sheehan, Vietta, Lacoue-Labarthe, Derrida, Bourdieu, Schwann, Janicaud, Zimmerman, Wolin, Thomä, etc.) has created a momentum of its own. It has been realized that Heidegger's Nazism raises important moral and political issues" (p. 3). Certainly, the Heidegger affair raises some extremely difficult questions, especially for academics. What are we to make of notions of academic responsibility and ethical sensibility in light of what we are know about Heidegger's complicity? What about Heidegger's silence? For me, it is this silence that is most troubling, not his philosophy.

Unlike Heidegger artists such as Thomas Mann, Klaus Mann, Heinrich Böll, Günter Grass, Christa Wolf, Ursula Hegi, Bernard Schlink and others write about the Nazi era and refuse to remain silent or sunk in denial. These German novelists, each in their own way, have broken through the pervasive numbness and repression that still haunts many Germans. Even 3rd-generation Germans are haunted by this uncanny feeling of numbness. Barbara Heimmansberg and Christoph Schmidt (1993) comment that psychotherapists encounter many Germans who are troubled by numbness and emptiness. These therapists tell us that

> often in psychotherapy we encounter people of a peculiar emotional numbness and emptiness; they can tell us nothing about the causes and precipitants of their sudden anxiety attacks, and if asked about their parents they reveal a broad field of ignorance ... diffuse anxiety and feelings of guilt can be the half-erased traces of the Nazi past. (p. 3)

Günter Grass (1959/1964), in his novel *The Tin Drum*, describes a ritual that Germans must undergo in order to shed a tear. Cutting an onion induces weeping, but what kind of weeping is this? It is artificially induced; this kind of grief is superficial. Or perhaps this is not grief at all.

However, early Holocaust novels, especially those by Thomas Mann, Heinrich Böll, and Günter Grass demonstrate a start, a struggle to at least begin the mourning process. Some may argue that their mourning is incomplete, but at least they have begun the process. Whether these novelists were driven by a sense of guilt or shame, or an ethical sense of responsibility, whether they were driven by their own sadness or numbness, they were driven, and that they were driven needs to be recognized.

The ways in which German novelists grapple with the Nazi past varies. Some novels demonize Germans, others do not. Thomas Mann's (1948/1992) *Doctor Faustus* tends to demonize. Ursula Hegi's (1994) *Stones from the River* does not demonize. Novels that attempt to portray East Germans as victims of history, like Christa Wolf's (1980) *Patterns of Childhood*, lack what I would consider an ethical responsibility. Grass's (1959/1964) *The Tin Drum*, on the other hand, is ethically sensitive, for he insists that individuals must take responsibility for their crimes.

One of the interesting connections that has been made by Judith Ryan (1983) around literary and historical representations of the Nazi era is that literary representations tend to parallel, in many ways, historical ones. Literature and history, that is, follow, similar trajectories.

> Changes in the novel form must be seen as a response to changes in conceptualized thought: if history is seen as determined by fate or necessity, by recurrent or archetypal configurations, this will be reflected in essentially self-contained literary structures; if on the other hand, history is seen as subject to change, as a process that can be influenced ... [literary] forms ... mirror this view. (Ryan, 1983, p. 21)

Fatalist views of history are nothing new. One might suggest that Hegel's was a fatalist view of history. Spirit moving through the world, killing anything in its way, determined the path of history. Subjects do not produce history, history produces subjects. Hegel had world history all sewn up. At the end of time, all contradictions would be solved. Interestingly, deterministic views of history seep into Thomas Mann's writings. He suggests that the Germany was doomed since, at the least, Martin Luther. Germany was waiting for a Hitler to come along. A turn in Holocaust historiography, since at least the Eichmann trial, suggested that arguments around so-called collective guilt of Germans would no longer be tenable. Historians have stressed over and over again that individuals are to blame and it is to individual guilt that we must turn. Subjects produce history. History is contingent on individual decision making and action. This is the intentionalist argument discussed previously. There is nothing deterministic about the rise of the Third Reich; it was created by individuals who made decisions to do what they did. We hear echoes of the intentionalist position in the writings of Günter Grass. Peoples' decisions shape history.

Let us begin these inquiries into German Holocaust fiction with Thomas Mann's (1948/1992) *Doctor Faustus*. This novel is about Germany's pact with the devil. Adrian Leverkühn declares that he is sought out by the devil. "But seen Him I have, at last, at last: He was with me, here in this hall, He sought me out" (p. 222). "The Lutheran Leverkühn" (p. 8) makes a pact with the devil, a pact that will ensure the composition of the most perfectly wicked piece of music that will flood the gates of hell. Serenus Zeitblom, the narrator, remarks that Adrian's "lamentation" named after Dürer's woodcut of the Apocalpse represents utter "soullessness! I will know that this is at bottom what they mean who apply the word "barbaric" to Adrian's creation" (p. 377). After Adrian's monstrous creation was written, Zeitblom comments that

> Germany had become a thick-walled underground torture-chamber, converted into one by a profligate dictatorship vowed to nihilism.... Now the torture-chamber has been broken open. (p. 481)

This pact Leverkühn made with the devil was an inevitable one. He was "destined" to do this, he was "so afflicted by fate" (p. 3). "Fate has crowded the German soul!" (p. 3) And this German fate suffered from "old-world, underground neurosis" (p. 37) which could be traced back to Luther.

Donna Reed (1985) points out Mann was familiar with the writings of Freud and like Freud believed in the "power of the unconscious" (p. 101). Reed claims that

> From Mann's point of view, potential hysteria is omnipotent, ready to repeat itself. He often makes no historical distinctions between the irrationalism of the Middle Ages, the pre-Nazi cult of instinct ... and the impassioned faces cheering Hitler. (p. 111)

Mann's Leverkühn, the melancholic, suffered from migraines. He was emotionally cold, ruthless, arrogant. "What is afoot betwixt me and Satan; not much to it after all" (p. 141). His pact with the devil enabled him to achieve what he called "the breakthrough" (p. 304). This so-called breakthrough was the path toward evil. Zeitblom says, "O Germany, thou art undone" (p. 388); Germany has become a "land self-maddened, psychologically burnt out" (pp. 481–482). "Our essential Germanness is stained" (p. 482), says the narrator.

Thomas Mann's novel pathologizes and demonizes Germans. But this pathology and demonization was determined beforehand, by fate. Germany was fated to do what it did. Like the *Sonderweg* thesis, which argues that basically Germany was seized by demons and therefore strayed down a deviant path, Mann argues that Germany was fated to become monstrous; that the monstrous path taken by Germans was sown into the soil of Germany from Luther on. Does Mann offer up an apologetic? Does the demonization of Germany serve as an exoneration? If being possessed by demons is beyond the control of individuals, who is responsible for Germany's crimes? Leverkühn, or Doctor Faustus, remarks "how little he was his own master" (p. 359). If a country has gone mad and is not its own master who is to blame? The insane cannot be judged; Germany cannot be judged. The demonization of the so-called German character is no longer thought to be tenable because there is no "essential Germanness" (Mann, p. 482). To suggest that there is something innately evil about all Germans is ridiculous. Germany was not fated to carry out the Holocaust. Germans carried it out because they wanted to. At least this is the message in Goldhagen's (1997) controversial historiography. Of course, things are much more complicated than that. Yet still human beings choose to take certain paths and must take responsibility for the path chosen. "Fate" is a mythological creature. History is not determined by fate, but its path is contingent. It is contingent on decisions people make.

Mann's notion of the troubled genius, the melancholy musician is highly problematic, for it signifies a romantic notion of a melancholy Germany. To romanticize over Germany's "fate," is an inadequate response to a Germany's failings. Julianna Schiesari (1992) explains that according to Aristotle, "all great men" must suffer from melancholia (p. 6). But women suffering from melancholia, Schiersari remarks, are thought to be merely hysterical and weepy. It is the mark of male genius to suffer. However, there is no necessary connection between genius and illness. There is no necessary connection between melancholia and genius. Günter Grass criticizes Mann's melancholic Germany because it implies a "stasis" and an inability to act and change the course of history. Judith Ryan (1983) explains that Grass

> Points out in the Dürer Lecture [in 1971] that melancholy is essentially a function of the belief in stasis; it is a response to the assumption that the course of history is not really open to change.... When resistance seems virtually impossible, melancholy becomes a substitute for action. (p. 69)

Melancholia sounds a certain stuckness in time. A depressed Germany cannot get out of its own way to do anything to stop the wheels of history. The melancholic is stuck, glued to one place and one thought, one feeling, trapped, immobile and helpless. Paula Salvio (1998) remarks that "What is dangerous about the gaze of the melancholic is that it causes life (time) to flow out of objects—it petrifies them ... one of the forgotten symbols of melancholy, Walter Benjamin (1977) reminds us, is stone" (p. 17). The stoney German character, Mann suggests, prevents the stopping of Hitler. Germany becomes, in Mann's eyes, the victim of its own melancholia. Zeitblom, the narrator of Mann's novel, comments on the "evils" of Germany. Hell is a German creation, he says.

> There were years in which we children of the dungeon, dreamed of a hymn of exultation, a Fidelio, a Ninth Symphony, to celebrate the dawn of a freed Germany—freed by herself. Now only this can avail us, only this will be sung from our very souls: the Lamentation of the Son of Hell, the Lamentation of men and God ... the most frightful lament ever set up on this earth. (p. 485)

I suggest that a pact with the devil has nothing to do with some mythological transcendent creature who comes to earth and possesses human souls. Making a pact with the devil is the act of banishing one's own devil, ones own bad objects, one's own heart of darkness from one's psyche. To banish the otherness within the self is an invitation for all sorts of projections. To banish one's heart of darkness within one's own soul is an invitation to the projection of hatred onto others. Germany could not manage difference and banished the other to concentration camps. Like a piece of music, Germany created the concentration camps, the Nazi, and the ordinary German who killed; Germany created its own hell and perfected it and therefore, Germany must be held responsible for its own creations. A creation is a human invention, not a monster, although Germany's was a monstrous creation.

> Adolf Bartelmas, a railway employee in Auschwitz said in his testimony at the Auschwitz trial that in Frankfurt many years later that flames could be seen at a distance of 15–20 kilometers and that it was known that human beings were burned there. (Laquer, 1981, p. 23)

The flames of the apocalypse are not mythological; the apocalypse was Auschwitz, it marked the end of the world for European Jews.

Unlike Thomas Mann, Günter Grass stressed that individuals in Germany made choices and that they were movers of history and that therefore they were responsible for the crimes of Germany. Choice and responsibility are themes that are found throughout Grass's Danzig Trilogy (*The Tin Drum* (1964/1991), *Cat and Mouse* (1961), and *Dog Years* (1963/1986). *The Tin Drum* caused terrific scandal in Germany when it was first published. John Reddick (1975) says that about 40 lawsuits were filed against Grass and this novel "was prominent amongst a number of books publicly burnt in Düseldorf by a religious youth organization" (p. 4). This novel was thought to be obscene and offensive to Germans. But I think the reverse is true; this novel is Grass's best and most gritty work. Salman Rushdie (1985) remarks that "what Grass learned on his journey across the frontiers of history was Doubt ... he is quintessentially the artist of uncertainty" (p. xiii). Further Rushdie comments that Grass is, "after all, a metaphorical being" (p. xiv).

What draws me to Grass is his metaphorical writing and his unabashed criticism of Germany. Frank Keele (1988) declares that "Grass's artistic search for the causes of evil ... concentrates on minutiae: on subtleties of language, of prejudice and political accommodation, of misplaced sexual and religious fervor" (pp. 4–5). Grass's uncanny ability to capture the minutiae of everyday experience in German life, the heaviness of the 1930s, the slowness in the *Dog Years*, the carnivalesque atmosphere of German society, the absurdity and seeming normality of what Grass (1985) calls "the great crime" (p. 86) draws me in as a reader. Frank Keele (1988) remarks that "Grass has said that in Danzig the Nazis 'rise to power occurred slowly, almost as a microcosmic model, so that one could take notes'" (p. 4). Unlike Mann, Grass sinks into the metaphors of ordinary life during the rise of the Third Reich. Mann transcends the ordinary by taking readers into an extra-ordinary transcendent, mythical realm. Conversely, Grass offers a picture of German complicity from a bottom-up perspective, akin to what historians call *Alltagsgechichte*. Grass's novels are not couched in historical realism, though, but they are rather situated within the realm of metaphorical absurdity. This metaphorical absurdity leaves traces of otherness, strangeness, and alienness that one does not necessarily feel when reading Thomas Mann. Normalcy and brutality, two creatures living side by side, alongside, and with each other are taken-for-granted modes of being in Grass's worldview. Grass's novels are quite chilling. Never does he lapse into sentimentality, romanticism, or nostalgia. Ever the harsh critic, Grass "does not exempt himself from guilt" (Keele, 1988, p. 5). Grass (1985) tells us that he became so bothered by his own complicity as member of the Hitler Youth that he suffered nightmares about the possibility of doing the unspeakable. "I could not swear that, if I had been six or seven years older, I would not have participated in the great crime" (p. 86). Against the backdrop of so much denial in Germany, Grass demonstrates a move away from denial, he demonstrates a grappling with the Nazi past in a way that is gritty. This gritty sense of responsibility Grass takes up is reflected in the *Danzig Trilogy*. Here I look at only *The Tin Drum*, because of the three novels in the trilogy, this one struck me the most. It is *The Tin Drum* that I think is Grass's best contribution to the German memory of the Holocaust.

The Tin Drum (1964/1991) is the story of a mentally ill Germany. In many ways, Grass's novel parallels early psychohistories and psychobiographies of the Nazi era. Recall, these early histories tended to pathologize Germans. When we turn to page one of Grass's novel, we are introduced to Oskar Matzerath, who is in a mental hospital. Oskar comments that

> Granted: I am an inmate of a mental hospital, my keeper is watching me, he never lets me out of his sight; and my keeper's eye is the shade of brown that can never see through a blue-eyed type like me. (p. 15)

This non-transparent blue-eyed type, has landed in a mental hospital because he had a breakdown on November 9, 1938, when the Nazis took the drum store owner, Sigsimund Marks, away. November 9, 1938 dates *Kristallnacht*, a day that signaled a turning point in German history, a day that begins the breakdown of German society, and the date that causes many Jews to commit suicide (Trunk, 1979).

Oskar's story begins at his painful birth when he decided that he did not want to progress past the age of three. "He had lost his enthusiasm even before this life beneath the light bulbs began" (p. 49). Oskar decided that the only thing that would keep him alive would be to acquire a tin drum. He wanted to arrest his growth nonetheless. Thus, he would fling himself down the stairs.

> I noticed that the trap door leading to the cellar was open.... Above all, no harm must come to my drum ... from the ninth step, I flung myself down, carrying a shelf laden with bottles of raspberry syrup. (p. 62)

Landing on his head, Oskar remained stunted and dwarfed forever. Oskar's first choice had been made. He chose to become dwarfed. As Judith Ryan (1983) remarks, "For Oskar, choice is the operative element.... He chooses not to renounce Satan just as he chooses not to grow up" (p. 61). Grass seems to suggest that Oskar's infantile regression is symptomatic of Germany's own infantilism. Although Oskar declares that he wanted to be a "resistance fighter" (p. 124) as he "disrupted six or seven rallies and threw three or four parades out of step with [his] drumming" (p. 174), he ultimately chooses to join Bebra's (or Satan's) circus. Bebra, another dwarf, continually tries to "justify" (p. 309) why he aligned himself with Goebbels and Göring. Bebra warns Oskar that the Nazis are coming and they will do whatever it takes to clear the way, including murder.

> They are coming, he whispered. They will take over the meadows where we pitch our tents. They will organize torchlight parades. They will build rostrums and fill them, and down from the rostrums they will preach our destruction. (p. 114).

Bebra's rationalization to align himself with the Nazis was this: kill or be killed. If he joined the Nazis, they would not have killed him. The truth of the matter, though, is that nobody was coerced to join the Nazi party, nobody was coerced to kill. In fact, as Christopher Browning (1998) teaches us, Pappa Trapp, leader of police battalion 101, gave his men a choice not to kill Jews, a choice to step out of the firing squad. But only 12 out of 500 made the choice not to kill. Those who stepped out were not punished at all. Certainly nobody was killed because they did not choose to kill.

Like Bebra, Oskar's mother and father chose to embrace the Nazis. When Oskar's father joined the party, he proceeded to hang a picture of Hitler above the piano. "The picture of the gloomy Beethoven ... was removed ... and Hitler's equally gloomy countenance was hung upon the same nail" (p. 115). Whereas Oskar's father wanted to "banish" (p. 115) Beethoven, his mother "insisted" (p. 115) that Beethoven be placed "over the sideboard" (p. 115). Oskar's father felt that the old culture of Germany replaced the new. Beethoven must be, therefore, banished from the chronicles of history.

But the banishment of Beethoven caused Oskar's mother to die. Her illness and death started with eels. Out of a dead, decapitated horse's head, "small light-green eels were darting" (p. 150). Meanwhile, Oskar's father "was too busy to see Mama turn green" (p. 150). Mr. Matzerath was too busy running around in his SA uniform to see that his wife was sickened by what had been transpiring in Germany. Oskar's mother intuited that Beethoven's move to the sideboard meant certain death for Germany. But what part did Oskar play in all of this? Oskar asks, "What had my drum in common with the blood of Poland?" (p. 226)

Oskar's part in spilling the blood of Jews began with his decision to join Bebra's circus. But his complicity and guilt could be traced back even earlier to the day he bought his tin drum. Our little drummer boy was very adept at "shattering glass" (p. 64) [read: *Kristallnacht*]. Initially, he only shattered glass when someone threatened to take away his tin drum. And then, Oskar screamed.

> Oskar, who until then had passed as a quiet, almost too well-behaved child, succeeded in emitting that first annihilating scream: the polished round crystal which protected the honey-colored dial of our clock from dust ... burst ... the destruction was complete. (p. 66)

As Oskar mastered his screaming talent, he could destroy more and more crystal, he could destroy more efficiently and more easily, even without any provocation. It is not insignificant that "Hitler was known as the drummer" (Keele, 1988, p. 140). When he gave speeches he screamed and pounded his fists. His speeches sounded completely and utterly hysterical. Such incredible, hideous rage emanated from the podium. This is probably why Binion (1976) suggests that Hitler suffered from "oral sadism" (p. 170). Film clips of Hitler's so-called speeches demonstrate this maniacal behavior. I have never heard anybody scream like Hitler. When anyone threatened to take his power away, Hitler shattered glass; *Kristallnacht* marked the first shattering. The killing sped up and became more efficient. Nobody dared challenge him, nobody dared to take his drum of power away.

Unlike Thomas Mann, Günter Grass suggests in this story that this everyday family, the Matzerath's, made choices and were complicit in the course that history would take in Germany. Germany was not fated to align itself with evil. For Grass, Germany chose that path. Grass's novel, along with early psychohistories, helps us to understand why people would so easily wish to diagnose and pathologize Germans. In a way it is easier for us to diagnose, to categorize, to suggest that they (Germans) are not like us (non-Germans). They went mad, we did not. This is a simple dichotomy which keeps people from thinking about the unthinkable. We want so to explain the Nazi phenomenon, or perhaps we want to explain it away with easy categorization. This is what pathologizing does, it explains things away. But the hideousness will not go away. This splitting off of us from them is a way to defend us against massive hideousness, which I think Grass tries to depict metaphorically. Eels squiggling around in a dead horse's head, winding up on the dinner table symbolizes the grotesque nature of what it was the Nazis were doing. Quite frankly, Grass's images are disgusting. Oskar's mother manically shoving eels down her throat until she dies [read: Germans shoving Jews into ovens] captures the disgusting and horrible things that the Nazis were doing. No need to be literal here. Grass drives his point home metaphorically and it is through the metaphor that readers experience a kind of pervasive horror. Some scholars, though, are opposed to the utilization of metaphor. Judith Ryan (1983) argues that it is appropriate for Jews to draw on metaphors when writing Holocaust fiction, but not for Germans. She suggests that when German writers utilize metaphor they obscure the "great crime" (Grass, 1985, p. 86). Again we hear the call to literalism. But as James Young (1988) points out that

> It becomes all the more puzzling when critics persist in trying to know the Holocaust without recourse to metaphor, as if it were possible to write about literature, talk about it, or even narrate its history without figurative language. (p. 89)

It is Grass's metaphorical bent that makes his work so dense, so layered over with unconscious traces. Eels, dead horse heads, dwarves, and tin drums may trigger unconscious responses in the reader that otherwise would lay dormant. Unconscious responses open the reader to the otherness of the text.

Like Oskar Matzerath, Trudi Montag, another dwarf, is the main character in Ursula Hegi's (1994) novel entitled *Stones from the River.* Through the eyes of a 4-year-old dwarf readers see another picture of everyday life in Germany during the Nazi era. Trudi, however, is very different from Oskar. Her dwarfedness gives her the power to "resist" "Hitler's gaze" (p. 167). Trudi does not demonize her fellow Germans for their complicity. Trudi comments that, "In real life it was not that easy to tell who the villains were, and even if you could identify them, they were not total villains. No one was entirely all of one thing" (p. 168). Trudi gathers and collects stories from the "people of Burgdorf" (p. 239). After the war she wanted to tell these stories, stories mainly of "complicity" (p. 239), but she realized that nobody would listen.

> Trudi would find very few who'd want to listen because the people of Burgdorf would be immersed in changing what had happened into a history they could sleep with, *eine heile welt*—an intact world they could offer to the next generation. (pp. 361–362)

This intact world is, thus, something that the people of Bavaria also wanted to offer to the next generation as depicted in the film *Schreckliche Mädchen* or the *Nasty Girl* (1990) directed by Michael Verhöeven. The English translation "Nasty Girl" is misleading, for *Schreckliche* suggests terrible, fearful, or dreadful. What is dreadful for the townspeople of Bavaria is that a young girl writes a book called *My Home Town During the Third Reich*. In the process of doing research for her book, this young girl, or nasty girl, uncovers all kinds of dirt about her neighbors' complicity during the rise of the Nazis. Everyone she encounters lies and tries to cover up their involvement during the Third Reich. The townspeople make it difficult for her to gain access to archives until she wins a lawsuit which enables her to get the information needed to complete her book. She ends up having to steal the files necessary to unlock the secrets of Bavarian complicity. In the meantime, her life was in danger. Thugs kill her cat and hang it on her front door. Thugs throw rocks through her car window. Thugs toss an explosive into her home and nearly kill her. The townspeople of Bavaria were determined to unwrite history. Director Michael Verhöeven states that this film is a mixture of fact and fiction and was inspired by Anja Rosmus who attempted to reveal the truth of her hometown. Anja Rosmus became very unpopular with her neighbors because she found out about her neighbors.

Like Verhöeven's film, Hegi's novel points to the ways in which Germans have tried to rearrange the past, so they could sleep better. Trudi Montag must have been considered a kind of nasty girl too, because she hid Jews in her cellar. I would think that this would be total anathema for Germans. Spying made this nearly impossible. Even children spied on their neighbors and informed the SS when Germans transgressed Nazi policy. Trudi, though, hid Erma and Konrad Neimann, Eva Sturm and others from the Nazis, while the rest of Burgdorf was busy attending

> parades and speeches—some like the taxidermist, because they genuinely believed in their leaders; others like Herr Blau because not to go would call attention to yourself. Most practiced the silence they were familiar with, a silence nurtured by fear and complicity. (p. 234)

Trudi stresses that it was obedience more than anything else that allowed Germans to become complicit. "You learned about obedience from your parents and all other adults, then obedience to your church, your teachers, your government" (p. 10). Daniel Goldhagen (1997) explains that the argument that Germans acted out a sense of obedience is nothing new. This theme, he tells us has been popular among historians and psychoanalysts. Accordingly, Stanley Milgram, Herbert C. Kelman, V. Lee Hamilton, Erich Fromm, and G. P. Gooch, says Goldhagen, suggest it was obedience that made Germans do what they did. However, Goldhagen takes them to task and says that obedience had nothing to do with it. Germans killed, he suggests, because they wanted to.

But Trudi Montag was not obedient and she was not duped by the Brown Shirt thugs who marched through Burgdorf. The problem was, Trudi declares, that nobody paid much attention.

> The Nazi time came upon Bergdorf like a *Dieb auf Schleichwegen*—a thief on sneaky paths—Herr Blau would say after the war. To him and to many others in the town, the men were *unsympathisch*, ridiculous even, but surely not dangerous. Who really paid much attention. (p. 194)

Grass claims that the Nazis moved in so slowly that one could almost take notes. Similarly, Hegi's character Trudi remarks that "The people of Burgdorf were drawn in gradually, almost imperceptibly" (p. 195).

In Hegi's (1997) work *Tearing the Silence* she remarks:

> Fifteen years ago I walked into a mail room at the University of New Hampshire, and when I overheard two of my colleagues talk about a Holocaust documentary, I backed away, unable to speak.... I was still within the silence, though I wouldn't have defined it that way. (p. 14)

Although born in Germany, Hegi now resides in the United States and declares that it is distance from Germany that has allowed her to "tear the silence" (p. 157). The past seemed erased for her as her parents, teachers and relatives were "reluctant" (p. 15) to tell her much. Analyst Sammy Speier (1993) claims that for Germans, "what is erased reappears in the children, who are patients today, as emptiness, identity diffusion, bewilderment and confusion" (p. 62). What kind of a silence has Hegi torn? Her protagonist and heroine Trudi Montag is the quintessential righteous Gentile who saves Jews by hiding them in her cellar. Of course, there were righteous Gentiles in Germany who did save Jews.

Certainly, theologian Dietrich Bonhoeffer and members of The Confessing Church were examples of righteous Gentiles. Bonhoeffer was murdered by the Nazis when it was discovered that he was involved in a plot to kill Hitler. Oskar Schindler was considered to be a righteous Gentile too. He saved many Jews by allowing them to work for him. Schlinder's list, the Jews who he summoned to his factory, was well over 1,000. But by and large, and this is the crucial point here, most Germans were not involved in any kind of resistance movement to save Jews. Saul Friedländer (1997) drives this point home:

> When pastor Umfried criticized the attacks on Jews in his town, no church authority supported him; when Jewish businesses were boycotted, no religious voice was heard ... when Jewish colleagues were dismissed, no German professor publicly protested; when the number of Jewish students was dramatically reduced, no university committees or faculty members experienced opposition. (pp. 59–60)

For the most part, Germany "cast a cold eye" (Yeats, 1938–1939/1989, p. 325). Trudi Montag, though, is an example of a righteous Gentile in Hegi's novel. Laypersons unfamiliar with Holocaust history may be misled reading Hegi's work. It might be misleading to think that Trudi Montag represented a vast sector of German society during the Nazi era. She would have been an exception.

Another possible interpretation of Hegi's novel is that Trudi sees herself as a victim of history. She had the power to see through the Brown Shirt thugs who marched through Burgdorf. Because she is a dwarf, we might take pity on her because she is ostracized and nobody would be willing to listen to the stories of complicity that she gathers throughout the novel. This interpretation, then, would suggest to me that Hegi has not torn the silence deeply enough. Hegi, it seems, has not fully mourned this history. It is mourning that enables one to tear the silence. However, analyst Sheldon Roth (1995a) declares

> that Germans will never be able to do this [mourn for Germany's past] and I will tell you why. They will be tortured and I think it will take generations for them. In order to mourn you have to go back to the past and openly feel! I think the mourning process for Germans is definitely different from what it is for us [Jews]. (pp. 233–235)

It seems to me that Hegi's novel lacks a sense of mourning and lacks a sense of grit, the kind of grit we see in Grass's work. One wonders how Germans can come to terms with the Nazi era, especially as many critics argue that former West Germany had many continuities with the Nazi regime. Markovits and Noveck (1996) write:

> Germans refer to 1945 as *Stunde Null*, a historical *tabula rasa* created by the end of the war and the reestablishment of democracy in the Federal Republic. But a number of Germans as well as foreign critics have questioned the validity of this.... They point to the many continuities between the Nazi regime and the Federal Republic. (p. 401)

Former Nazis were put in power positions after 1945. Some became judges. Imagine that. Like the former West Germany, the former East Germany is still trying to come to terms with its past and is still trying to undo the rhetoric of anti-Fascism. It was in 1991 that former East Germany officially took responsibility for the Holocaust. Until then, this was completely denied. But just because rhetoric has changed, actions have not. In Germany anti-Semitism is on the rise again. Peck (1996) claims that:

> Programmatic GDR State doctrine against anti-Semitism, racism, xenophobia seems to have had little effect on either the GDR's own citizenry or those in the former West Germany, since Jewish cemeteries continue to be desecrated. (p. 449)

Many scholars worry that the strength of a reunified Germany will unleash even more hatred. The tensions between former East and West Germany have resulted in the current atmosphere where Turks and others have been killed and brutalized. A stronger Germany does not necessarily mean a better one.

Someone who was opposed to reunification is Christa Wolf, a former East German. Wolf (1980) wrote the novel *Patterns of Childhood*. This novel has captured the attention of many who are interested in the power of autobiography, memory, and storytelling. The novel has been praised for its gripping narrative, but criticized for its politics. Julia Hell (1997) explains that:

> Critics have called *Kindheitsmuster* the autobiography of a "victorious subject," a metaphor resonating with the novel's psychological and historical dimensions ... the novel demonstrates the "victorious" emergence of the subject out of all those components that are repressed, denied, split off ... the novel plays with the SED's self-characterization as victims of history. (p. 199)

Christa Wolf's story is narrated by Nelly. She looks back and recalls what it was like as a five year old child to watch the rise of the Third Reich. What can a 5-year-old child do? Protest? Children were victims of "Fascism" (p. 36). Recall, former East Germans engaged in what is referred to as *Staatlich Verordnete anti-Faschismus* (state sanctioned program of anti-Fascism), (Wegner, 1995, p. 175). The former East German government has traditionally only honored Communist resistors of Fascism. It would seem that Wolf embraces this ideology and injects it into her story. Wolf's fictional testimonial, however, is powerful. Her novel from the start is quite evocative. Much of the subject matter turns on problems of repressed memory. For me, this novel was particularly interesting. At first, though, I did not understand what it was that Wolf was doing because I read her novel before researching East German politics. I had no idea why the critics were skeptical of Wolf's underlying message. It was on my reading around East German politics that drove home the point again that it is so important to read both historiography and literature, otherwise, one does not fully understand what one reads. I think, at first, I was duped by Wolf's writing. Still, I think that Wolf's understanding of repressed memory is important.

Nelly, the heroine of Wolf's novel, remarks that "The present intrudes upon remembrance, today becomes the last day of the past. Yet we could suffer continuous estrangement from ourselves if it weren't for our memory of the things we have done" (p. 4). Nelly comments that she has "encapsulated vaults of memory" (p. 69). Memory is imprisoned and hovers right below the surface of awareness. Germans, says Nelly, "Ignore, overlook, neglect, deny, unlearn, obliterate, forget" (p. 149) the past. These denials cannot be maintained. "Suddenly a wall to one of the well-sealed vaults of memory breaks down" (p. 69). When the vault breaks open, Germans remember. Most Germans, though, cannot break open this vault. So they engage in the narrative of, 'we did not know.' But when repressed memory is lifted, "suddenly you know that everyone knew" (p. 69). Historians point out that Auschwitz was no secret. Workers coming home from a day at the crematorium talked. Walter Laquer (1981) explains that:

> Hundreds of civilian employees, Germans as well as Poles, worked at Auschwitz, arriving in the morning leaving in the afternoon.... Many technicians and workers from various parts of Germany and the occupied countries came to Auschwitz. (p. 24)

Nelly struggles to break through repressed memory, to break through the fog of the present to get at this horrific past. She wonders if she is successful. Nelly asks "Has memory done its duty?" (p. 406) Has she admitted her own "guilt and concealment" (p. 57) enough? If one admits complicity is that enough? Can repressed memory, once lifted, exonerate? Has Nelly conquered her memory? Does she emerge as the "victorious subject" after all? (Hell, 1997).

The novel does seem to suggest that Nelly conquers repressed memory. But is repression that simple? A complex look at the nature of repression, though, might suggest that repression never fully goes away. As Jean Laplanche (1999) argues, most everything is "partly translated and partly repressed" (p. 94). For Germans especially it would seem that repressed memory is interminable. There is no getting rid of repression in a clean sense. It is impossible for Germans to think of this past without not thinking of it at the same time. It is never clear how much of this past Germans can actually take in psychologically. It is not as if one suffers from repressed memory, remembers what one has forgotten through therapy or novel writing, and then puts the past to sleep once and for all. Traces of repression remain.

Studying the Holocaust through literature is crucial for grappling with this event. It is not enough to just read historiography. A more balanced curriculum, one that examines both fictional and historical accounts broadens readers' perspectives. As Mary Aswell Doll (2000) points out, curriculum theorists "have long called for what writers do best: create fictions, ... metaphorical ways of expressing the life of the mind" (p. x). Holocaust Fiction, when it is metaphorical, is especially powerful. But docu-realist novels serve their purpose as well. When people argue that the Holocaust as represented in literary form is inappropriate, perhaps they should listen to Aharon Appelfeld (1994) as he teaches that:

> One sometimes hears this argument and warning: "Keep literature out of the fire zone. Let the numbers and the well-established facts speak." I have no wish to belittle that claim, but I do wish to point out that the numbers and the facts were the murderers' own well-proven means. Man as a number is one of the horrors of dehumanization. (pp. 27–28)

SEVEN

Under the Sign of a Dystopic Curriculum

In previous chapters, I argue that doing work around the Holocaust requires us to examine both historiography and fiction. I stress that studying these two competing forms of representation does not mean that we can get a complete picture of this horrific event called the Holocaust. A partial picture is all we can ever get. Our understanding of the Holocaust also concerns the nature of thinking, generally speaking. Thus, this final chapter will take a turn toward thinking in general. The question I raise here is, what kind of thinking conceals or reveals the wish to murder 6 million people? I suggest that utopian thinking, the wish phantasy for the perfect place, the wish phantasy for the perfect world may conceal a murderous intent. In this chapter, I trace a brief history of utopian thinking to show how this thinking, in part, created conditions to enable the Holocaust to occur. I argue that educators might embrace what I call a dystopic curriculum. Dystopic thinking is skeptical of happy places and happy worlds. Happy places and happy worlds conceal othering. Those who do not fit into happy places are exiled or annihilated. Before turning to utopic and dystopic thinking it is important, at this juncture, to ask generally why we do curriculum work in the first place.

Interpreting one's own curriculum theorizing requires memory work. To remember why one does curriculum theory in the first place becomes key to doing self-reflexive scholarship. Several possibilities might emerge. One possibility might be that one does curriculum theory to offer hope to students and colleagues in the academy; another reason is more despairing. One might do curriculum work to offer warnings. These warnings concern the dangers and worries of living in the world, the troubles of lived experience. I want to offer warnings about hope. In order to do this, though, I choose an inbetween place from which to speak. Distance from hope and despair allows the curriculum worker to examine the dangers of each. Being mired in hope blinds; being mired in despair causes deafness. I despair about hope. To understand this, I stand in the middle; I take the middle way between both. This is the way of the Buddha, the place situated between the extremes. However, unlike the Buddha, I am not offering enlightenment; I am merely attempting to get distance from the extremes of hope and despair in order to better despair about hope. When I recall why I do curriculum work, it turns on this paradox. To despair about hope becomes my mantra.

Brent Davis (1996) suggests that "our schooling system can no longer robe itself in the rhetoric of benevolence of hope" (p. xxii). To disrobe the concept of hope to find out what it conceals, then, is my task. I attempt to discover why words like hope turn dangerous. Ernst Bloch (1938/1986) says "It is a question of learning hope" (p. 3). Bloch's magisterial work, entitled *Principle of Hope*, is meant to convince readers of the necessity of hope. To live a better life and create a better world one must, Bloch insists, learn hope. But I am not convinced that learning hope necessarily leads to good things. If hope is something that is, in fact, learned, can it be unlearned? Should it be unlearned? What would it mean to live without hope?

What monster hides beneath the concept of hope? Utopianism. And it is this that demands interrogation. Utopianism is a way of being-in-the-world that embraces a rainbow at the end of each thunderstorm, that sees good in everything and everyone, and that makes claims to innocence. Utopianism is the dream of equality, liberty, and justice for all. Utopianism reaches toward heaven and paradise.

The utopic teacher believes she can make the world a better place; a utopic curriculum worker believes she can make the academy a better, happier place. But wishing for this better, happier place tends to reduce the complexities of lived experience into a recipe, or a method, for happiness. That is, the purpose of school, for the utopic teacher, is to teach young people how to achieve happiness, how to create a better life. Toni Morrison (1998) warns: "How exquisitely human [is] the wish for permanent happiness, and how thin human imagination [becomes] trying to achieve it" (p. 306).

Unexamined utopianism, the wish for happier places, is dangerous and can even become deadly. Utopianism is dangerous because it may perpetuate what I term *the evil of innocence*. Innocence is a refusal to hear the four horsemen of the apocalypse descending, to acknowledge that bad people do exist, to understand that equality is often gotten at the expense of liberty, or that justice is often incompatible with law. Utopianism offers up a deadly, naive phantasy about an earthly paradise. School, for instance, as a possible haven/heaven is the utopic teacher's dream. To create a safe place for young people to learn is the dream. But more often than not, school is like prison; school is a deadly place where murders occur, where drugs are exchanged, where lives are destroyed. Even if school seems to be a safe place where none of these activities occur, even if school seems far from the mad world outside, violence, discontent, and despair still seep through the school walls. There is no haven/heaven on earth, and school is not a haven, for it is part of the larger culture, the larger world, and this world can be a frightening place for young people who are already involved in drug cultures or death cults. Further, when teachers attempt to protect students from the world outside they are unwittingly creating more difficulties for them. Protecting students presupposes that school and society are distinct. John Dewey (1909/1975) teaches that school and society are not separate. School walls are an illusion because culture and society are already inside the school walls. Protecting students is a way of controlling them. It is this that is especially worrisome. John Weaver (In press) points out, "From a controlled and manipulated curriculum, young adults leave schools wondering why the world does not fit the one that was created at school."

A utopic curriculum, whether conceived as a blueprint, a static plan with objectives and goals, or as a dynamic current of lived experience, runs the risk of blinding and thwarting understanding. I argue that understanding the complexities of life has little to do with rainbows and paradise; understanding the complexities of what it means to be an educated person has little to do with becoming happy or feeling better. If the goal of education is making citizens happy, and making them feel better about themselves, I think it is a thin and unproductive enterprise. Certainly education should offer more than the dreams of kindergarten, a child's garden, an Eden. A dystopic curriculum seems more adequate to the task of becoming an educated person. Dystopia is not myopia. Dystopia is a way of looking suspiciously at happy texts, happy histories, and happy memories. A dystopic curriculum seeks out monsters robed in the rhetoric of utopian thinking. People who do not fit into happy histories, those who suffer and are persecuted, slip into what George Orwell (1949/1977) terms *memory holes*. Memories that slip through holes have disappeared and are forgotten. Recalling them becomes key. So too, recalling what utopic thinking is, what creates memory holes to begin with becomes crucial. Utopic thinking cannot manage the other, cannot manage difference, so it thrusts unhappy memories in holes and forgets to retrieve them. There is no place for the other in utopias. Thus, a dystopic curriculum looks for what Alan Block (1997) terms "lost articles." "A lost article is unrealized, it requires the other to exist.... In discovering lost articles, we engage in relationships which bear unique responsibilities" (p. 7). The responsibility for dystopic curriculum workers is partly to remember how and why the other got lost to begin with. What was it that forced the other out of the picture, outside the frame? Utopias force others out. Utopias make others faceless. Utopias turn the other into a number.

Utopias create happy places for those who fit the utopic dream. Those who do not fit in are shut out. Schooling, then, built on utopian thinking, forces students and teachers into a "homogenizing process [which] can become totalitarian in its demands for conformity" (Egan, 1997, p. 11). Utopianism can become a form of totalitarianism because it offers a total vision, a grand metanarrative of the perfect life, a life without glitches or idiosyncracies. Further utopianism offers up "the illusion of order" (Weaver, in press). Weaver (in press) reminds us, moreover, that illusions limit understanding. Weaver remarks that the "forms of knowledge we sanction through our work and the illusions we impose upon the world [limit] what can be created and imagined in schools and in universities." If curriculum is ordered only around orthodox canonical readings, orthodox ways of thinking emerge. If a Holocaust curriculum is ordered only around canonical historical texts and historical debates, only one kind of thinking emerges, the historical. I argue for a broadening of texts when studying the Holocaust. Reading Holocaust fiction, as I point out, is considered inappropriate for some. Fiction, for some, is thought to be less important than historical texts; it is considered mere fluff. Some argue that the Holocaust should not be represented by fictional texts because we cannot learn anything from them. But these are orthodox views which I think too narrow and limit, ultimately, our understanding and memory of this event.

One of the issues here turns on the importance of imagination and the ways in which imagination enriches memory rather than depletes it. Orthodox canonical ways of thinking squash out imagination. What is squashed out of imagination are other ways of thinking about the world, ways that might admit ambiguity or paradox. These other ways of thinking might allow for more heterodox, idiosyncratic knowledges to appear on the scene.

If, however, curriculum is ordered around orthodox texts, whereby young people read only how Plato's cave people emerge in the sun finally to be enlightened, how Rousseau's Emile lives happily ever after in his natural solitude, how Aristotle's Nichomacheaus finally becomes the happy ethicist bravely walking through life, then we have limited what students can imagine by offering up these grand utopic visions, these grand narratives of happy endings. If we turn the Holocaust into a happy ending, a light at the end of the tunnel, a story of bravery and courage, a story of faith and love, we have done a great injustice to the reality of this event. Brought up on utopian stories, raised on grand metanarratives, inculcated into Plato's brand of enlightenment masks darkness that surrounds real events lived in real time in real lives. The storyline that suggests that at the end time redemption is at hand only serves to conceal that tragic sense of life, that darkness, and the black sun of Auschwitz. Let us think again.

It is so difficult to rid our psyches of these utopian metanarratives because of transference. The themes and plots of these narratives get transferred onto narratives that are horrific. I stress that we must work to undo these deeply ingrained beliefs in happy endings, especially when we are dealing with Holocaust texts. There is nothing happy about the Holocaust. I stress that my position is not nihilistic. Memory work is the work of justice. It is an ethical project that dares to take the plunge into the unthinkable. Memory work is a way of coping. There is nothing liberating about it. Liberation, emancipation, and hope belong to grand myth-o-narratives. Educators might feel much resistance to thinking through what it is that utopias conceal, yet thinking through this resistance is crucial.

Curriculum workers need to remember why they might be mired in utopian thinking. How did they "learn hope" (Bloch, 1938/1986, p. 3)? What are the consequences of this learned hope? Hope is, after all, a social construction. It is to texts that I turn to grapple with these questions, because it is the always already of texts that are handed down to us in culture that produce and influence the ways one might think about life. It seems to me that there is something deeply psychological about buying into the myth-o-narratives of hope, benevolence, emancipation, and liberation. Psychological transference might explain, in part, why many are wedded to these kinds of concepts. There is something deeply psychological about the investments one has to a particular way of viewing the world. Thus, this question about utopianism is not just an epistemological one; it is a psychological one, too. The unconscious transference of one kind of story (e.g., a fairytale where the princess is rescued by the prince) onto another (that the Holocaust is a story of rescue and resistance, which has been the pervasive myth of France's Vichy until the 1970s), is key to understanding why interpretations of a most hideous event can become yet another story with a happy ending.

In this chapter, I examine utopianism briefly in order to come to a more adequate understanding of some of the philosophical underpinnings of this way of thinking. Secondly, and more specifically, I will review the writings of Charles Fourier, Pierre Tielhard de Chardin, H. G. Wells, and Adolf Hitler. I argue that utopian thinking, overwhelmingly, others. And for these writers, whether implicitly or explicitly, it is Jewish bodies that are othered. So Jewish bodies are shoved down "memory holes" (Orwell, 1949/1977, p. 35) in order that they be forgotten, erased, mutilated, or murdered. Moreover, and most importantly, I contend that 2,000 years of utopian thinking in the West has created the conditions, in part, for a Hitler to emerge and to write a blueprint for the perfect killing dream.

REMEMBERING UTOPIANISM

Michael Clifford Spencer (1981) explains that the word *utopia* "was first used by Thomas More in 1516 [and is] the Greek derivation [of] ou-topos ... and means ... "nowhere" or "happy place" (p. 126). Immediately one might wonder about the contradictory nature of the term. The term *utopia* means at once a happy place that is a no place. If utopia is a place, it is someplace, located in time and space; if utopia is a no place it is a nowhere, found neither in time nor space, but rather only in imagination. Ruth Shklar (1966) suggests that classical utopias, perhaps traceable back to Plato's *Republic*, are no place; that is, they are "contemplative only" (p. 105), whereas modern utopias, which Shklar dates around the nineteenth century, are a "summons to action" (p. 109). Thus, Shklar contends that from Plato to Rousseau, utopias are thoughts about no place. After Rousseau, utopias are thoughts in some place.

More generally, David Higgs (1978) summarizes trends in utopian thinking from the 16th to the 19th century.

> In the 16th and 17th centuries this longing [for no place] was often a desire to return to religious sources; 18th century utopias were moral critiques, and the utopias produced from the middle of the 19th century onward draw much inspiration from science. (p. 25)

These broad trends can be found in different writings such as political philosophies, religious texts, fiction, and science fiction. Curiously, Western culture has been replete with utopic writings. In fact, Frank and Fritzie Manuel (1979) explain that "the profusion of Western utopias has not been equaled in any other culture" (p. 1). What is it about utopias that so fascinate the West? Here there are at least two avenues of thought concerning this question. First, some believe that human beings have a certain "utopian propensity" (Manuel & Manuel, 1979, p. 5) which "springs from deep within the psyche" (Richter, 1975, p. 45). That is, dreaming of a better place is part of the human psyche. It is an innate something that is embedded in the core of being. It is, in other words, natural to hope for a better life. However, this so-called natural way of thinking essentializes. It presupposes that everyone, at bottom, has an essential longing for better things. But pessimists and spoilers have always lived alongside eternal optimists.

A more adequate way of thinking about the why of utopianism might be captured by Ruth Levitas. She claims that utopian thinking is a social construction. There is, then, nothing natural about it. Levitas (1990) declares that:

> Utopia is a social construct which arises not from a 'natural' impulse subject to social mediation, but as a socially constructed response to an equally socially constructed gap between the needs and wants generated by a particular society. (pp. 181–182)

Thus, Levitas argues that utopia is an invention of Western thought, not a natural disposition. Still, the question as to why utopian thinking is so prevalent in the West is shrouded in mystery. Why are so many invested in this type of thinking? The answer is far from clear. From Plato through Rousseau, from Charlotte Perkins Gilman to H. G. Wells, utopian ideas abound.

A shift in utopian thinking began to occur with the advent of World War I. Erich Fromm (1977) comments that the First World War was to "destroy a 2,000 year old western tradition of hope" (pp. 258–259). In fact, Albert Soboul (1978) reminds us that "according to Ernst Bloch, utopia is born from the 'principle of hope" (p. 176). And if utopias spring from the principle of hope, what happens when the West becomes less hopeful? One would think that utopias might wane or disappear altogether. Although they have waned, they have not disappeared. Some even call for the re-conceptualizing of utopias by making them more feminist, open-ended and dynamic (Goodwin & Taylor, 1982). But still, utopias like these involve some sort of quest for perfection. As Isaiah Berlin (1991) warns, "the search for perfection does seem ... a recipe for bloodshed" (p. 18). Perfect societies are a call to uniformity and conformity. This call causes othering. And so, as Adam Ulam (1966) suggests, "perhaps we have reached a moratorium, if not indeed the end of utopias, and perhaps this is not altogether a bad thing" (p. 134). According to Richter, Nikolas Berdyaev (1975) says that "the pressing problem of today is not how to reach utopia but how to avoid it" (p. 7). I agree that utopias and utopian thinking should be left behind with the dinosaurs. These old crusty, awkward, naive creatures are dangerous and sometimes deadly. I do not argue that one should attempt to rescue them by making them more feminist or open-ended, but I contend that they be interrogated, dismantled, and finally demolished.

In order to demolish utopianism, one might consider how utopian thinking is connected to memory. As I have earlier explained, what I call personal memory text is elusive, hard to pin down. When I remember something, I look back and I conjure up images in my mind of an event that is distanced from me. Memories seem cloudy sometimes. Memories of yesterday will differ from memories, say, of two years ago because time plays tricks on memory. Sometimes yesterday's memories are more cloudy than that of two years ago; sometimes older memories are more cloudy than yesterday's memories. Amos Funkenstein (1993) reminds us that "personal memory—as first shared by Augustine of Hippo—is likewise never pure memory. Most of our personal memories are … also the memories of memories" (p. 7). Thus, what I re-member is a re-experiencing of an event through a filter of memories. This complicates things. This does not mean, though, that I cannot grasp my past lived experience at all. I can, but it is mediated through complex re-presentations of memories.

Collective memory involves many intersecting memories, many people's memories across time and place. Funkenstein (1993) comments that collective memory "can be characterized as a system of signs, symbols, and practices: memorial dates, names of places, monuments … museums and texts" (p. 6). The collective and personal are interwoven and mediated through culture. Further, memories change over time, and consequently, the meanings of our memories of places and texts change. How I understand memory effects how I think about the past, present, and future. Much of utopian thinking tends to drive a wedge between past, present and future. Utopian thinking cuts a clear line between time, as if time could be clearly demarcated. It is this assumed demarcation that sets up many difficulties for utopianism. Memory and time, however, do not seem to be bifurcated in this way. As Henri Bergson (1946) suggests "there is simply the continuous melody of our inner life" (p. 176). Bergson claims that events happen in a duration of time, a fluidity of past and present. However, utopian thinking bifurcates past from present, and present from future.

Not only is the present separated from the past, in utopian thought, it is denigrated. Utopian thinkers often feel that the "Now" is hell. It is curious that Alighieri Dante (1307/1982) begins *Divine Comedy* in hell, in *The Inferno*. "Abandon Every Hope, who enters here" (p. 21). Hell is a place without hope and the Now is this place. Utopian thinkers attempt, therefore, to escape the Now, escape the present, in order to reclaim lost hope. The *Divine Comedy* is the upward journey from hell to paradise. For Dante, it is only possible to pull oneself out of hell through

God's grace. Although Dante was critical of the corruption of the popes, he offered a traditional Christian position, which is a form of utopian thinking.

Utopian thinkers who have unhappy memories of the past often tend to construct futuristic utopias. Dante's is a futuristic tale because one enters paradise after death, after a long struggle in hell and purgatory. Utopias like H. G. Wells' (1967) *A Modern Utopia*, Charles Fourier's (1808/1996a; 1808/1996b; 1808/1996c; 1808/1996d) *The Theory of the Four Movements*, and Pierre de Chardin's (1964) *The Future of Man* are all types of futuristic utopias. For all of these writers, the future is idealized because the present is hell and the past is backward. Looking to the future while denigrating the past and the present becomes problematic. The future seems golden.

Contrarily, utopian thinkers who remember the past as a golden age, tend to construct utopias that attempt to claim the happy past. Nostalgic longings for things remembered past are captured in the writings of Doris Lessing's (1981) *Briefing for a Descent into Hell*, Charlotte Perkins Gilman's (1915/1979) *Herland*, Rousseau's (1750/1938) *Social Contract*, and his (1755/1938) *Discourses on Inequality*, and most disturbingly, Adolf Hitler's (1923) *Mein Kampf*. Bertrand Russell (1972) comments that, in fact, "Hitler is an outcome of Rousseau" (p. 685). I argue that not only is Hitler an outcome of Rousseau, he is more broadly an outcome of 2,000 years of utopian thinking.

What is it that goes wrong when the past or future is idealized? Most obviously, it is naive to think that things were better in the past or that things would be better in the future if I can just create a new world. Transgressing the present is impossible. I cannot step outside of the Now, I am steeped in it. The past is always already influencing me; the future seeps into the present as well. More importantly, though, it seems that transgressing involves violence. That is, in order to create a new world which idealizes past or future, I may have to commit violence. Therefore, utopian thinking nearly always moves through an apocalyptic phase to reach its objectives. As Darrell Fasching (1993) teaches:

> The modern mythos is at one and the same time both apocalyptic and utopian. It is apocalyptic in that it demands a decisive break with the past; a break that in its more radical manifestations is conceived of as requiring a revolutionary battle between the forces of light and darkness. It is utopian in that what is imagined to follow this radical break ... is a new utopian order. (p. 23)

A brave new world requires transgression either from the old or from the new. This brave new/old world, then, may require violence to achieve its ends. Hence, utopian thinking intersects and crosses over with apocalyptic thinking.

This kind of thinking is even older than modernity. It may even be pre-modern. New Testament scholar Earl Richard (1988) points out that apocalyptic literature (which has both apocalyptic and utopian elements in it) can be traced back through "Exilic and post-exilic prophets, in the Book of Daniel, in intertestamental literature, in the synoptic tradition" (p. 398). Even further back, Lewis Hopfe (1991) points out that already in Zoroastrianism, a tradition older than that of Judaism, we find notions of heaven and hell. It is possible that the utopian tradition may date back 3,000 years in the West.

Utopian thinking, generally speaking, falls in two broad categories. Some utopias are framed in static terms (Plato, Rousseau, Gliman, Lessing, Hitler); some in dynamic terms (Fourier, Wells, de Chardin, Hitler). Hitler's (1923) *Mein Kampf*, and its subsequent realization in National Socialism, can be considered both a static and a dynamic utopia. It was static in the blueprint of *Mein Kampf* and dynamic in its actuality in National Socialism. Joseph Goebbels commented that Nazism "like all living beings, is in a state of becoming" (cited in Hermand, 1992, p. 170). And as Saul Friedländer (1997) remarks, the Nazis were "masters of improvisation" (p. 326). What must be emphasized here is that utopias that are dynamic, that admit of change and process, are not necessarily better than static ones. In fact, it may be the case that dynamism is even more dangerous. There is always room to change the blueprint in order to justify killing more people who do not conform to the utopian way of life.

Is there any harm, one might wonder, in having phantasies about a better, happier place? Perhaps phantasies are harmless enough. When phantasies become realized as prescriptions for living and are acted out in the world, danger looms near. When the images of utopias become realized in the flesh, something happens that tends to lead to ruin. A phantasy island becoming real hardens to stone something that was once dreamy. Are dreamy phantasies innocent? Perhaps not.

Utopian thinking is a form of Pelagianism. Dystopic thinking is a form of Augustinianism. Krishan Kumar (1987) explains that:

> Part of the interwoven story of utopia and anti-utopia can indeed be interestingly told as the long standing clash between Augustinianism and Pelagian traditions.... The utopian ... is a Pelagian. He denies original sin, and believes that men can perfect themselves by creating the right environment. The anti-utopian ... is Augustinian. He sees weak human creatures constantly succumbing to the sins of pride, avarice and ambition. (p. 100)

Pelagius, an eternal optimist, believed that human beings could pull themselves up by their own bootstraps. Augustine, the eternal pessimist, was more concerned with why people sin. Like Augustine, I do believe that what is worth worrying about is why people do bad things. Unlike Augustine, though, I do not believe that there is such a thing as "original sin," for this presupposes some sort of enduring character that is passed along generations. Certainly, I do believe people sin, but there is nothing original about it, because sin is not innate.

Utopian discourse is often trotted out in theological contraries such as hope–despair, salvation–perdition, paradise–apocalypse. To achieve hope, salvation, and paradise, stages of the apocalypse must be acted out or experienced along the way. To help citizens achieve utopian goals, utopias nearly always include some sort of educational blueprint which is meant to inculcate citizens. But this utopian vision is usually achieved by wiping out, eliminating, or annihilating whoever gets in the way of its final objective. Those who are considered weak, impure, dirty, or nonconforming must be controlled, manipulated, or killed. Purity, strength, and conformity are the keys to sustaining a utopian world. At bottom, then, utopias concern the manipulation and surveillance of bodies. As Foucault (1979) reminds us, "It is always the body that is at issue" (p. 25).

THE FOUR HORSEMEN OF UTOPIANISM

I now turn to the "four horsemen" of utopianism. I first examine Fourier, de Chardin, and Wells, and finally, I address Hitler's (1923) *Mein Kampf.* Charles Fourier (1808/1996c; 1808/1996a) in *The Theory of the Four Movements*, robes his utopian scheme in theological discourse. The four movements of the "social, animal, organic, and material" (p. 3), and what Fourier calls the "destinies … [of] past, present and future" (p. 6), evolve and are determined by "God's mathematical laws" (p. 36). Of the four movements, Fourier (1808/1996a) calculates that the social "will progress uninterruptedly in two ages of ascending and descending combinations … which will take about 7,000 years" (p. 44). Presently, we are living in an age of "ascending incoherence" (p. 41) in which there is much "suffering" (p. 41). Fourier suggests that this suffering is due to capitalism, modern industry, and poverty. Fourier believes that the earth and the other planets are created in cycles. These cycles are moving, ever evolving. He tells us that the planets "can copulate" (p. 45). Thus, planet earth was created out of a sexual act. The "first creation" (pp. 45–46), of which there are many, Fourier compares to hell:

> The first creation … filled land and sea with an immense quantity of harmful animals … what could hell in its fury invent that would be worse than rat-

tle-snakes, bed-bugs, the legions of insects and reptiles, sea-monsters. (pp. 45–46)

Unlike Fourier's account of creation, the biblical account in Genesis 2:4 of the creation of the world was not hellish, but was a paradise, at least in the beginning. With the advent of the Fall, of course, things went badly and the world began to flood and plagues rolled over the children of God.

Central to Fourier's utopian world is the concept of God. God is both transcendent and immanent, but he is mostly transcendent. God "reign[s] [over] the combined order ... which is the most beautiful of the divine conceptions" (p. 67). The order of things are progressing in what Fourier terms a *progressing series*. God is also immanent. Nicholas Riasanovsky (1969) explains that for Fourier, "God, like man had both body and soul ... he did sometimes appear as a personality" (p. 35). Thus, for Fourier, God is both immanent and transcendent.

Further, God organizes society by what Fourier (1808/1889c) calls "passionate attraction" (p. 15). These attractions are sexual. So it is sex that orders the world. Sexual relations are most healthy, says Fourier, if they are free. Therefore, marriage is not part of this utopian world. Communal living and free love are key to sustaining utopia. Communities called "phalanxes" (p. 15) would be ideal. Michael Clifford Spencer (1981) explains that for Fourier a phalanx is "the basically agricultural economic and social unit in harmony usually containing about 1600 [people]" (p. 181). Fourier thought that civilization and modern industry brought about decline and disharmony. He blamed this decline on the Jews. Fourier (1808/1889c) states that "civilized industry was ... a calamity invented by God as a punishment" (p. 7). Thus, salvation involved living in harmony free from disorder and "incoherence" (p. 13). What he really means to say here is that salvation is life without Jews. Fourier's Jew hatred permeates his texts; in fact, Fourier was a rabid anti-Semite, as I point out later.

For now, we move on to another brand of utopian thinking. Here let us turn to utopian thinking, that is also couched in theological language, that of Pierre Tielhard de Chardin. In his *The Future of Man*, de Chardin (1964) offers a utopian vision which departs little from traditional Christian theology, except that de Chardin attempts to combine pseudo-scientific talk about evolution (read: social Darwinism) with eschatology. De Chardin's utopia ends up justifying racism and supersessionism. The future of man, for de Chardin, is really about the future of White supremacy and Christian imperialism.

De Chardin's obfuscating language is cluttered with neologisms like "noosphere" and "neogenesis" which confuses more than not and conceals a very conservative kind of christological position. Like classical christology, de Chardin's work exalts Christ as the last and final savior, and Christianity as the final word on religion. Christianity, for de Chardin, is the only right and true religion. At least this is the impression I get from reading *The Future of Man*. The only difference between de Chardin's position and that of the classical one turns on the notion of evolution. Evolution of the species, says de Chardin (1964), involves greater and greater love for Christ. In fact, he claims that "there is only one evolution ... the whole of the world's industrial, aesthetic, scientific and moral endeavor serves physically to complete the body of Christ" (p. 23). It becomes hard to understand how the world can complete the body of Christ, when de Chardin's Christ has no body to begin with. De Chardin's Christ is cosmic, not embodied. He says Christ's spirit, which is different from his body, can "radiate through all centuries and all beings" (p. 94). This brand of what is termed *high christology* leaves Jesus, the human being, out of the picture, while emphasizing the Christ part of Jesus, which is his divinity. A *low christology*, which stresses that Jesus was a human being who suffered and wept while participating in the divinity of God, seems to make more sense to me. But this is not what de Chardin is offering.

De Chardin's eschatological vision is that, at the end time, all people will psychologically merge to agree on the fact that Jesus was the Son of God. Moreover, all human beings will become more and more alike in spirit, mind, and body in this belief. De Chardin declares that "psychic centration, phyletic intertwining, and planetary envelopment ... give birth to the noosphere" (p. 159). The noosphere is the mind of the world which will enfold on itself around the belief in Christ when evolution is complete.

Like Fourier, de Chardin's vision is dynamic, progressive and evolving. But these qualities do not make it more adequate than another more static utopia. I wonder what happens to those who do not merge into the noosphere? Not everyone believes that Jesus was the Son of God. Not all Christians believe in a cosmic Christ, and not all theologians agree that high christology is an adequate way to conceptualize Jesus. De Chardin allows no room for difference. What happens to non-Christians in his utopic vision? De Chardin is silent on this issue, and it is this silence that worries me. In one way or another, many utopias, whether explicitly Christian or not, set up schemes that do not allow for otherness. There is only one way to salvation, one possible path toward the good, one way to God. As Asher Moore (1978) points out "utopia involves standardization" (p. 1).

Like de Chardin and Fourier, H. G. Wells (1967) in his *Modern Utopia* robes his vision in theological discourse. Wells describes the leaders of this futuristic society as "samurai" (p. 159). Samurai are priests who administer and run the modern utopia. "The Samurai will be forbidden the religion of dramatically lit altars, organ music, and Catholic ritual" (pp. 300–301). Wells sounds like Martin Luther in his dislike for embellishment and ritual. For the Samurai, God must be transcendent. Recall, for both de Chardin and Fourier, God is a transcendent one, although Fourier sometimes images God in an immanent way. The image of a transcendent God is a theologically conservative one. More liberal theologians, such as John Cobb (1975) and David Griffin (1973), talk about God as being both immanent and transcendent. This position is termed *panentheism*. Unlike pantheism, whereby God is completely immanent in the world after the fashion, say, of Spinoza, panentheism suggests that God is both in the world and beyond it. If God is completely immanent, how then do theologians solve the problem of evil? For if God is wholly immanent, then God creates evil. If God, on the other hand, is completely transcendent, how can I relate to him? But if God is both immanent and transcendent, the problem of evil gets lodged in the heart of humankind. Thus, the construction of the notion of God is inextricably tied to theodicy.

H. G. Wells (1967) remarks that "the leading principle of the utopian religion is the repudiation of original sin" (pp. 299–300). Wells echoes Shklar's (1966) claim that all classical utopias are rejections of original sin. Recall, Shklar dates classical utopias from Plato to Rousseau. Thus, it seems that Wells's utopia fits in with this classical model. What is it about the concept of sin that bothers utopian thinkers? Looking into one's heart of darkness is completely antithetical to utopian projects. I wonder how one can build a utopia without doing a little self work? How can citizens of utopias become better if they do not admit that they have fallen somewhere along the way? Why is it that many who do not look into their heart of darkness become wicked? Wells's utopian dream is monstrous, perhaps because he could not integrate his own badness in himself. His description of the leaders of utopia conjure up, in my mind, images of Nazis. A Samurai is a "clean-shaven," lean, muscular type who likes to engage in combat. A Samurai is a warrior, a hero, a dashing, young, healthy swashbuckler. Wells describes the samurai as a:

> well-built man of perhaps five and thirty, with the easy movement that comes with perfect physical condition, his face is clean shaven and shows the firm mouth of a disciplined man.... His general effect reminds me ... of the knights templars. (1967, p. 159)

Hitler dreamt the knights templars into existence. Already in 1933, Hitler had an "idealized image of the knight, the German knight, or the knight of the Teutonic order" (Hermand, 1992, p. 239).

It is curious that all three of these writers robe their discussions in theological language. What is disturbing is that this language serves as a gloss. This gloss attempts to cover over and conceal violence. The paradox of slippery theological and eschatological visions is that they offer up a hopeful picture, yet it is only through oppression that this picture can be completed.

All three of these writers discuss how to better inculcate the citizens of their utopian worlds through some sort of educational blueprint. This educational blueprint ensures that citizens know how to fit in. Thus, education means standardization. Standardized objectives and goals are key to inculcating citizens, for everyone learns precisely the same things for precisely the same reasons. While reading these utopian writers, I was reminded of Alan Bloom's (1987) *The Closing of the American Mind*.

Bloom comments that "America tells one story: the unbroken, ineluctable progress of freedom and equality" (p. 55). Like many utopian writers, Bloom (1987) declares that:

> Idealism as it is commonly conceived should have primacy in an education, for man is a being who must take his orientation by his possible perfection. To suppress the most natural of all inclinations ... is ... to throw out the baby with the bath. Utopianism is, as Plato taught us ... the fire with which we might play because it is the only way we can find out what we are. (p. 67)

Bloom's position, not unlike most utopian thinkers, is naive, exclusionistic, conservative, and dangerous. First, Bloom's assumption that America has one story to tell is naive. American history is made up of many competing and conflicting stories. Secondly, his insistence on the "primacy" of ideals in education may serve oppressive ends. Whose ideals should we teach and why? And for what purpose should we teach ideals? Thirdly, why should perfection be an "orientation" at all? The goal of producing perfect students fosters the worst sort of competition. Furthermore, perfection is not a natural inclination, it is a social construction. Perfectionism is dangerous for the soul. Recall, Isaiah Berlin (1991) said that the quest for perfection means bloodshed.

Like Bloom, Fourier wants standardized educational objectives which serve to inculcate citizens into the utopia of the four movements. Like Rousseau, Fourier suggests that children should avoid cultural influences as long as possible so as to not be corrupted by them. Unlike Rousseau, Fourier (1808/1996a) declares that children should have no teachers. "The children teach themselves without any external prompting or surveillance" (p. 69). The children will learn to become "constantly active" (p. 69) so as to build up their bodies at a young age. Thus, education means activity, not reflection for Fourier. And activity is standardized. Activities are done in a so-called natural environment away from the dangers of culture. Fourier's educational blueprint is anti-intellectual, like Rousseau's. Anti-intellectualism is dangerous because it fosters all sorts of prejudices. An unreflective mind has difficulty working through tough issues. Further, Fourier suggests that culture can be split off from nature. But there is no way to jump outside of culture. Nature is cultural. Even the way we talk about nature is socially constructed. The always already of culture shapes us even before we arrive on the scene. These sorts of romantic, nostalgic visions of education fail because they begin on false premises and are mired in illusions.

For both de Chardin and Wells, the goal of education in their utopian worlds is singular. Citizens must learn standardized visions to realize the goals of their societies. For de Chardin (1964), Christian education is the only correct kind. In fact, he says, "there is no institution other than Christianity" (p. 36). The institution of Christianity must be run by Christian teachers. Wells (1967), like de Chardin, declares that "the whole world will surely have a common language" (p. 17). This common language is a common vision. Education must have a "clear common purpose" (p. 128). Alan Bloom echoes in the background here. I wonder how education can have a clear common purpose when people have little in common to begin with. Why are these thinkers so invested in the quest for commonalities? Further, it is not clear what educating citizens means in the first place. If anything, education is a highly complex and ambiguous process. Common purposes and standardized bodies of knowledge, more often than not, serve oppressive ends. Brent Davis (1996) points out that, for instance, standardized mathematics education has traditionally been

> an enabler of scientific "advances," of military technologies, of normalizing statistical reductions, mathematics has been associated with the establishment and maintenance of power imbalances contributing to large-scale destruction of the planet; and the disenfranchizing and depersonalizing the citizenry of Western cultures ... all in the name of progress.... Mathematical knowledge has ... become coterminous with masculinist, Western, bourgeois, and modernist regimes of power. (p. xxii)

It seems that standardized bodies of knowledge attempt to conceal their real objectives, which are military and scientific imperialisms.

What is colonized, especially, in utopian writings, are bodies. Bodies are colonized, controlled, and manipulated to fit the utopian ideal. Those who call for standardized bodies, like those who call for standardized bodies of knowledge, do not allow for differences. Nonconforming bodies, therefore, get squashed. Recall, Fourier's utopia is a perfect universe where harmony, peace, and love reign. However, certain bodies do not fit into this picture. And these are Jewish bodies. Fourier (1808/1996d) declares, "Jews are parasites" (p. 261); they are "the secret enemy of all nations" (p. 233).

> Has there ever been a more contemptible nation than the Hebrews, who never made a single advance in the arts and sciences, and who were distinguished only by their habitual crimes and brutality. (p. 64)

Leon Poliakov (1975) comments that nearly all of Fourier's writings contain Jew hating diatribes like these. As a matter of fact, Poliakov (1985) states that along with Fourier, many other French socialists (Fourier was a socialist) were anti-Semites. For instance, P. J. Proudon (1969) writes in his diaries that he would have liked to have called

> for the expulsion of the Jews from France, the abolition of all their synagogues; denial to them of all employment; the abolition of their cult.... The Jew is the enemy of the human race. This race must be sent back to Asia, or exterminated. (p. 228)

The legacy of socialist utopias are deadly. F. A. Hayek (1994) draws a connection between Nazism and utopian socialism. Certainly, Proudhon and Fourier buttress Hayek's thesis, although of course there are many brands of socialism which do not. At any rate, Jewish bodies bug socialist utopic discourse.

Like Fourier, Wells deals with bodies that do not fit into his utopian scheme. And his "solution" to the "problem" of bodies that bug him, echoes Hitler's Final Solution. Wells (1967) cannot tolerate dirt or mess. Bodies that seem dirty must be "punished" (p. 110). In this utopia, apartments will have "no corners to gather dirt" (p. 104). Moreover, those who are considered dirty or odd will be dealt with.

> It is our business to ask what utopia will do with its congenital invalids, its idiots and madmen, its drunkards and men of vicious mind, its cruel and furtive souls, its stupid people ... its lumpish and unimaginative people. (p. 136)

Wells declares that the way to deal with these lumpish, stupid people is simply to get rid of them. "The species must be engaged in eliminating them" (p. 136). Wells remarks, "Utopia will kill all deformed and evilly monstrous births" (p. 143). Hitler did just this. Daniel Goldhagen (1997) explains that in October of 1939, Hitler initiated what he called the "euthanasia program" (p. 143) whereby he gassed to death the "congenitally infirm and insane" (p. 143). This so-called euthanasia program was a sort of trial run to see how effective gas would be. The trial run prepared that Nazis for the Jews. By the time the gas chambers were up and running in 1941, Hitler had perfected his poison gas machines. Some could kill up to 2,000 people at once. Imagine that!

Along with eliminating the "insane" and "lumpish" people, Wells also advocated that all members of the utopia be accounted for at all times by a keeper of an index. Bentham's panoptican lives. Wells (1967) comments that "a little army of attendants would be at work upon this index day and night" (p. 165). Lucy Dawidowicz (1975/1986) remarks that, similarly, Reinhard Heydrich, who was appointed Gestapo chief in 1936, headed an "intelligence gathering agency" (p. 77) that began to "organize a card index of NSDAP opponents [read: Jews]" (p. 78).

At this juncture, I examine Hitler's (1923) *Mein Kampf.* Disturbingly, Werner Maser (1974) explains that Hitler "had serious plans to become a priest" (p. 6). In fact, many historians comment on the religious/theological nature of Hitler's vision of a National Socialist utopia. Saul Friedländer (1997) claims that Hitler's was a "decidedly religious vision, that of a German (or Aryan) Christianity" (pp. 86–87). Amos Funkenstein (1993) and Robert Wistrich (1991) comment on the apocalyptic quality of Hitler's writings. And Jost Hermand (1992) comments on Hitler's "religious belief in the "resurrection" of the volk" (p. 171). *Mein Kampf* is shrouded in theological discourse and reveals the "blueprint" (Dawidowicz, 1975/1986; Goldhagen, 1997) for the Holocaust. It is a utopian vision that serves to inculcate through the destruction of bodies. Educating citizens of the Third Reich that the Jews must be slayed was Hitler's dream. This dream was couched in religious language. Hitler (1923) says "Thus did I believe that I must act in the sense of the Almighty Creator: by fighting against the Jews I am doing the Lord's work" (p. 25). Hitler really believed that he had been called, like a prophet, to carry out the will of God. He uses words like "providence" over and over again to suggest that the Final Solution was fated by God. Consequently, Germans, says Hitler, had a "mission appointed for them by the Creator of the universe" (p. 94). The mission entailed a "National resurrection" (p. 99) of "race ... [and] purity of blood" (p. 94). This mission could only be completed in "the spirit of fanaticism and intolerance in which it attacks all others" (p. 141). Hitler called for "Salvation for the German nation" (p. 54).

To inculcate the German nation's citizens into his Third Reich, Hitler offered up an educational blueprint that would focus on the practical. Hitler remarks that "there were a great number of weak points in German education before the war ... a view to mere knowledge and very little with a view to producing practical ability" (p. 107). Anti-intellectualism is Hitler's brand of education. Hitler declared that education should teach young boys the value of strong bodies, particularly through boxing. "There is no sport which encourages the spirit of attack as this one does" (p. 167). In other words, education should teach violence. Attacking opponents is the sport of learning. And education "must be directed toward giving them [young people] a conviction that they are superior to others" (p. 168). Here Hitler is talking about young, so-called Aryan youth. They should, in other words, feel superior to so-called Semitic, or Jewish, youth.

Jewish bodies, for Hitler (1923), are diseased beings whose "spiritual pestilence … [was what] the nation was being inoculated [with]" (p. 21). To "fight with poison gas" (p. 11) against the Jews will return Germany to more "healthy social conditions" (p. 10). It is this passage about poison gas that has led some historians, like Lucy Dawidowicz (1975/1986), to claim that Hitler intended all along to kill the Jews.

Even right before Hitler committed suicide, he continued to believe that he had been called by God to murder 6 million Jews. He felt totally justified in doing what he did. He justified his actions in theological gloss. In 1944, Hitler declared:

> The gods love those … of whom they ask the impossible and who ask them the impossible of them. And when we do the impossible we shall assuredly win the approval of Providence.
>
> I may not be a light in the Church, a pulpiteer, but deep down I am a pious man and believe that whoever fights bravely in defense of the natural laws of God and never capitulates will never be deserted by the law giver, but will, in the end receive the blessings of Providence. (cited in Maser, 1974, p. 208)

Bromberg (cited in Rappaport, 1975); Waite (1977); and Erikson (1976) each suggest that Hitler suffered from borderline personality disorder. Laplanche and Pontalis (1973) explain that the "Term [*borderline* is] most often used to designate psychopathological troubles lying on the frontier between neurosis and psychosis, particularly latent schizophrenia presenting an apparently neurotic set of symptoms" (p. 54). Borderline personality disorder, in other words, signals that the individual's psyche founders somewhere on a continuum between madness and sanity. This is a person who can function in the world, but may have periodic lapses of schizophrenia. But, some borderline patients are more neurotic than psychotic, and do not regress to a schizoid state. Borderline personalities exhibit severe mood swings and unpredictable behavior. They tend to swing "between sadism and masochism, destruction and creativity, cruelty and kindness" (Waite, 1977, p. 168). But again, what good does it do to pathologize Hitler? What do we learn about him by doing this? What does this category of borderline personality disorder keep us from thinking about?

In the book *The Soul's Code: In Search of Character and Calling*, post-Jungian psychologist James Hillman (1996) argues that Hitler was "possessed" by the demonic (p. 216). The demonic, Hillman suggests, is a "timeless" (p. 216) "transcendence" (p. 235). This "particular demon selected Hitler for its host" (p. 215). This demonic spirit was both "genius" and "evil" (p. 215). Hillman goes on to argue that Germans suffered from a "collective demonization" (p. 216). Hillman explains:

> The idea of a demon or evil genius helps account for his appeal to the substrate of shadow in the German Volk, and to the formation of that group ethos which, blinded by his demonic visions, complied with and executed them ... the fascinating power in Hitler changed millions into a collective demonization. (p. 216)

Hillman's thesis echoes that of Thomas Mann's (1948/1992) in *Doctor Faustus*. A transcendent, mystical, demonic force possessed Adrian Leverkühn and he made a pact with the devil because the devil sought him out. Adrian's pact with the devil marked the end of Germany, for Germany had gone astray.

Hillman is certainly out of step with current trends in psychohistory and Holocaust scholarship. In contrast to Hillman, Ernst Rappaport (1975) argues that

> Hitler was neither a genius nor a demonic personality.... His intellect was below average and his "soaring" imagination was that of an ambulatory schizophrenic who was obsessed with his paranoid delusions. (p. 210)

To contend that Hitler was possessed by some kind of transcendent spirit, and that Germans were blinded by this spirit, functions as an apologetic. Germans' egos were quite intact, as Roth (1995a) points out. Germany knew what it was doing (Hilberg, 1961/1985). Christopher Browning (1998) suggests that legitimate Holocaust scholarship must avoid demonizing. Hillman's argument that Germans suffered from "collective demonization" (p. 216) implies the notion of collective guilt. But the notion of collective guilt has been dismissed by historians at least since the Eichmann trial in 1961. Disturbingly, Hillman (1996) criticizes the prosecutors of the Nuremberg trial and actually compares them to Inquisitors.

> The labored, obsessive methods used from the Inquisition through the trial of Adolf Eichmann in Israel, Klaus Barbie in France, and in the Nuremberg trials themselves. This controlling carefulness of step-by-step rationalism defends against the demonic force. (p. 230)

These so-called step-by-step rational judicial methods were necessary to demonstrate that individuals, not transcendent demons or forces, were guilty. Individuals who made choices, committed crimes, and carried out mass murder were guilty. And what was at stake in these trials was individual guilt and responsibility. Jeffrey Herf (1997) drives this point home:

> The message of the Nuremberg trials was that human beings and their political decisions had made Auschwitz possible—not being, fate destiny [or demons], instrumental reason, the Enlightenment, modernity or the West. (p. 208)

Hillman offers up an argument shrouded in mystical language that I think is dangerous. The demon in Hitler was nothing transcendent; it was Hitler's own badness that he projected onto Jews. He needed scapegoats, although we do not really know why. Some psychobiographers blame Hitler's tyrannical behavior on his alcoholic father (Waite, 1977); and others blame his overbearing mother (Rappaport, 1975; Binion, 1976). Binion (1976) declares that after Hitler's mother died from cancer, he "saw Germany's fateful enfeeblement as due to the Jewish cancer" (p. 21). A Jewish doctor tended to Hitler's mother and, possibly, Hitler blamed him for her death. Hence, his scapegoat was born. But of course there was more to it than that.

Whoever Hitler was, he was a man of his culture and of his time. I do not believe that he was possessed by demons, or by an evil spirit hovering around the universe waiting to take somebody over, to steal someone's soul. I believe that Hitler was little more than an ordinary German. Robert Waite (1977) comments that:

> A thoughtful writer in the Frankfurt *Allgemeine Zeitung* (11 Oct. 1972) who warned his countrymen against "demonizing Hitler" . . . for to do so would be to diminish their own responsibility. The German journalist concluded that the terrifying thing about Hitler was not his uniqueness but his banality. (p. xvii)

Hitler, Eichmann, Roehm, Mengele, and Heydrich, architects of the Holocaust, were all ordinary men, mortal men who made choices, who killed willingly, and who were responsible for the "great crime" (Grass, 1985, p. 86). A Germany fated to become possessed by demonic forces does not explain, but explains away. A demonic Germany conceals more than it reveals.

I offer a dystopic curriculum as a warning against hope. It is a curriculum that demands that happy texts be dismantled. I offer a dystopic curriculum as a warning so that one may understand, in a more adequate way, how texts handed down through culture may fool us into believing that utopias are good things. Two thousand years of utopian thinking led, in part, to the murder of 6 million Jews. But it was not just utopian thinking that led to Hitler's killing dream: the causes of this terrible event are highly complex. Dahlia Beck (1997) suggests that "curriculum is the battered sub-/emerging carriage of memory, it is what makes verses of the vanished possible" (p. 17). What has been forgotten is that in happy places (utopias), people tend to vanish. If curriculum is to "tap the current within" (Doll, 2000), memories must be stirred up a bit in order that curriculum workers get some understanding of why it is they want happy endings. Must we despair of hope? Since Auschwitz, yes.

Under the sign of a dystopic curriculum, I struggle to make sense of this research against the background of my Jewishness. I struggle to make sense of my life in the midst of the memory of this horrific event. I struggle because even the sense that I have made is continually interrupted and ruptured by the enormous wound left in my psyche. Every day seems split by the present post-Holocaust era and the black sun of Auschwitz. The paradox is that the Holocaust is not "post" at all; it is here every day. Not only is it in my psyche, it is in the public eye as well. Every day in the newspaper, yet another article related to the Holocaust appears. There have been more books published on the Holocaust than on any other event in history, and books keep proliferating. Holocaust memories are so haunting that they demand continual re-thinking. Doing research on this Jewish tragedy has unnerved me. The past bursts into the present at every turn. Anti-Semitism is alive and well, not just in Germany, but in the United States; synagogues were recently burned in California. On August 10, 1999, Buford O. Furrow walked into a Jewish community center in Granada Hills, Los Angeles and fired 70 rounds of bullets at children! Five were wounded. Luckily, most of the children were outside playing. Rabbi Marvin Hier, dean of the Simon Wisenthal Center, reports that about 20 children from the Jewish community center were taking a tour of the Wiesenthal Center's Museum of Tolerance at the time of the shootings. Rabbi Hier remarks that "it's ironic that the 20 children were here learning about man's inhumanity to man, when their own day camp became a target of such hatred" (1999, p. A-4). In New Orleans, since August 10, there has been a police presence at the Jewish Community Center and at local synagogues. It is so disturbing to me that children are targets of hate. And it is so disturbing to me that when I attend the synagogue I see police outside of the building. This is no time for complacency.

The *Jewish News* reports that approximately 30,000 Jews have fled Russia due to rising anti-Semitism and 30,000 more are expected to emigrate by the end of the year. Leopold Kaimovsky, the manager of Moscow's Jewish Arts center, was stabbed by a neo-Nazi who, when caught by the police, said "There are 50,000 of us. We will kill all of you anyway" (1999, p. 24). Lev Krichevsky (1999) claims that in Russia there are, in fact, about 50,000 neo-Nazis who belong to a group called Russian National Unity. This is alarming because there is a tremendous sense of lawlessness in Russia today. The Russian Mafia does as it pleases, while the hard-liners, according to Krichevesky, make "inflammatory statements" (p. 24) against Jews. And to top it off, the economy in Russia is at rock bottom. Scapegoating worsens in such climates. This is no time for complacency.

Remembering the Holocaust is an international issue. Intercultural dialogue and the internationalization of curriculum studies might open avenues for further discussion and debate cross-culturally. I urge open and democratic discussions between Germans and Jews, especially. I urge open and democratic discussions cross-culturally. More academic projects which foster this kind of exchange might help second-, third-, and fourth-generation Jews and Germans to cope. Work around race, class, gender, and sexuality in Holocaust studies needs to be deepened. Queer memories demand more visibility too. More work needs to be done on transgenerational trauma. Some of our students and colleagues in the academy may suffer from a transgenerational haunting. As teachers and researchers, educators need to become more aware of this. Broader and more interdisciplinary approaches to Holocaust research are needed. Popular culture is also crucial to understanding this event. Young people may get introduced to the Holocaust through film. Film, art, dance, theater, poetry, and museums all have something to offer to the future generations.

The important issue for educators to focus on is to keep this memory alive. "Never again" is the chant Jews utter. But can we be so sure? Who is to say what the new millennium will bring? The Holocaust lives in a present absence. It is simultaneously here and not here. But educators might take up the responsibility to make this "great crime" (Grass, 1985, p. 86) known, and re-known again. For too soon the next generation will forget. How many have forgotten already? I remember when I was in the 6th grade and Mrs. G. came to our class to show us the numbers on her arm. She came to our 6th grade class to tell us that every time she hears a train she mourns. But I did not understand what she was talking about. What does a 12-year-old know? However, the memory of Mrs. G. has stuck with me all these years; in fact, it has haunted me. And so whenever I hear a train I think of Auschwitz. Another haunting is this one: At the beginning of my graduate program at Louisiana State University, I wrote a letter to Elie Wiesel asking him if I could study with him, and fly to Boston a few times a semester to work on his novels (I forgot I had done this, and I do not understand why I forgot: Repression works in uncanny ways.) Wiesel wrote back a lovely letter to me, saying that he just did not have extra time to take on another student. But Wiesel has taken on another student. I am a student to this memory. My work has just begun.

References

Ackerman, N., & M. Jahoda (1950). *Anti-Semitism and emotional disorder: A psychoanalytic interpretation.* New York: Harper & Brothers.

Adorno, T. W., Frenkel-Brunswik, E., Levinson, D. J., Sanford, R. N., Aron, B., Hertz Levinson, M., & Morrow, W. (1950). *The authoritarian personality.* New York: Harper & Brothers.

Adorno, T. W. (1966/1995). *Negative dialectics* (A. B. Ashton, Trans.). New York: Continuum.

Albin, M. (1980). Preface. In M. Albin (Ed.), *New directions in psychohistory: The adelphi papers in honor of Erik Erikson* (pp. xi–xvii). Lexington, MA: Lexington, D.C.: Heath.

Anger, P. (1981). *With Raul Wallenberg in Budapest: Memories of the wars in Hungary.* New York: Holocaust Library.

Antze, P., & Lambek, M. (1996). Preface. In P. Antze & Lambek M. (Eds.), *Tense past: cultural essays in trauma and memory* (pp. vii–ix). New York: Routledge.

Appelbaum, P., & Kaplan, R. (1998). An other mathematics: Object relations and the clinical interview. *Journal of Curriculum Theorizing, 14*(2), 35–42.

Appelfeld, A. (1994). *Beyond despair: Three lectures and a conversation with Philip Roth* (J. M. Green, Trans.). New York: Fromm.

Atwell-Vasey, W. (1998). *Nourishing words: Bridging private reading and public teaching.* Albany: State University of New York Press.

Avni, O. (1995). Beyond psychoanalysis: Elie Wiesel's night in historical perspective. In L. Kritzman (Ed.), *Auschwitz and after: Race, culture, and "the Jewish question"* (pp. 203–218). New York: Routledge.

Bar-On, D. (1993). Holocaust perpetrators and their children: A paradoxical morality. In B. Heimmansberg & C. Schmidt (Eds.), *The collective silence: German identity and the legacy of shame* (pp. 195–208). (C. O. Harris & G. Wheeler, Trans.). San Francisco: Jossey-Bass.

Barrow, R. (1981). *The philosophy of schooling.* New York: Wiley.

Barthes, R. (1981). *Camera lucidia: Reflections on photography* (R. Howard, Trans.). New York: Farrar, Straus & Giroux.

Bartov, O. (1997). German soldiers and the holocaust: Historiography, research and implications. In *History and Memory, 9*(1/2), 162–188.

Bauer, Y. (1989). Forms of Jewish resistance during the holocaust. In J. K. Roth & M. Berenbaum (Eds.), *Holocaust: Religious and philosophical implications* (pp. 137–155). St. Paul: MN: Paragon.

Bauer, Y. (1997). Daniel J. Goldhagen's view of the Holocaust. In F. Littel (Ed.), *Hyping the Holocaust: Scholars answer Goldhagen* (pp. 59–72). Merion Station, PA: Merion Westfield.

Bauman, Z. (1995). *Life in fragments: Essays in postmodern morality.* Oxford: Blackwell.

Beck, D. (1997). The living fabric of memory. In T. R. Carson & D.

Sumara (Eds.), *Action research as a living practice* (pp. 11–23). New York: Peter Lang.

Becker, C. (1935). *Everyman his own historian: Essays on history and politics.* New York: Appelton Century Crofts.

Bellamy, E. (1997). *Affective genealogies: Psychoanalysis, postmodernism, and the "Jewish question" after Auschwitz.* Lincoln: The University of Nebraska Press.

Benzaquen, A. (1998). Freud, little Hans, and the desire for knowledge. *Journal of Curriculum Theorizing, 14*(2), 43–52.

Berenbaum, M., & Roth, J. K. (1989). Why? In J. K. Roth & M. Berenbaum (Eds.), *Holocaust: Religious & philosophical implications* (pp. 371–373). St. Paul, MN: Paragon.

Bergman, M., & Jucovy, M. (1990). Prelude. In M. Bergmann & M. Jucovy (Eds.), *Generations of the Holocaust* (pp. 3–29). New York: Columbia University Press.

Bergson, H. (1946). *The creative mind* (M. L. Andison, Trans.). New York: The Philosophical Library.

Bergson, H. (1988). *Matter and Memory* (N. M. Paul & W. S. Palmer, Trans.). New York: Zone.

Berlin, I. (1991). The pursuit of the ideal. In H. Hardy (Ed.), *The crooked timber of humanity: Chapters on the history of ideas* (pp. 1–19). New York: Knopf.

Bettelheim, B. (1971). *An informed heart: Autonomy in a mass age.* New York: Avon.

Bhabha, H. (1994). *The location of culture.* New York: Routledge.

Binion, R. (1976). *Hitler among Germans.* New York: Elsevier.

Bird, B. (1990). Notes on transference: Universal phenomenon and hardest part of analysis. In A. Esman (Ed.), *Essential papers on transference* (pp. 331–361). New York: New York University Press.

Blake, Cohen, M. (1988). Countertransference and anxiety. In B. Wolstein (Ed.), *Essential papers on countertransference* (pp. 64–83). New York: New York University Press.

Bloch, E. (1938–1947/1986). *The principle of hope. Volume one* (N. Plaice & S. Plaice Trans.). Cambridge, MA: MIT Press.

Bloch, M. (1954). *The historian's craft: Reflections on the nature and uses of history and the techniques and methods of historical writing* (P. Putnam, Trans.). London: Manchester University Press.

Block, A. (1997). Finding lost articles: The return of curriculum. *Journal of Curriculum Theorizing: An Interdisciplinary Journal of Curriculum Studies, 13*(3), 5–12.

Bloom, A. (1987). *The closing of the American mind.* New York: Simon & Schuster.

Bloom, J. (1993). Introduction: The technology of modern wonder. In J. Bloom (Ed.), *Photography at bay: Interviews, essays and reviews* (pp. 3–7). Albuquerque: The University of New Mexico Press.

Boguslawska, A. (1975). *Food for the children.* London: Leo Cooper.

Bollas, C. (1996). *Cracking up: The work of unconscious experience.* New York: Hill and Wang.

Bollas, C. (1997). An interview. In A. Molino (Ed.), *Freely associated: Encounters in psychoanalysis* (pp. 5–52). New York: Free Association Books.

Bower, T. (1998). *Nazi gold.* New York: Harper Perennial.

Boyarin, J. (1992). *Storm from paradise: The politics of Jewish memory.* Minneapolis: The University of Minnesota Press.

Breines, P. (1990). *Tough Jews: Political fantasies and the moral dilemma of American Jewry.* New York: Basic.

Britzman, D. (1995). Teachers under suspicion: Is it true that teachers aren't as good as they used to be? In J. L. Kincheloe & S. R. Steinberg (Eds.), *Thirteen questions: Reframing educational conversations* (pp. 69–76). New York: Peter Lang.

Britzman, D. (1998). *Lost subjects, contested objects: Toward a psychoanalytic inquiry of learning.* New York: State University Press.

Brooks, P. (1987). The idea of a psychoanalytic literary criticism. In S. Rimmon-Kenan (Ed.), *Discourse in psychoanalysis and literature* (pp. 1–18). London: Methuen.

Browning, C. (1992). *The path to genocide: Essays on launching the final solution.* New York: Cambridge University Press.

Browning, C. (1996). German memory, Judicial Interrogation, and historical reconstruction: Writing perpetrator history from postwar testimony. In S. Friedländer (Ed.), *Probing the limits of representation: Nazism and the "final solution"* (pp. 22–36). Cambridge, MA: Harvard University Press.

Browning, C. (1998). *Ordinary men: Reserve police battalian 101 and the final solution in Poland.* New York: Harper Perennial.

Broszat, M. (1969/1981). *The Hitler state: The foundation and development of the internal structure of the third reich* (J. W. Hiden, Trans.). New York: Longman.
Brunner, J. (1997). Pride and memory: Nationalism, narcissism and the historian's debate in Germany and Israel. In *History and Memory, 9*(1/2), 256–300.
Burgoyne, B., & Sullivan, M. (1997). *The Klein-Lacan dialogues.* B. Burgoyne & M. Sullivan (Eds.). London: Rebus.
Carmichael, J. (1992). *The satanizing of the Jews: Origin and development of mystical anti-Semitism.* New York: Fromm.
Carpi, D. (1994). *Between Mussolini and Hitler: Jews and Italian authorities in France and Tunisia.* Hanover: Brandeis University Press.
Casey, E. S. (1987). *Remembering: A phenomenological study.* Bloomington: Indiana University Press.
Cesarani, D. (1996). Great Britain. In D. Wyman (Ed.), *The world reacts to the holocaust* (pp. 599–641). Baltimore: The Johns Hopkins University Press.
Cholowski, S. (1980). *Soldiers from the ghetto.* San Diego, CA: A. S. Barnes.
Cobb, J. (1975). *Christ in a pluralistic age.* Philadelphia: Westminster.
Cohen, J. (1982). *The friars and the Jews: The evolution of medieval anti-Judaism.* Ithaca, NY: Cornell University Press.
Collingwood, R. G. (1922/1965) Are history and science different kinds of knowledge? In W. Debbins (Ed.), *Essays in the philosophy of history by R. G. Collingwood* (pp. 23–33). Austin: The University of Texas Press.
Collingwood, R. G. (1924/1925, 1965). The nature and aims of a philosophy of history. In W. Debbins (Ed.), *Essays in the philosophy of history by R. G. Collingwood* (pp. 34–56). Austin: The University of Texas Press.
Collingwood, R. G. (1946). *The idea of history.* Oxford: Clarendon.
Columbo, F. (1996). Introduction. In S. Zuccotti, *The Italians and the holocaust: Persecution, rescue and survival* (pp. ix–xvii). Lincoln: The University of Nebraska Press.
Cooper, A. (1990). Changes in psychoanalytic ideas: Transference interpretation. In A. Essman (Ed.), *Essential papers on transference* (pp. 511–528). New York: New York University Press.
Cornwell, J. (1999). *Hitler's Pope: The secret history of Pope Pius XII.* New York: Viking.
Crowley, R. (1988). Human reactions of analysts to patients. In B. Wolstein (Ed.), *Essential papers on countertransference* (pp. 84–90). New York: New York University Press.
Danieli, Y. (1989). Mourning in survivors and children of survivors of the Nazi holocaust: The role of group and community modalities. In D. Dietrich & P. Shabad (Eds.), *The problem of loss and mourning: Psychoanalytic perspectives* (pp. 427–460). Madison, CT: International Universities Press.
Dante, A. (1307/1982). *The divine comedy of Dante Alighieri, inferno* (A. Mandelbaum, Trans.). New York: Bantam.
Davis, B. (1996). *Teaching mathematics: Toward a sound alternative.* New York: Garland.
Dawidowicz, L. (1975/1986). *The war against the Jews.* New York: Holt Reinhart.
Dawidowicz, L. (1982). *On equal terms: Jews in America 1881–1981.* New York: Winston.
de Castell, S. (1996). On finding one's place in the text: Literacy as a technology of self-formation. *Journal of Curriculum Theorizing: An Interdisciplinary Journal of Curriculum Studies, 12*(4), 27–31.
de Chardin, P. T. (1964). *The future of man.* New York: Harper & Row.
de Lange, N. (1991). The origins of anti-Semitism: Ancient evidence and modern interpretation. In S. L. Gilman & S. T. Katz (Eds.), *Anti-Semitism in times of crisis* (pp. 21–37). New York: New York University Press.
Delbo, C. (1990). *Days and memory* (R. Lamont, Trans.). Vermont: The Marlboro Press.
Derrida, J. (1991). Psyche: Inventions of the other. In Peggy Kamuf (Ed.). (P. Kamuf, Trans.) *A Derrida reader: Between the blinds* (pp. 200–220). New York: Columbia University Press.
Derrida, J. (1996). *Archive fever: A Freudian impression* (E. Prenowitz, Trans.) Chicago: The University of Chicago Press.
Dewey, J. (1909/1975). *Moral principles in education.* Carbondale: Southern Illinois University Press.

The diary of Anne Frank. (1989). The critical edition, D. Barnouw & G. Van Der Stroom (Eds.; A. J. Poermans & B. M. Mooyart, Trans.). New York: Doubleday.

The diary of Eva Heyman: Child of the Holocaust (1988). (M. M. Kohn, Trans.). New York: Yad Vashem.

Dilthey, W. (1907–1910/1962). *Pattern and Meaning in History: Thoughts on history and society.* New York: Harper Torch.

Dinnerstein, L. (1994). *Antisemitism in America.* New York: Oxford University Press.

Dobroszycki, L. (1984). *The chronicle of the Lodz ghetto, 1941–1944* (R. Lourie & J. Neugroshel, Trans.). New Haven, CT: Yale University Press.

Docherty, T. (1996). *Alterities: Criticism, history, representation.* Oxford: Clarendon.

Doll, M. A. (2000). *Like letters in running water: A mythopoetics of curriculum.* Mahwah: NJ: Lawrence Erlbaum Associates.

Donat, A. (1979). *The death camp treblinka.* New York: Holocaust Library.

Dwork, D. (1991). *Children with a star: Jewish youth in Nazi Europe.* New Haven, CT: Yale University Press.

Eagelton, T. (1967). *Marxism and literary criticism.* Berkeley: University of California Press.

Edgerton, S. (1996). *Translating the curriculum: Multiculturalism and cultural studies.* New York: Routledge.

Eagan, K. (1997). *The educated mind: How cognitive tools shape understanding.* Chicago: Chicago University Press.

Eisen, G. (1988). *Children and play in the holocaust.* Cambridge, MA: University of Massachusetts Press.

Ellsworth, E. (1997). *Teaching positions: Difference, pedagogy and the power of the holocaust.* New York: Teachers College Press.

Erikson, E. (1962). *Young man Luther: A study in psychoanalysis and history.* New York: Norton.

Erikson, E. (1976). The legend of Hitler's childhood. In G. Kren & L. Rappoport (Eds.), *Varieties of psychohistory* (pp. 99–110). New York: Springer.

Fairbairn, R. (1941/1954). A revised psychopathology of the psychoses and psychoneuroses. In R. Fairbairn, *An object-relations theory of the personality* (pp. 28–58). New York: Basic.

Fairbairn, R. (1943/1954). The repression and the return of bad objects (with special reference to the 'war neuroses'). In R. Fairbairn, *An object-relations theory of the personality* (pp. 59–81). New York: Basic.

Fairbairn, R. (1944/1954). Endopsychic structure considered in terms of object-relationships. In R. Fairbairn, *An object-relations theory of the personality* (pp. 82–132). New York: Basic.

Fairbairn, R. (1946/ 1954). Object-relationships and dynamic structures. In R. Fairbairn, *An object-relations theory of the personality* (pp. 137–151). New York: Basic.

Fasching, D. J. (1993). *The ethical challenge of Auschwitz and Hiroshima: Apocalypse or Utopia?* Albany: State University of New York Press.

Feingold, H. (1995). *Bearing witness: How America and its Jews responded to the holocaust.* New York: Syracuse University Press.

Felman, S., & Laub, D. (1992). *Testimony: Crises of witnessing in literature, psychoanalysis and history.* New York: Routledge.

Ficowski, J. (1977). Introduction. In B. Schulz's *The street of crocodiles* (pp. 13–24). New York: Penguin.

Fink, I. (1997). *Traces: Stories* (P. Boehm & F. Prose Trans.). New York: Henry Holt.

Fletcher, J. (1999). Introduction: Psychonanalysis and the question of the other (pp. 1–51). In *Jean Laplanche's essays on otherness* (pp. 1–51). New York: Routledge.

Foucault, M. (1966/1994). *The order of things: An archaeology of the human sciences.* New York: Vintage.

Foucault, M. (1979). *Discipline and punish: The birth of the prison* (A. Sheridan, Trans.). New York: Vintage.

Fourier, C. (1808/1996a). First part: Exposition of some branches of the general destinies. In G. Stedman & I. Patterson (Eds.), *The theory of the four movements by Charles Fourier* (pp. 33–101). New York: Cambridge University Press.

Fourier, C. (1808/1996b). Second part: Description of the various branches of the private or domestic destinies. In G. Stedman & I. Patterson (Eds.), *The theory of the four movements by Charles Fourier* (pp. 107–181). New York: Cambridge University Press.

Fourier, C. (1808/1996c). The theory of the four movements and of the general destinies. In G. Stedman & I. Patterson (Eds.), *The theory of the four movements by Charles Fourier* (pp. 1–29). New York: Cambridge University Press.

Fourier, C. (1808/1996d). Third part: Confirmation derived from the inadequacy of the inexact sciences to deal with all the problems that the civilized mechanism presents. In G. Stedman & I. Patterson (Eds.), *The theory of the four movements by Charles Fourier* (pp. 191–310). New York: Cambridge University Press.

Freire, P. (1990a) My respect for the soul of culture. In B. Ball, J. Gauenta & J. Peters (Eds.), *We make the road by walking: Conversations on education and social change Myles Horton and Paulo Freire* (pp. 131–137). Philadelphia: Temple University Press.

Freire, P. (1990b). We make the road by walking. In B. Ball, J., Gauenta & J. Peters (Eds.), *We make the road by walking: Conversations on education and social change Myles Horton and Paulo Freire* (pp. 3–8). Philadelphia: Temple University Press.

Freud, A. (1966/1993). *The ego and the mechanisms of defense*. Connecticut: International Universities Press.

Freud, S. (1957/1995). *The standard edition of the complete psychological works of Sigmund Freud* (J. Strachey, Ed. and Trans). In collaboration with Anna Freud. Assisted by A. Strachey & A. Tyson, 24 Vols. London: Hogarth Press and Institute for Psychoanalysis.

Freud, S. (1893–1899). The neuro-psychoses of defense. *Standard Edition, 3* (pp. 45–61). London: Hogarth.

Freud, S. (1899/1989). Screen memories. In P. Gay (Ed.), *The Freud Reader* (pp. 117–128). New York: Norton.

Freud, S. (1894–1895). On the grounds for detaching a particular syndrome from neaurasthenia under the description 'anxiety neurosis.' *Standard Edition, 3* (pp. 90–116). London: Hogarth.

Freud, S. (1900a). The interpretation of dreams (first part). *Standard Edition, 4* (pp. 10–327). London: Hogarth.

Freud, S. (1900b). The interpretation of dreams (second part). *Standard Edition, 5* (pp. 340–601). London: Hogarth.

Freud, S. (1909–1910). Five lectures on psycho-analysis. *Standard Edition, 11* (pp. 9–55). London: Hogarth.

Freud, S. (1911–1913). Remembering, repeating and working-through (Further recommendations on the techniques of psycho-analysis II). *Standard Edition, 12* (pp. 145–156). London: Hogarth.

Freud, S. (1914–1916). Instincts and their vicissitudes. *Standard Edition, 14* (pp. 117–140). London: Hogarth.

Freud, S. (1915). The unconscious. *Standard Edition, 14* (pp. 166–204). London: Hogarth.

Freud, S. (1920–1922). Group psychology and the analysis of the ego. *Standard Edition, 18* (pp. 69–143). London: Hogarth.

Freud, S. (1920/1989). Beyond the pleasure principle. In P. Gay (Ed.), *The Freud Reader* (pp. 594–625). New York: Norton.

Freud, S. (1925/1989). Negation. In P. Gay (Ed.), *The Freud Reader* (pp. 666–669). New York: Norton.

Freud, S. (1930/1961). *Civilizations and its discontents* (J. Strachey, Trans.). New York: Norton.

Freud, S. (1932–1936a). New introductory lectures on psycho-analysis and other works: Revision of the theory of dreams. *Standard Edition, 22* (pp. 7–30). London: Hogarth.

Freud, S. (1932–1936b). The dissection of the psychical personality. *Standard Edition, 22* (pp. 57–80). London: Hogarth.

Freud, S. (1936/1963). *The problem of anxiety* (H. A. Bunker, Trans.). New York: Norton.

Freud, S. (1937/1991). Analysis terminable and interminable. In J. Sandler (Ed.), *On Freud's Analysis terminable and interminable* (pp. 3–40). New Haven, CT: Yale University Press.

Freud, S. (1937–1939). Constructions in analysis. *Standard Edition, 23* (pp. 257–269). London: Hogarth.

Freud, S. (1959). *Inhibitions, symptoms and anxiety* (A. Strachey, Trans.). New York: Norton.

Freud, S. (1966). *Introductory lectures on pyscho-analysis* (J. Strachey, Trans.). New York: Norton.

Freud, S. (1966/1990). The dynamics of transference. In A. Essman (Ed.), *Essential papers on transference* (pp. 28–36). New York: New York University Press.

Friedländer, S. (1978). *History and psychoanalysis: An inquiry into the possibilities and limits of psychohistory* (S. Suleiman, Trans.). New York: Homes & Meier.

Friedländer, S. (1993). *Memory, history, and the extermination of the Jews of Europe.* Bloomington: Indiana University Press.

Friedländer, S. (1997). *Nazi Germany and the Jews volume 1: The years of persecution, 1933–1939.* New York: HarperCollins.

Fromm, E. (1941/1969). *Escape from freedom.* New York: Avon.

Fromm, E. (1977). Afterward. In *George Orwell's 1984* (pp. 257–267). New York: Harcourt Brace Jovanovich.

Funkenstein, A. (1993). *Perceptions of Jewish history.* Berkeley: University of California Press.

Gay, P. (1985). *Freud for historians.* New York: Oxford University Press.

Gay, P. (1989). Introduction. In P. Gay (Ed.), *The Freud reader* (pp. xiii–xxix). New York: Norton.

Gay, P. (1989). Sigmund Freud: A chronology. In P. Gay (Ed.), *The Freud Reader* (pp. xxxi–xlvii). New York: Norton.

Gay, P. (1998). *My German question: Growing up in Nazi Berlin.* New Haven, CT: Yale University Press.

Gerber, D. (1986). Anti-Semitism and Jewish–Gentile relations in American. In D. Gerber (Ed.), *Anti-Semitism in American history* (pp. 3-54). Chicago: University of Chicago Press.

Geve, T. (1987). *Guns and barbed wire: A child survives the Holocaust.* Chicago: Academy Chicago.

Gilbert, J. (1998). Reading colorblindness: Negation as an engagement with social difference. *Journal of Curriculum Theorizing, 14*(2), 29–34.

Gilbert, M. (1985). *The Holocaust: A history of the Jews of Europe during the second world war.* New York: Henry Holt.

Gill, M. (1988). The interpersonal paradigm and the degree of the therapist's involvement. In B. Wolstein (Ed.), *Essential papers on countertransference* (pp. 304–338). New York: New York University Press.

Gilman, C. P. (1915/1979). *Herland.* New York: Pantheon.

Gilman, S. (1986). *Jewish self-hatred: Anti-semitism and the hidden language of the Jews.* Baltimore, MD: The Johns Hopkins University Press.

Gilman, S. (1995). *Jews in today's German culture.* Bloomington: Indiana University Press.

Goldhagen, D. (1997). *Hitler's willing executioners: Ordinary Germans and the holocaust.* New York: Vintage.

Goodwin, B., & Taylor, K. (1982). *The politics of utopia: A study in theory and practice.* London: Hutchinson.

Grass, G. (1961). *Cat and mouse* (R. Manheim, Trans.). New York: Harcourt Brace.

Grass, G. (1963/1986). *Dog years* (R. Manheim, Trans.). New York: Fawcett Crest.

Grass, G. (1964/1991). *The tin drum* (R. Manheim, Trans.). New York: Vintage.

Grass, G. (1985). *On writing and politics 1967–1983* (R. Manheim, Trans.) New York: Harcourt Brace Jovanovich.

Green, A. (1986). *On private madness.* London: Hogarth.

Green, A. (1994). Prologue: The psycho-analytic reading of tragedy. In M. Ellman (Ed.), *Psychoanalytic literary criticism* (pp. 39–75). New York: Longman.

Greenberg, J. R., & Mitchell, S. (1983). *Object relations in psychoanalytic theory.* Cambridge, MA: Harvard University Press.

Greene, M. (1995). *Releasing the imagination: Essays on education, the arts and social change.* San Francisco: Jossey-Bass.

Greenson, R. (1990). The working alliance and the transference neurosis. In A. Essman (Ed.), *Essential papers on transference* (pp. 150–171). New York: New York University Press.

Griffin, D. (1973). *A process christology.* Philadelphia: Westminster.

Griffin, S. (1992). *A chorus of stones: The private life of war.* New York: Doubleday.

Grossman, L. (1990). *Between history and literature.* Cambridge: Harvard University Press.

Grotstein, J. (1994). Notes on Fairbairn's metapsychology. In J. Grostein & D. Rinsley (Eds.), *Fairbairn and the origins of object relations* (pp. 112–148). London: Guildford.

Grotstein, J., & Rinsley, D. (1994). Editors' introduction. In J. Grotstein & J. Rinsely (Eds.), *Fairbairn and the origins of object relations* (pp. 3–16). London: Guilford.

Grubrich-Simitis, I. (1996). *Back to Freud's texts: Making silent documents speak* (P. Slotkin, Trans.). New Haven, CT: Yale University Press.

Grumet, M. (1988). *Bitter milk: Women and teaching.* Amherst: The University of Massachusetts Press.

Grumet, M. (1995). The curriculum: What are the basics, and are we teaching them? In J. L. Kincheloe & S. R. Steinberg (Eds.), *Thirteen questions: Reframing education's conversation* (pp. 15–21). New York: Peter Lang.

Grumet, M. (1999). Word worlds: The literary reference for curriculum criticism. In W. F. Pinar (Ed.), *Contemporary curriculum discourse: Twenty years of JCT* (pp. 233–245). New York: Peter Lang.

Gur-Ze'ev, I. (1998). Toward a nonrepressive critical pedagogy. In *Educational Theory, 48*(4), 463–486.

Gutman, I. (1989). *The Jews of Warsaw 1939-1943. Ghetto, underground revolt* (I. Friedman, Trans.). Bloomington: Indiana University Press.

Halbwachs, M. (1992). *On collective memory.* Chigaco: The University of Chicago Press.

Hampl, P. (1997). Memory and imagination. In I. Railu & G. Grewell (Eds.), *Transitions: Lives in America* (pp. 58–69). Mountain View, CA: Mayfield.

Hartmann, G. (1986). Introduction 1985. In G. Hartman (Ed.), *Bitburg in moral and political perspective* (pp. 1–12). Bloomington: Indiana University Press.

Hartmann, G. (1996). *The longest shadow in the aftermath of the holocaust.* Bloomington: Indiana University Press.

Hass, A. (1996). *In the shadow of the Holocaust: The second generation.* New York: Cambridge University Press.

Hegel, G. W. F. (1837/1987). *Reason in history: A general introduction to the philosophy of history* (R. S. Hartman, Trans.). New York: Macmillan.

Heger, H. (1980). *The men with the pink triangle: The true life and death story of homosexuals in the nazi death camps* (D. Fernbach, Trans.). New York: Alyson.

Hegi, U. (1994). *Stones from the river.* New York: Scribner's.

Hegi, U. (1997). *Tearing the silence: Being German in America.* New York: Simon & Schuster.

Heidegger, M. (1981). Only a God can save us: The Spiegel interview (1966) with Martin Heidegger. In T. Sheehan (Ed.), *Heidegger the man and the thinker* (pp. 45–76). Chicago: Precedent.

Heimannsberg, B., & Schmidt, C. (1993). Psychological symptoms of the nazi heritage: Introduction to the German edition. In B. Heimmansberg & C. Schmidt (Eds.), *The collective silence: German identity and the legacy of shame* (pp. 3–10). (C. O. Hanis & G. Wheeler, Trans.). San Francisco: Jossey-Bass.

Hell, J. (1997). *Post-Fascist fantasies: Psychoanalysis, history, and literature of East Germany.* Durham: Duke University Press.

Herf, J. (1984). *Reactionary modernism: Technology, culture, and politics in Weimar and the Third Reich.* New York: Cambridge University Press.

Herf, J. (1997). *Divided memory: The nazi past in the two Germanys.* Cambridge, MA: Harvard University Press.

Hermand, J. (1992). *Old dreams of a new reich: Völkisch utopias and national socialism* (P. Levesque & Soldovieri, Trans.). Bloomington: Indiana University Press.

Heydrecker, J. (1990). *The Warsaw ghetto.* London: I. B. Tauris.

Heyek, F. A. (1994). *The road to serfdom.* Chicago: University of Chicago Press.

Hick, J. (1978). *Evil and the god of love.* San Francisco: Harper & Row.

Hier, M. (1999). Wire reports. New Orleans, LA: *The Times Picayune* (pp. A1–A6).

Higgs, D. (1978). Nostalgia, utopia and the French revolution. In M. Allain (Ed.), *France and North America: Utopias and utopians* (pp. 25–32). Lafayette, LA: The Center for Louisiana Studies.

Hilberg, R. (1961/1985). *The destruction of the European Jews volume one, revised and definitive edition.* New York: Holms and Meier.

Hilberg, R. (1986). Bitburg as symbol. In G. Hartman (Ed.), *Bitburg in moral and political perspective* (pp. 15–26). Bloomington: Indiana University Press.

Hilberg, R. (1992). *Perpetrators, victims, bystanders: The Jewish catastrophe 1933–1945.* New York: Harper Perennial.
Hilberg, R. (1996). *The politics of memory: The journey of a Holocaust historian.* Chicago: Ivan R. Dee.
Hillesum, E. (1983). *An interrupted life: The diaries of Etty Hillesum 1941–1943.* New York: Washington Square Press.
Hillman, J. (1996). *The soul's code: In search of character and calling.* New York: Random House.
Hitler, A. (1923). *Mein Kampf* (E. T. S. Dugas, Trans.). New York: Houghton Mifflin.
Hoffman, S. (1981). Forward. In M. Marrus & R Paxton, *Vichy France and the Jews* (pp. ix–xii). California: Stanford University Press.
Holliday, L. (1995). *Children in the Holocaust and world war II: Their secret diaries.* New York: Pocket Books.
Holocaust Museum of Washington Photoarchives (1997). [Online]. www.ushmm.org/research/photoarc.html.
Hopfe, L. (1991). *Religions of the world.* New York: Macmillan.
Horkheimer, M. (1950). Preface. In Adorno et al. (Eds.), *The authoritarian personality* (pp. ix–xii). New York: Harper & Brothers.
Horton, M. (1990). Is it possible just to teach biology? In B. Bell, J. Gaventh & J. Peters (Eds.), *We make the road by walking: Conversations on education and social change, Myles Horton and Paulo Freire* (pp. 102–108). Philadelphia: Temple University Press.
Horowitz, S. (1992). *Voicing the void: Muteness and memory in holocaust fiction.* New York: State University of New York Press.
Horowitz, S. (1998). Women in Holocaust literature: Engendering trauma memory. In D. Ofer & L. Weitzman (Eds.), *Women in the holocaust* (pp. 364–377). New Haven, CT: Yale University Press.
Iggers, G. (1997). *Historiography in the twentieth century: From scientific objectivity to the postmodern challenge.* Hanover, NH: Wesleyan University Press.
Irwin-Zarecka, I. (1994). *Frames of remembrance: The dynamics of collective memory.* New Brunswick: NJ: Transaction.
Iser, W. (1978). *The act of reading: A theory of aesthetic response.* Baltimore, MD: The Johns Hopkins University Press.
Iser, W. (1989). *Prospecting: From reader response to literary anthropology.* Baltimore: The Johns Hopkins University Press.
Isherwood, C. (1959). *Berlin stories.* New York: A New Directions Paper Book.
Jagodzinski, J. (1997). *Postmodern dilemmas: Outrageous essays in art & and art education.* Mahwah, NJ: Lawrence Erlbaum Associates.
James, W. (1890/1950). *The principles of psychology volume one.* New York: Dover.
Jardine, D. (1995). The profession needs new blood. *The Journal of Curriculum Theorizing: An Interdisciplinary Journal of Curriculum Studies, 11*(3), 105–130.
Kafka, F. (1916/1972). *The metamorphosis* (S. Corngold, Trans.). New York: Bantam.
Kamenetsky, C. (1984). *Children's literature in Hitler's Germany.* Athens: Ohio University Press.
Kaplan, M. (1998). *Between dignity and despair: Jewish life in nazi* Germany. New York: Oxford University Press.
Katz, M. (1970). *Poland's ghettos.* New York: Twayne.
Keele, F. (1988). *Understanding Günter Grass.* Charleston: University of South Carolina Press.
Kellner, H. (1989). *Language and historical representation: Getting the story crooked.* Madison: University of Wisconsin Press.
Kempster, N. & Chen, E. (1999, June). NATO must be a 'living buffer,' Wiesel says (pp. A–22). New Orleans, LA: *The Times Picayune.*
Kelman, H. (1976). Violence without moral restraint: Reflections on the dehumanization of victims and victimizers. In G. Kren & L. Rapporport (Eds.), *Varieties of psychohistory* (pp. 282–314). New York: Springer.
Kernberg, O. (1992). *Aggression in personality disorders and perversions.* New Haven, CT: Yale University Press.
Kernberg, O. (1998). Foreword. In J. Sandler & A.M. Sandler, *Internal objects revisited* (pp. xv–xx). Madison, CT: International Universities Press.

Kestenberg, J. (1989). Coping with losses and survival. In D. Dietrich & P. Shabad (Eds.), *The problem of loss and mourning: Psychoanalytic perspectives* (pp. 381–403). Madison, CT: International Universities Press.

Kestenberg, J. (1990). Survivor-parents and their children. In M. Bergman & M. Jucovy (Eds.), *Generations of the Holocaust* (pp. 83–101). New York: Columbia University Press.

Kestenberg, J., & Kestenberg, M. (1990). The background of the study. In M. Bergman & M. Jucovy (Eds.), *Generations of the Holocaust* (pp. 33–46). New York: Columbia University Press.

Klarsfeld, S. (1996). *French children of the Holocaust: A memorial.* New York: New York University Press.

Klein, M. (1940/1975). Mourning and its relation to manic-depressive states. In M. Klein, *Love, guilt and reparation and other works* (pp. 344–369). New York: Delacourte Press/Seymore Lawrence.

Klein, M. (1946/1984). Notes on some schizoid mechanisms. In M. Klein, *Envy and gratitude and other works 1946–1963* (pp. 1–24). New York: The Free Press.

Klein, M. (1950/1975). On the criteria for the termination of a psycho-analysis. In M. Klein, *Envy and gratitude and other works 1946–1963* (pp. 43–47). New York: The Free Press.

Kogan, E. (1975). *The theory and practice of hell: The German concentration camps and the system behind them.* Berkeley: The University of California Press.

Kogan, I. (1995). *The cry of mute children: A psychoanalytic perspective of the second generation of the Holocaust.* New York: Free Association Books.

Kohut, H. (1996a). The question of drive psychology and some thoughts on technique. In P. Toplin & M. Toplin (Eds.), *Heinz Kohut: The Chicago Institute Lectures* (pp. 211–226). Hillsdale, NJ: The Analytic Press.

Kohut, H. (1996b). Varieties of aggression, possibilities of self. In P. Toplin & M. Toplin (Eds.), *Heinz Kohut: The Chicago Institute Lectures.* Hillsdale, NJ: The Analytic Press.

Kren, G., & Rappoport, L. (1976). Cleo and psyche. In G. Kren & L. Rappoport (Eds.), *Varieties of psychohistory* (pp. 63–77). New York: Springer.

Krichevsky, L. (1999, July). Prominent Moscow Jew stabbed: Attacker threatens to "kill all of you" (p. 24). In *The Jewish News.*

Kritzman, L. (1995). Critical reflections: Self portraiture and the representation of Jewish identity. In L. Kritzman (Ed.), *Auschwitz and after: Race, culture, and 'the Jewish question'* (pp. 88–117). New York: Routledge.

Kumar, K. (1987). *Utopia and anti-utopia in modern times.* New York: Blackwell.

Kurtzweil, E. (1988). *The Freudians: A comparative perspective.* New Brunswick, NJ: Transaction.

Kushner, T. (1984). *The Holocaust and the liberal imagination: A social and cultural history.* New York: Oxford University Press.

LaCapra, D. (1985). *History and criticism.* Ithaca, NY: Cornell University Press.

LaCapra, D. (1994). *Representing the Holocaust: History, theory, trauma.* Ithaca, NY: Cornell University Press.

Lang, B. (1990). *Act and idea in the nazi genocide.* Chicago: The University of Chicago Press.

Langbein, H. (1996). *Against all hope: Resistance in the Nazi concentration camps, 1938–1945* (H. Zohn, Trans.). New York: Continuum.

Langer, L. (1975). *The Holocaust and the literary imagination.* New Haven, CT: Yale University Press.

Langer, L. (1991). *Holocaust testimonies: The ruins of memory.* New Haven, CT: Yale University Press.

Langer, L. (1995). *Admitting the Holocaust: Collected essays.* New York: Oxford University Press.

Langer, L. (1998). *Preempting the Holocaust.* New Haven, CT: Yale University Press.

Langer, S. (1953). *Feeling and form: A theory of art development from philosophy in a new key.* New York: Scribner's.

Langmuir, G. I. (1990). *History, religion, and anti-semitism.* Berkeley: University of California Press.

Laplanche, J., & Pontalis, J.-B. (1973). *The language of psychoanalysis* (D. Nicholson-Smith, Trans.). New York: Norton.

Laplanche, J. (1985). *Life and death in psychoanalysis.* Baltimore: The Johns Hopkins University Press.

Laplanche, J. (1999). *Essays on otherness.* New York: Routledge.

Laquer, W. (1981). *The terrible secret: Supression and the truth about Hitler's 'final solution.'* Boston: Little, Brown.

Laska, V. (1993). Women in the resistance and in the holocaust. In C. Rittner & J. Roth (Eds.), *Women and the Holocaust: Different voices* (pp. 250–269). St. Paul: MN: Paragon.

Laub, D., & Auerhann, N. (1984). Reverberations of genocide: Its expression in the conscious and unconsciousness of post-holocaust generations. In S. Luel & P. Marcus (Eds.), *Psychoanalytic reflections on the Holocaust: Selected essays* (pp. 151–167). New York: KYAV.

Lawton, H. (1988). *The psychohistorian's handbook.* New York: The Psychohistory Press.

Lazar, M. (1991). The lamb and the scapegoat: The dehumanization of the Jews in medieval propaganda imagery. In S. Gilman & S. Katz (Eds.), *Anti-semitism in times of crisis* (pp. 38–80). New York: New York University Press.

Le Chene, E. (1971). *Mauthausen—The history of a death camp.* London: Methuen.

LeGoff, J. (1992). *History and memory* (S. Randall & E. Claman, Trans.). New York: Columbia University Press.

Lerner, E. (1996). American anti-semitism and the Jewish question. In D. Gerber (Ed.), *Anti-semitism in American history* (pp. 57–78). Chicago: The University of Chicago Press.

Lessing, D. (1981). *Briefing for a descent into hell.* New York: Vintage.

Levi, P. (1996). *Survival in Auschwitz: The nazi assault on humanity.* New York: Simon & Schuster.

Levinas, E. (1969). *Totality and infinity: An essay on exteriority* (A. Lingis, Trans.). Pittsburgh: Duquesne University Press.

Levinas, E. (1995). Difficult freedom. In L. Kritzman (Ed.), *Auschwitz and after: Race, culture, and the "Jewish question" in France* (pp. 180–200). New York: Routledge.

Levinas, E. (1996a). Is ontology fundamental? In A. T. Peperzak, S. Critchley & R. Bernasconi (Eds.), *Emmanuel Levinas: Basic Philosophical Writings* (pp. 1–10). Bloomington: Indiana University Press.

Levinas, E. (1996b). Transcendence and Height. In A. T. Peperzak, S. Crithchley & R. Bernasconi (Eds.), *Emmanual Levinas: Basic Philosophical Writings* (pp. 11–32). Bloomington: Indiana University Press.

Levitas, R. (1990). *The concept of utopia.* New York: Syracuse University Press.

Lifton, B. J. (1988). *The king of children. A biography of Janusz Korczak.* New York: Farrar & Strauss.

Lifton, R. J. (1986). *The nazi doctors: Medical killing and the psychology of genocide.* New York: Basic.

Linden, R. (1993). *Making stories, making selves: Feminist reflections on the Holocaust.* Columbus: Ohio State University Press.

Lipstadt, D. (1993). *Denying the Holocaust: The growing assault on truth and memory.* New York: The Free Press.

Lister, M. (1995). Introductory essay. In M. Lister (Ed.), *The photographic image in digital culture* (pp. 1–26). New York: Routledge.

Little, M. (1981). *Transference neurosis and transference psychosis: Toward basic unity.* New York: Aronson.

Loewenberg, P. (1983). *Decoding the past: The psychohistorical approach.* New York: Knopf.

Loewenberg, P. (1995). *Fantasy and reality in history.* New York: Oxford University Press.

Löwith, K. (1995). *Martin Heidegger and European Nihilism* (Trans. G. Steiner). New York: Columbia University Press.

Lukas, R. (1994). *Did the children cry: Hitler's war against Jewish and Polish children, 1939–1945.* New York: Hippocrene.

Luther, M. (1523/1962). That Jesus Christ was born a Jew, 1523. In W. I. Brandt (Ed. & Trans.), *Luther's work volume 45. The Christian in Society II* (pp. 195–230). Philadelphia: Muhlenberg.

Luther, M. (1538/1971). Against the sabbatarians: Letter to a good friend, 1538. In F. Sherman (Ed.). (M. Bertram, Trans.), *Luther's works volume 47. The Christian in society IV* (pp. 57–98). Philadelphia: Fortress.

Luther, M. (1543/1971). On the Jews and their lies. In F. Sherman (Ed.), (M. Bertram, Trans.), *Luther's works volume 47. The Christian in Society IV* (pp. 121–307). Philadelphia: Fortress.

Macdonald, J. (1995). Theory, practice and the hermeneutic circle. In B. J. Macdonald (Ed.), *Theory as a prayerful act: The collected essays of James B. Macdonald* (pp. 173–186). New York: Peter Lang.

MacKenzie, R. J. (1988). The transference phenomenon in psychoanalytic therapy. In B. Wolstein (Ed.), *Essential papers on* countertransference (pp. 36–50). New York: New York University Press.

Maier, C. (1988). *The unmasterable past: History, Holocaust and German national identity.* Cambridge, MA: Harvard University Press.

Mann, T. (1948/1992). *Doctor Faustus: The life of the German composer* (H. T. Lowe-Porter, Trans.). New York: Vintage.

Mannoni, M. (1999). *Separation and creativity: Refinding the lost language of childhood* (S. Fairfield, Trans.). New York: The Other Press.

Manuel, F. E., & Manuel, F. P. (1979). *Utopian thought in the western world.* Cambridge: Harvard University Press.

Marcuse, H. (1976). No title. In S. Wiesenthal, *The sunflower with a symposium* (p. 169). New York: Schocken.

Markovits, A., & Reich, S. (1997). *The German predicament: Memory and politics in the new Europe.* Ithaca, NY: Cornell University Press.

Markovits, S., & Noveck, S. (1996). West Germany. In D. Wyman (Ed.), *The world reacts to the Holocaust* (pp. 391–446). Baltimore: The Johns Hopkins University Press.

Marks, B. (1975). *Uprising in the Warsaw ghetto.* New York: Schocken.

Marrus, M. (1987). *The Holocaust in history.* Hanover: University Press of New England.

Marrus, R., & Paxton, R. (1981/1995). *Vichy France and the Jews.* California: Stanford University Press.

Marty, M. E. (1976). No title. In Simon Wiesenthal, *The sunflower with a symposium* (pp. 170–175). New York: Schocken.

Marwick, A. (1984). *The nature of history.* New York: Garland.

Maser, W. (1974). *Hitler's letters and notes* (A. Pomerans, Trans.). New York: Harper & Row.

Marx, K., & Engels, F. (1844/1987). *Economic and philosophic manuscripts of 1844 and the communist manifesto* (M. Milligan, Trans.) New York: Prometheus.

Marx, K., & Engels, F. (1845–1846/1978) The German ideology part one. In R. C. Tucker (Ed.), *The Marx-Engels reader* (pp. 146–200). New York: Norton.

Marx, K. (1846/1978). Society and economy in history. In R. C. Tucker (Ed.), *The Marx-Engels Reader* (pp. 136–142). New York: Norton.

Mead, G. H. (1913/1964). The social self. In A. Reck (Ed.), *Selected writings of George Herbert Mead* (pp.142–149). Chicago: University of Chicago Press.

Memmi, A. (1966). *The liberation of the Jew* (J. Hyuan, Trans.). New York: Orion.

Milton, S. (1993). Women and the holocaust: The case of German and German-Jewish women. In C. Rittner & J. Roth (Eds.), *Women and the Holocaust: Different voices* (pp. 213–249). St. Paul, MN: Paragon.

Mink, L. O. (1987). *Historical understanding.* Ithaca, NY: Cornell University Press.

Mitchell, S. (1994). The origin and nature of the "object" in the theories of Melanie Klein and Fairbairn. In J. Grotstein & D. Rinsely (Eds.), *Fairbairn and the origins of object relations* (pp. 66–87). London: Guilford.

Mitchell, S. (1998). Letting the paradox teach us. In J. G. Teichholz & D. Kriegman (Eds.), *Trauma, repetition and affect regulation: The work of Paul Russell* (pp. 49–58). New York: The Other Press.

Mitchell, W. J. T. (1994). *Picture theory: Essays on verbal and visual representation.* Chicago: University of Chicago Press.

Mitscherlich-Nielsen, M. (1989). The inability to mourn—today. In D. Dietrich & P. Shabad (Eds.), *The problem of loss and mourning: Psychoanalytic perspectives* (pp. 405–426). Madison, CT: International Universities Press.

Mommsen, H. (1966). *Officialdom in the third reich.* Stuttgart: Germany.

Mommsen, H. (1997). Conditions for carrying out the holocaust: Comments on Daniel Goldhagen's book. In F. Little (Ed.), *Hyping the Holocaust: Scholars answer Goldhagen* (pp. 31–43). Merion Station, PA: Merion Westfield.

Moore, A. (1978). The use and abuse of utopia. In M. Allain (Ed.), *France and North America: Utopias and Utopians* (pp. 1–10). Lafayette, LA: The Center for Louisiana Studies.

Morrison, T. (1998). *Paradise*. New York: Knopf.

Moses, R. (1995). Introduction. In R. Moses (Ed.), *Persistent shadows of the Holocaust: The meaning to those not directly affected* (pp. xv–xxii). Madison, CT: International Universities Press.

Müller, K. (1980). Introduction. In H. Heger, *The men with the pink triangle: The true life and death story of homosexuals in the nazi death camps* (pp. 7–16), (D. Fernbach, Trans.) New York: Alyson.

Munro, P. (1997). *Dislocating the family plot: Engendering curriculum history.* Paper presented at the meeting of the American Educational Research Association. Chicago.

Munro, P. (1998). *Subject to fiction: Women teacher's life history narratives and the cultural politics of resistance.* Philadelphia: Open University Press.

Musil, R. (1990/1914). Commentary on a metapsychics In B. Pike & D. S. Luft (Eds. and Trans.), *Robert Musil. Precision and soul: Essays and addresses* (pp. 54–58). Chicago: University of Chicago Press.

Nasio, J. D. (1998). The causes of hysteria. In J. Feher Gurewich & S. Fairfield (Eds.), *Juan-David Nasio: Hysteria from Freud to Lacan: The splendid child of psychoanalysis* (pp. 13–31). New York: The Other Press.

Nicolls, W. (1993). *Christian antisemitism. A history of hate.* New Jersey: Jason Armstrong.

Nir, Y. (1989). *The lost childhood.* New York: Harcourt Brace.

Nochlin, L. (1995). Introduction: Starting with the self: Jewish identity and its representation. In L. Nochlin & T. Garb (Eds.), *The Jew in the text: Modernity and the construction of identity* (pp. 1–19). London: Thames & Hudson.

Noddings, N. (1989). *Women and evil.* Berkeley: University of California Press.

Oberman, H. A. (1984). *The roots of anti-semitism in the age of renaissance and reformation* (J. I. Porter, Trans.). Philadelphia: Fortress.

Ocshe, K. (1994). What could be more fruitful, more healing, more purifying? Representations of Jews in the German media after 1989. In S. L. Gilman & K. Rimmler (Eds.), *Reemerging Jewish culture in Germany: Life and literature since 1989* (pp. 113–129).

Ofer, D & Weitzman, L. (1998). Introduction: The role of gender in the holocaust. In D. Ofer & L. Weitzman (Eds.), *Women in the Holocaust* (pp. 1–18). New Haven, CT: Yale University Press.

Ogden, T. (1994). The concept of internal object relations. In J. Grotstein & D. Rinsely (Eds.), *Fairbairn and the origins of object relations* (pp. 88–111). London: Guilford.

Orwell, G. (1949/1977). *1984*. New York: Harcourt Brace Jovanovich.

Ostow, M. (1996). *Myth and madness: The psychodynamic of anti-semitism.* New Brunswick, NJ: Transaction.

Ozick, C. (1989a) *Rosa*. New York: Knopf.

Ozick, C. (1989b). *The shawl*. New York: Knopf.

Pajak, E. (1998). Exploring the "shadow side" of teaching. *Journal of Curriculum Theorizing, 14*(2), 8–14.

Paulson, W. (1988). *The noise of culture: Literary texts in a world of information.* Ithaca, NY: Cornell University Press.

Paxton, R. (1975). *Vichy France: Old guard and new order 1940–1944.* New York: Norton.

Peck, J. (1996). East Germany. In D. S. Wyman (Ed.), *The world reacts to the Holocaust* (pp. 447–472). Baltimore: The Johns Hopkins University Press.

Perl, G. (1993). A doctor in Auschwitz. In C. Rittner & J. Roth (Eds.), *Women and the Holocaust: Different voices* (pp. 104–118). St. Paul: MN: Paragon.

Pinar, W. F. (1991). Curriculum as social psychoanalysis: On the significance of place. In J. Kincheloe & W. Pinar (Eds.), *Curriculum as social psychoanalysis: The significance of place* (pp. 165–186). New York: SUNY Press.

Pinar, W. F. (1994). *Autobiography, politics and sexuality: Essays in curriculum theory 1972–1992.* New York: Peter Lang.

Pinar, W. F. (1995). The curriculum: What are the basics, and are we teaching them? In J. L. Kincheloe & S. R. Steinberg (Eds.), *Thirteen questions: Reframing education's conversation* (pp. 23–30). New York: Peter Lang.

Pinar, W., Reynolds, W., Slattery, P., & Taubman, P. (1995). *Understanding curriculum.* New York: Peter Lang.

Pinar, W. F. (1999). Farewell and celebrate. In W. Pinar (Ed.), *Contemporary curriculum Discourses: Twenty years of JCT* (pp. xi–xx). New York: Peter Lang.

Pitt, A., Robertson, J., & Todd, S. (1998). Psychoanalytic encounters: Putting pedagogy on the couch. *Journal of Curriculum Theorizing, 14*(2), 2–7.

Plant, R. (1986). *The pink triangle: The nazi war against homosexuals.* New York: Henry Holt.

Poliakov, L. (1975). *The history of anti-semitism volume three: From Voltaire to Wagner* (M. Kochan, Trans.). New York: Vanguard.

Poliakov, L. (1985). *The history of anti-semitism volume four: Suicidal Europe: 1870–1933.* New York: Vanguard.

Pollefeyt, D., & Colijn, G. (1997). Leaving evil in Germany: The questionable success of Goldhagen in the low countries. In F. Little (Ed.), *Hyping the Holocaust: Scholars answer Goldhagen* (pp. 3–8). Merion Station, PA: Merion Westfield.

Proudhon, P. J. (1969). Part three: Philosophy and morality. In S. Edwards (Ed.), (E. Fraser, Trans.), *Selected writings of P. J. Proudhon* (pp. 219–263). New York: Doubleday.

Rapaport, L. (1997). *Jews in Germany after the Holocaust: Memory, identity and Jewish–German relations.* Cambridge, MA: Cambridge University Press.

Rappaport, E. (1975). *Anti-Judaism: A psychohistory.* Chicago: Perspective.

Rashkin, E. (1992). *Family secrets and the psychoanalysis of narrative.* New Jersey: Princeton University Press.

Reddick, J. (1975). *The 'Danzig trilogy' of Günter Grass: A study of the tin drum, cat and mouse and dog years.* New York: Harcourt Brace Jovanovich.

Reed, D. (1985). *The novel and the nazi past.* New York: Peter Lang.

Reich, W. (1933/1945). *The mass psychology of fascism* (T. Wolfe, Trans.). New York: Orgone Institute Press.

Reik, T. (1948/1998). *Listening with the third ear: The inner experience of a psychoanalyst.* New York: Noonday Press; Farrar, Straus & Giroux.

Riasanovsky, N. V. (1969). *The teaching of Charles Fourier.* Berkeley: University of California Press.

Richard, E. (1988). *Jesus: One and many. The christological concept of new testament authors.* Wilmington, DE: Michael Glazier.

Richter, P. (1975). Utopia/Dystopia?: Threats of hell or hopes of paradise. In P. Richter (Ed.), *Utopia/Dystopia?* (pp. 1–28). Cambridge, MA: Schenkman.

Ricoeur, P. (1990). *Time and narrative* (K. Blamey & D. Pellauer, Trans.). Chicago: The University of Chicago Press.

Ringelblum, E. (1974). *Notes from the Warsaw ghetto. The journal of Emmanuel Ringelblum.* New York: Schocken.

Ringelheim, J. (1993). Women and the Holocaust: A reconstruction of research. In C. Rittner & J. Roth (Eds.), *Women and the Holocaust: Different voices* (pp. 373–418). St. Paul, MN: Paragon.

Rittner, C., & Roth, J. (1993). Prologue: Women and the Holocaust. In C. Rittner & J. Roth (Eds.), *Women and the Holocaust: Different voices* (pp. 1–20). St. Paul, MN: Paragon.

Robins, K. (1995). Will images still move us? In M. Lister (Ed.), *The photographic image in digital culture* (pp. 30–45). New York: Routledge.

Rockmore, T. (1997). *On Heidegger's Nazism and philosophy.* Berkeley: University of California Press.

Rorty, R. (1991). *Objectivity, relativism, and truth: Philosophic papers volume one.* New York: Cambridge University Press.

Rose, P. L. (1990). *Revolutionary antisemitism in Germany: From Kant to Wagner.* New Jersey: Princeton University Press.

Rosenberg, M. (1994). *Hiding to survive: Stories of Jewish children rescued from the Holocaust.* New York: Clarion.

Rosenfeld, A. (1980). *A double dying: Reflections on Holocaust literature.* Bloomington: Indiana University Press.

Roth, S. (1995a). Final panel plenary discussion. In R. Moses (Ed.), *Persistent shadows of the Holocaust: The meaning to those not directly affected* (pp. 221–243). Madison, WI: International Universities Press.

Roth, S. (1995b). Shadows of the Holocaust. In R. Moses (Ed.), *Persistent shadows of the Holocaust: The meaning to those not directly affected* (pp. 37–64). Madison, WI: International Universities Press.

Rousseau, J. J. (1750–1755/1938). *The social contract and discourses* (G. D. H. Cole, Trans.). New York: E. P. Dutton.

Rubenstein, W. (1997). *The myth of rescue: Why the democracies could not have saved more Jews from the Nazis.* New York: Routledge.

Ruether, R. (1974). *Faith and fratricide: The theological roots of anti-semitism.* New York: Seabury.

Rüsen, J. (1997). The logic of historicization: Metahistorical reflections on the debate between Friedländer and Broszat. In *History and Memory, 9*(1 & 2), 113–146.

Rushdie, S. (1985). Introduction. In G. Grass, *On writing and politics 1967–1983* (R. Manheim, Trans.), (pp. ix–xv). New York: Harcourt Brace Jovanovich.

Russell, B. (1972). *A history of western philosophy.* New York: Simon & Schuster.

Russell, P. (1998). Trauma and the cognitive function of affects. In J. G. Teicholz & D. Kriegman (Eds.), *Trauma, repetition, and affect regulation in the work of Paul Russell* (pp. 23–47). New York: The Other Press.

Ryan, J. (1983). *The uncompleted past: Postwar German novels and the third reich.* Detroit, MI: Wayne State University Press.

Salvio, P. (1997). On keying pedagogy as an interpretive event. In T. R. Carson & D. Sumara (Eds.), *Action research as a living practice* (pp. 247–264). New York: Peter Lang.

Salvio, P. (1998). The teacher/scholar as melancholic: Excavating scholars and pedagogic (s)crypts in fugitive pieces. *Journal of Curriculum Theorizing: An Interdisciplinary Journal of Curriculum Studies, 14*(2), 15–23.

Salvio, P. (1998). On using the literacy portfolio to prepare teachers for "willful world traveling." In W. Pinar (Ed.), *Curriculum: Toward New Identities* (pp. 41–74). New York: Garland.

Salvio, P. (1999). Reading beyond narratives of cure in curriculum studies: Introductory notes. *The Journal of Curriculum Theorizing, 15*(2), 185–188.

Sandler, J., & Sandler A. M. (1998). *Internal objects revisited.* Madison, CT: International Universities Press.

Sartre, J. P. (1946). *Anti-Semite and Jew* (G. J. Becker, Trans.). New York: Schocken.

Sartre, J. P. (1948). *The psychology of imagination.* New York: The Philosophical Library.

Sartre, J. P. (1968). *Search for a method* (H. Barnes, Trans.). New York: Vintage.

Schiesari, J. (1992). *The gendering of melancholia: Feminism, Psychoanalysis, and the symbolism of loss in renaissance literature.* Ithaca, NY: Cornell University Press.

Schulz, B. (1934/1977). *The street of crocodiles* (C. Wieniewska, Trans.). New York: Penguin.

Schulz, B. (1939/1979). *Sanatorium under the sign of the hourglass* (C. Wieniewska, Trans.). New York: Penguin.

Seel, P. (1997). *Liberation was for others: Memoirs of a gay survivor of the Nazi Holocaust* (J. Neugroshel, Trans.). New York: DeCapo.

Serres, M. (1982). *Hermes: Literature, science, philosophy* (J. V. Havari & D. F. Bell, Trans.) Baltimore: The Johns Hopkins University Press.

Shklar, J. (1966). The political theory of utopia: From melancholy to nostalgia. In F. E. Manuel (Ed.), *Utopias and utopian thought* (pp. 101–115). Boston: Houghton Mifflin.

Sicher, E. (1998). Introduction. In E. Sicher (Ed.), *Breaking crystal: Writing and memory after Auschwitz.* Chicago: Illinois University Press.

Slattery, P., & Morris, M. (1999). Simone de Beauvoir's ethics and postmodern ambiguity: The assertion of freedom in the face of the absurd. In *Educational Theory, 49*(1), 21–36.

Simon, R. (1998, June). The contribution of holocaust audio-visual testimony to remembrance, learning and hope. *International Journal on Audio-Visual Testimony*, 141–152.

Smith, D. G. (1999). *Pedagon: Interdisciplinary essays in the human sciences, pedagogy, and culture.* New York: Peter Lang.

Smith, M. J. (1995). *Dachau: The narrowing of hell.* New York: SUNY Press.

Soboul, A. (1978). Notes toward a history of utopia in France in the 18th century. In M. Allain (Ed.), *France and North America: Utopias and Utopians* (pp. 175–186). Lafayette: The Center for Louisiana Studies.

Sontag, S. (1977). *On photography.* New York: Farrar, Strauss & Giroux.

Speier, S. (1993). The psychoanalyst without a face: psychoanalysis without a history. In B. Heimannsberg & C. Schmidt (Eds.), (C. Oudejans Harris & G. Wheeler, Trans.), *The collective silence: German identity and the legacy of shame* (pp. 61–72). San Francisco: Jossey-Bass.

Spencer, M. C. (1981). *Charles Fourier.* Boston: Twayne.

Stammelman, R. (1995). The writing of catastrophe: Jewish memory and the poetics of the book in Edmond Jabes. *In Auschwitz and after: Race, culture, and "the Jewish question"* (pp. 264–279). New York: Routledge.

Stannard, D. (1980). *Shrinking history: on Freud and the failure of psychohistory.* New York: Oxford University Press.

Stanton, M. (1997). *Out of order: Clinical work and unconscious process.* London: Rebus.

Stein, A. (1994). *Hidden children: Forgotten survivors of the Holocaust.* New York: Penguin.

Stern, R. (1973). *The varieties of history: From Voltaire to the present.* New York: Vintage.

Stone, L. (1988). The transference-countertransference complex. In B. Wolstein (Ed.), *Essential papers on countertransference* (pp. 270–281). New York: New York University Press.

Strachey, J. (1961). Notes (J. Strachey, Trans.). In S. Freud, *Civilizations and its discontents* (p. 104). New York: Norton.

Sucher, C. (1997). *The rescue of memory.* New York: Scribner's.

Talburt, S. (1999). Unfitting Subjects. *Journal of Curriculum Theorizing, 15*(2), 59–68.

Tauber, E. (1988). Exploring the therapeutic use of countertransference. In B. Wolstein (Ed.), *Essential papers on countertransference* (pp. 111–119). New York: New York University Press.

Terry, J. (1984). The damaging effects of "survivor syndrome." In S. Luel & P. Marcus (Eds.), *Psychoanalytic reflections on the Holocaust: Selected essays* (pp. 135–148). New York: KTAV.

Thompson, P. (1988). *The voice of the past: Oral history.* New York: Oxford University Press.

Tower, L. (1988). Countertransference. In B. Wolstein (Ed.), *Essential papers on countertransference* (pp. 131–157). New York: New York University Press.

Trunk, I. (1979). *Jewish responses to nazi persecution: Collective and individual behavior in extremis.* New York: Stein & Day.

Ulam, A. (1966). Socialism and utopia. In F. E. Manuel (Ed.), *Utopias and utopian thought* (pp. 116–136). Boston: Houghton Mifflin.

Updike, J. (1979). Introduction. In B. Schulz, *Sanatorium under the sign of the hourglass* (pp. xii–xix). New York: Penguin.

Van Alphen, E. (1997). *Caught by history: Holocaust effects in contemporary art, literature, and theory.* California: Stanford University Press.

Verhöeven, M. (1990). *Schreckliche Mädchen.* Miramax Films.

Vidal-Naquet, P. (1992). *Assassins of memory: Essays on the denial of the Holocaust* (J. Mehlman, Trans.). New York: Columbia University Press.

Waite, R. (1977). *The psychopathic god: Adolph Hitler.* New York: Basic.

Wangh, M. (1984). On obstacles to the working-through of the Nazi holocaust experiences and on the consequences of failing to do so. In S. Luel & P. Marcus (Eds.), *Psychoanalytic reflections on the Holocaust: Selected essays* (pp. 197–205). New York: KTAV.

Wardi, D. (1996). *Memorial candles: Children of the Holocaust* (N. Goldblum, Trans.). New York: Routledge.

Warnock, M. (1987). *Memory.* London: Faber & Faber.

Wasserstein, B. (1988). *Britain and the Jews of Europe 1939–1945.* New York: Oxford University Press.

Weaver, J. (in press). *Rethinking academic politics in (Re)Unified Germany and the United States.* New York: Routledge/Falmer.

Weaver, J. (in press). Curriculum theorists as spawns from hell: SF as a metaphor for curriculum theorizing. In J. Weaver, T. Daspit & K. Anijar (Eds.), *Science fiction curriculum, cyborg teachers and youth culture(s).* New York: Peter Lang.

Webster, P. (1991). *Petain's crime: The full story of French collaboration in the Holocaust.* Chicago: Ivan R. Dee.

Wegner, G. (1995). Buchenwald concentration camp. Holocaust education for youth in the new Germany. *Journal of Curriculum and Supervision, 10*(2), 171–188.
Weil, G. (1984). *My sister, my Antigone* (K. Winston, Trans.). New York: Avon.
Weinberg, D. (1996). France. In D. Wyman (Ed.), *The world reacts to the Holocaust* (pp. 3–44). Baltimore: The Johns Hopkins University Press.
Weiss, J. (1996). *Ideology of death: Why the Holocaust happened in Germany.* Chicago: Ivan R. Dee.
Well, H. G. (1967). *A modern utopia.* Lincoln: The University of Nebraska Press.
Weatherill, R. (1998). *The sovereignty of death.* London: Rebus.
Wiesel, E. (1982). *Night.* New York: Bantam.
Wiesel, E. (1986). *The trial of God* (M. Wiesel, Trans.). New York: Schocken.
Wiesel, E. (1995). *All rivers run to the sea/memoirs.* New York: Knopf.
Wiesenthal, S. (1976). *The sunflower with a symposium.* New York: Schocken.
White, H. (1978). *Tropics of discourse.* Baltimore: The Johns Hopkins University Press.
White, H. (1990). *The content of the form: Narrative discourse and historical representation.* Baltimore: The Johns Hopkins University Press.
Wistrich, R. (1990). *Between redemption and perdition: Modern anti-semitism and Jewish identity.* New York: Routledge.
Wistrich, R. (1991). *Antisemitism: The longest hatred.* New York: Pantheon.
Wolf, C. (1980). *Patterns of childhood* (U. Molinaro & H. Rappolt, Trans.). New York: Farrar & Giroux.
Wyman, D. (1984/1998). *The abandonment of the Jews: America and the Holocaust.* New York: The New Press.
Wyschogrod, E. (1998). *An ethics of remembering: History, heterology, and the nameless others.* Chicago: University of Chicago Press.
Wyss, D. (1961/1973). *Pyschoanalytic schools from the beginning to the present* (G. Onn, Trans.). New York: Aronson.
Yardeni, M. (1990). *Anti-Jewish mentalities in early modern Europe.* New York: University of America Press.
Yeats, W. B. (1938–1939/1989). Ben bulen. In R. J. Finneran (Ed.), *The collected poems of William Butler Yeats* (pp. 325–328). New York: Macmillan.
Yerushalmi, Y. H. (1982). *Zakhor: Jewish history and Jewish memory.* Seattle: The University of Washington Press.
Young, J. (1988). *Writing and rewriting the Holocaust: Narrative and the consequence of interpretation.* Bloomington: Indiana University Press.
Young, J. (1993). *The texture of memory: Holocaust memorials and meaning.* New Haven, CT: Yale University Press.
Young-Bruehl, E. (1996). *The anatomy of prejudice.* Cambridge, MA: Harvard University Press.
Zeiger, H. A. (1960). *The case against Adolf Eichmann.* New York: Signet.
Zimmerman, M. (1990). *Heidegger's confrontation with modernity: Technology, politics, art.* Bloomington: Indiana University Press.
Zipes, J. (1991). *The operated Jew: Two tales of anti-semitism.* New York: Routledge.
Zuccotti, S. (1993). *The Holocaust, the French, and the Jews.* New York: Basic.
Zuccotti, S. (1996). *The Italians and the Holocaust: Persecution, rescue, and survival.* Lincoln: The University of Nebraska Press.

Author Index

R

S

T

Subject Index

A

B

C

H

I

N

O

R